Schema Therapy in Practice

Schema Therapy in Practice

An Introductory Guide to the Schema Mode Approach

ARNOUD ARNTZ, PhD[*]

Department of Clinical Psychological Science,
Maastricht University,
The Netherlands & Netherlands Institute for Advanced
Study in the Humanities and Social Sciences,
Wassenaar, The Netherlands

GITTA JACOB, PhD

Department of Clinical Psychology and Psychotherapy,
Freiburg University, Germany

[*]The order of authors is based on alphabetical order

A John Wiley & Sons, Ltd., Publication

This edition first published in English in 2013

© 2013

This book is a translated version of: Gitta Jacob and Arnoud Arntz, *Schematherapie in der Praxis*
© 2011 BELTZ Psychologie in der Verlagsgruppe Beltz • Weinheim, Basel

Wiley-Blackwell is an imprint of John Wiley & Sons, formed by the merger of Wiley's global Scientific, Technical and Medical business with Blackwell Publishing.

Registered Office
John Wiley & Sons Ltd, The Atrium, Southern Gate, Chichester, West Sussex, PO19 8SQ, UK

Editorial Offices
350 Main Street, Malden, MA 02148-5020, USA
9600 Garsington Road, Oxford, OX4 2DQ, UK
The Atrium, Southern Gate, Chichester, West Sussex, PO19 8SQ, UK

For details of our global editorial offices, for customer services, and for information about how to apply for permission to reuse the copyright material in this book please see our website at www.wiley.com/wiley-blackwell.

The right of Arnoud Arntz and Gitta Jacob to be identified as the authors of this work has been asserted in accordance with the UK Copyright, Designs and Patents Act 1988.

Library of Congress Cataloging-in-Publication Data

Arntz, Arnoud.
  Schema therapy in practice : an introductory guide to the schema mode approach / Arnoud Arntz, Gitta Jacob.
     p. cm.
  Includes bibliographical references and index.
  ISBN 978-1-119-96285-4 (cloth) – ISBN 978-1-119-96286-1 (pbk.) 1. Schema-focused cognitive therapy. 2. Personality disorders–Treatment. I. Jacob, Gitta. II. Title.
  RC489.S34A76 2013
  616.89′1425–dc23

                                                                              2012017512

A catalogue record for this book is available from the British Library.

Cover image © cosmin4000/iStockphoto
Cover design by www.cyandesign.co.uk

Set in 10.5/13pt Minion by Thomson Digital, Noida, India.
Printed in Malaysia by Ho Printing (M) Sdn Bhd

3   2014

Contents

About the Authors

Arnoud Arntz is Professor of Clinical Psychology and Experimental Psychopathology at Maastricht University, the Netherlands. He is Scientific Director of the University's Research Center of Experimental Psychopathology. He studies psychological theories and therapies for anxiety and personality disorders, and is the principal investigator for a series of multicenter trials investigating the effectiveness of schema therapy for various personality disorders. He also practices CBT and schema therapy.

Gitta Jacob is a Clinical Psychologist, Cognitive and Schema Therapist in the Department of Clinical Psychology and Psychotherapy, University of Freiburg, Germany. She is a founding board member of the International Society for Schema Therapy, and a past Chair of the Working Group on Borderline Personality Disorders at the Department of Psychiatry and Psychotherapy, University Hospital Freiburg.

Acknowledgments

The authors want to express their thanks to Jeffrey Young, the developer of Schema Therapy, for his teaching and deep insights; as well as to other prominent Schema Therapists who influenced their thinking, including Joan Farrell, Ida Shaw, Hannie van Genderen, and David Bernstein; to their collegues with whom they collaborated in applying and further developing Schema Therapy; and last but not least to their patients who helped them to develop the methods and techniques described in this book. This work was supported by a grant from the Netherlands Institute for Advanced Study in the Humanities and Social Sciences (NIAS) (A.A.) and by the European Social Fund and the Ministry of Science, Research and the Arts Baden-Württemberg (G.A.).

Introduction

Schema therapy is increasingly attracting the attention of therapists and consumers. This is partly based on the good effects reported by various studies, and partly on its appealing basis in the idea that children require fundamental needs to be met in order to develop in a psychologically healthy way. The integration of insights, methods, and techniques derived from a range of schools, including attachment theory, cognitive behavior therapy, and experiential therapies into a comprehensive model formulated in terms of the most prominent current psychological paradigm, the cognitive model, also plays a role. The promise of schema therapy that it can deal with psychological problems largely ignored by mainstream cognitive behavior therapy, such as recurrent problems in intimate relationships and the processing of troublesome memories and patterns from childhood, is attractive. Finally, the finding that schema therapy contributes to real recovery, defined not only by a reduction of symptoms, but by the creation of a life that is satisfying and of high quality, is undoubtedly appealing.

In teaching the model, methods, and techniques, we felt that a book presenting the practical basics of schema therapy for those that want to learn it as a generic method, and not in a specialized form for one disorder, was missing. We therefore decided to write such a book. This book does not compete with other publications on schema therapy, as it doesn't focus on theory or on a specific disorder. It aims to present the basics of the schema-therapy model based on the relatively new schema mode concept. It is basically an extension of our work with schema modes in almost all personality disorders. As we felt that the mode approach could also have application in some axis-I problems, and in milder personality issues, we decided to present the model, methods, and techniques in a generic way, and to use case examples of various disorders and problems.

The book is divided into two parts. The first deals with case conceptualization and consists of three chapters: Chapter 1, "Basics," summarizes the original schema approach by describing schemas and schema coping through the use of case examples; Chapter 2, "The Mode Concept," describes the schema mode concept in general terms, then goes on to provide descriptions of the specific mode models for various personality disorders that have been developed so far; finally, Chapter 3, "Communicating the Mode Concept to the Patient," explains how an individual mode model can be introduced in therapy.

The second part deals with treatment, in six chapters. Each chapter is devoted to one group of modes and is subdivided into sections on cognitive, emotional, and behavioral interventions and the therapeutic relationship. Chapter 4, "Treatment Overview," summarizes the central treatment goals and strategies of schema therapy based on the mode concept. Chapter 5, "Overcoming Coping Modes," describes how to deal with coping modes. It covers avoiding (detached protector, avoiding protector, etc.), surrender, and overcompensating coping modes (self-aggrandizer, bully & attack, etc.). Chapter 6, "Treating Vulnerable-child Modes," describes how to deal with vulnerable-child modes. It contains a long section on imagery rescripting and discusses the caring part of the therapeutic relationship in depth. Chapter 7, "Treating Angry and Impulsive Child Modes," describes how to deal with angry, enraged, impulsive, undisciplined, and obstinate child modes. Chapter 8, "Treating Dysfunctional-parent Modes," describes how to deal with both demanding- and punitive-parent modes. It contains a long section on chair dialogues as a therapeutic technique. Chapter 9, "Strengthening the Healthy-adult Mode," summarizes how the healthy adult mode is explicitly and implicitly developed in schema therapy. It also addresses how the treatment should develop when completion is near, and how to relate with the patient after formal completion of treatment.

I

CASE CONCEPTUALIZATION

1

Basics

Schema therapy, which was developed by Jeffrey Young (1990; Young et al., 2003), stems from cognitive behavioral therapy (**CBT**) and has been attracting increasing attention since it was first proposed. Young created schema therapy predominantly for patients who did not respond well to "classical" CBT treatment. These patients often experience a variety of symptoms and typically display complex interpersonal patterns, which may be either fluctuating or persistent; they usually meet the criteria for one or more personality disorders. Compared to CBT, schema therapy has a more intensive focus on the following three issues:

1 *Problematic emotions*, which are in the foreground, alongside the cognitive and behavioral aspects of the patient's problems and symptoms. Schema therapy makes intensive use of experiential or emotion-focused interventions — ones that have previously been developed and used in gestalt therapy or psychodrama. The main experiential intervention techniques consist of chair dialogues or imagery exercises. This focus on emotions is important, since problematic patterns in patients with personality disorders are usually maintained by problematic emotional experiences. For example, patients with borderline personality disorder (**BPD**) typically experience intense self-hatred; they can hardly distance themselves from this self-hatred on an emotional level, even if they do understand that such hatred is not appropriate. In such cases, the influence of cognitive insight into the connected emotional issues is very low. Such kinds of problem can be treated well by emotional interventions.

Schema Therapy in Practice: An Introductory Guide to the Schema Mode Approach,
First Edition. Arnoud Arntz and Gitta Jacob.
© 2013 John Wiley & Sons, Ltd. Published 2013 by John Wiley & Sons, Ltd.

2   *Childhood issues*, which are of much greater importance than in standard CBT, enabling schema therapy to integrate approaches or concepts that have so far been mainly considered psychodynamic or psychoanalytic. Biographical information is mainly used to validate patients by enabling them to understand the childhood origin of their problematic behavioral patterns. One goal is to help patients understand their current patterns as a result of dysfunctional conditions during their childhood and youth. However, in contrast to psychoanalysis, "working through" the biography is not considered to be the most important therapeutic agent.

3   The *therapeutic relationship*, which plays a very important role in schema therapy. On the one hand, the therapeutic relationship is conceptualized as "limited reparenting," which means that the therapist takes on the role of a parent and displays warmth and caring behavior towards the patient—within the limits of the therapeutic relationship, of course. It is important to note that the style of this reparenting relationship should be adapted to the patient's individual problems or schemas. Particularly for patients with personality disorders, the therapeutic relationship is regarded as the place in which the patient is allowed to and dares to open up and show painful feelings, try out new social behaviors, and change interpersonal patterns for the first time. Thus the therapeutic relationship is explicitly regarded as a place for patients to work on their problems.

Schema therapy offers both a complex and a very structured approach to conceptualizing and treating a variety of problem constellations. Thus schema therapy has been developed not for specific disorders, but rather as a general transdiagnostic psychotherapeutic approach. However, during its ongoing development, specific models for treatment of various personality disorders have emerged and been developed within schema therapy, which are introduced later in this book (Section 2.3). In this chapter, we will first give an overview of the original schema concepts, describing each maladaptive schema briefly and illustrating it with a case example. We will then introduce the development of the schema mode concept and the character of schema modes and their assessment. Finally, we will describe schema-therapy interventions based on the schema mode approach. Simply put, most interventions can be used during treatment both with the original schema and with the schema mode approach. Take for example a "chair dialogue" with two different chairs, where the patient's perfectionist side holds a discussion with the healthier and more relaxed side. This intervention can be regarded both as a dialogue between the modes of the demanding parent and the healthy adult, and as a dialogue between the schema "unrelenting standards" and the healthy side of the patient. Therefore, the interventions described with the schema mode model could also be used in therapy applying the original schema model.

1.1   Maladaptive Schemas

The so-called early maladaptive schemas (**EMS**s) are broadly defined as pervasive life patterns which influence cognitions, emotions, memories, social perceptions, and interaction and behavior patterns. EMSs are thought to develop during childhood. Depending on the life situation, individual coping mechanisms, and interpersonal patterns of an individual, EMSs may fluctuate throughout the course of life, and often they are maintained by these factors. When an existing schema is activated, intensive negative emotions appear, such as anxiety, sadness, and loneliness. Young et al. (2003) defined 18 schemas, which are ordered into five so-called "schema domains." The definition of these EMSs is mainly derived from clinical observations and considerations, and is not empirically or scientifically developed, although research supports their existence.

Any person can have either a single schema or a combination of several schemas. Generally all human beings do have more or less strong schemas. A schema is considered pathological only when associated with pathological emotional experiences and symptoms, or impairments in social functioning. Patients with severe personality disorders typically score highly on many of the schemas in the Young schema questionnaire (Schmidt et al., 1995). In contrast, therapy clients with only circumscribed life problems who do not fulfill the diagnostic criteria of a personality disorder and who have a higher level of social functioning usually score highly only on one or two of the schemas. Table 1.1 gives an overview of Young's schema domains and schemas.

Case example

Susan is a 40-year-old nurse. She takes part in day treatment, with the diagnosis of chronic depression. Susan reports severe problems at work, mainly bullying by her colleagues, which has resulted in her "depressive breakdown." Susan's most conspicuous feature is her inconspicuousness. Even 2 weeks after her admission, not every team member knows her name; she does not approach therapists with personal concerns and does not make contact with other patients. In group therapies, she is very quiet. When the group therapist explicitly asks for her contributions, she tends to confirm what everybody else has already said, and generally reacts very submissively and obediently. When faced with a more challenging situation, such as appointments with the social worker to discuss her complicated job situation, she avoids them. However, when confronted with her avoidance, Susan may unexpectedly react in an arrogant manner. After a couple of weeks in treatment, Susan's antidepressive psychotherapy seems to become stale, as she ostensibly avoids active behavior changes.

In the schema questionnaire, Susan has a high score on the "subjugation" schema. She always orients towards the needs of other people. At the same time, she feels powerless, helpless, and suppressed by others. She does not have any idea how to act more autonomously or how to allow herself to recognize her own needs. Diagnostic imagery exercises are applied, starting from her current feeling of helplessness and lack of power. In the imagery exercises, Susan remembers very stressful childhood situations. Her father was an alcoholic who often became unpredictably aggressive and violent. Her mother, on the other hand, was very submissive and avoidant, and suffered from depressive episodes, and thus was unable to protect Susan from her father. Moreover, as the family managed a small hotel, the children were always required to be quiet and inconspicuous.

In the imagery exercise, "Little Susan" sits helpless and submissive on the kitchen floor and does not dare to talk about her needs with her parents—she is too afraid that this will make her mother feel bad and that her father will become aggressive and dangerous. In the following schema therapy, imagery exercises are combined with imagery rescripting. In imagery rescripting exercises, an adult (first the therapist, later Susan herself) enters the childhood scenario to take care of Little Susan and her needs. Concomitantly, it becomes easier to confront Susan empathically with the negative consequences of her overly shy, obedient, and submissive behavior patterns. Disadvantages of this behavior are discussed: she acts against her own interests, she is not able to care for her own needs, other people become annoyed by her avoidance. Therefore, she must attempt to find the courage to behave more in line with her own interests and needs. With the combination of imagery rescripting and empathic confrontation, Susan becomes increasingly less withdrawn and more engaged and present in the day clinic; she opens up more and starts to articulate her needs. After discussing and analyzing her problematic schema-driven patterns, she reports further problems, which she had hidden at the start of therapy. She starts talking about a sexual relationship with a seasonal worker. She separated from him 2 years ago, as he continuously acted aggressively towards her, but he still gets in contact with her whenever he works in the city. Although she clearly knows that she dislikes this contact, he convinces her time and again to meet and engage in sexual relations, clearly against her needs. After learning about her schemas, Susan herself becomes able to relate this behavior to her overall patterns.

Table 1.1 Early maladaptive schemas (Young et al., 2003) and schema domains

Schema domain	Schemas
Disconnection and rejection	Abandonment/instability
	Mistrust/abuse
	Emotional deprivation
	Defectiveness/shame
	Social isolation/alienation
Impaired autonomy and achievement	Dependency/incompetency
	Vulnerability to harm and illness
	Enmeshment/undeveloped self
	Failure
Impaired limits	Entitlement/grandiosity
	Lack of self-control/self-discipline
Other-directedness	Subjugation
	Self-sacrifice
	Approval-seeking
Hypervigilance and inhibition	Negativity/pessimism
	Emotional inhibition
	Unrelenting standards
	Punitiveness

1.1.1 Schemas in the "disconnection and rejection" domain

This schema domain is characterized by attachment difficulties. All schemas of this domain are in some way associated with a lack of safety and reliability in interpersonal relationships. The quality of the associated feelings and emotions differs depending on the schema—for example, the schema "abandonment/instability" is connected to a feeling of abandonment by significant others, due to previous abandonment in childhood. Individuals with the schema "social isolation/alienation," on the other hand, lack a sense of belonging, as they have experienced exclusion from peer groups in the past. Patients with the schema "mistrust/abuse" mainly feel threatened by others, having been harmed by people during their childhood.

(1) Abandonment/instability Patients with this schema suffer from the feeling that important relationships which they have formed will never last and thus they are constantly worried about being abandoned by others. They typically report experiences of abandonment during their childhood; often one parent left the family and ceased to care about them, or important people died early. Patients with this schema often start relationships with people who are unreliable, who thus confirm their schema over and over again. But even in stable relationships, which are not threatened by abandonment, the most minor of events (such as the partner's return home from work an hour later than expected) may trigger exaggerated and unnecessary feelings of loss or abandonment.

Case example: abandonment/instability

Cathy, a 25-year-old college student, comes to psychotherapy to get treatment for her panic attacks and strong dissociative symptoms. Both symptoms increase when she has to leave her father after staying over at his house during weekends. She studies in another city, but visits her father nearly every weekend and at holidays. While her relationships with members of her family are very close, her relationships with others are typically rather superficial. She rarely feels truly close to other people, and has never been in a committed romantic relationship. She also reports being unable to imagine having a truly intimate relationship. When she ponders the reasons behind this, she starts feeling very upset. She breaks into tears, overwhelmed by the feeling that nobody will ever stay with her for long. This feeling is connected to her own biographical history. Her biological mother became severely ill and died when Cathy was 2 years old. Her father married again 2 years later, and the stepmother became a real mother for her. However, her stepmother died rather young herself, very suddenly from a stroke, when Cathy was 16 years of age.

(2) Mistrust/abuse People with this schema expect to be abused, humiliated, or in other ways badly treated by others. They are constantly suspicious, because they are afraid of being deliberately harmed. When they are treated in a friendly way, they often believe that the other person has a hidden agenda. When they get in touch with the feelings associated with this schema, they usually experience anxiety and threat. In severe cases, patients feel extremely threatened in nearly all social situations. The "mistrust/abuse" schema typically develops because of childhood abuse. This abuse is often sexual; however, physical, emotional, or verbal abuse can also cause severe abuse schemas. In many cases, children were abused by family members, such as a parent or a sibling. However, it is important to keep in mind that cruel acts performed by peers, such as bullying by classmates, can cause extreme abuse schemas as well, often combined with strong failure or shame.

Case example: mistrust/abuse

Helen, a 26-year-old nurse, was sexually and physically abused by her stepfather during her childhood and teens. As an adult she generally mistrusts men and is convinced that it is impossible to find a man who will treat her nicely. She cannot even imagine a man treating a woman nicely. Her intimate relationships are usually short-lived sexual affairs with men whom she meets on the Internet. Sadly, within these affairs she sometimes experiences abuse and violence again.

(3) Emotional deprivation   Patients with this schema typically refer to their childhood as a smooth and OK one, but they commonly did not experience much warmth or loving care, and did not feel truly safe, loved, or comforted. This schema is typically not characterized by feelings of much intensity. Instead, the affected patients don't feel as safe and as loved as they should when others do love them and do want to make them feel safe. Thus, people with this schema often do not suffer strongly from it. Others in the affected persons' environment, however, often sense this schema quite clearly, because they feel that they cannot get close to them or that they cannot reach them with love and support. People with the emotional deprivation schema seem somehow unable to perceive and acknowledge when others like them. This schema often remains quite unproblematic until the life circumstances of the affected person become in some way overwhelming.

Case example: emotional deprivation

Sally, a 30-year-old office clerk, has a high level of functioning: she is good at her job, she is happily married, and she has nice friends and interpersonal relationships. However, none of her relationships give her a real sense of being close to others and being truly loved by them. Although she does know that her husband and her friends care for her a lot, she simply does not feel it. Sally had been functioning very well for most of her life. Only during the last year, when her responsibilities at work and general workload increased considerably, did she begin to feel increasingly exhausted and lonely, and find herself unable to act in order to change her situation. The therapist suggested she should attempt a better work–life balance and try to integrate more relaxing and positive activities into her life. However, Sally does not regard these issues as very important, as she somehow does not feel herself to be significant or worthy enough. She reports that everything "was OK" in her childhood. However, both parents had busy jobs and therefore were often absent. She says that it was often simply too much for her parents to take care of their children after a long day at work.

(4) Defectiveness/shame This schema is characterized by feelings of defectiveness, inferiority, and being unwanted. People with this schema feel undeserving of any love, respect, or attention, as they feel they are not worthy—no matter how they actually behave. This experience is typically connected to intense feelings of shame. This schema is frequently seen in patients with BPD, often combined with mistrust/abuse. People with this schema typically suffered from intense devaluation and humiliation in their childhood.

Case example: defectiveness/shame

Michael, a 23-year-old male nurse, starts psychological treatment for his BPD. He reports severe problems at work due to pervasive feelings of shame. He regards himself as completely unattractive and uninteresting, despite the fact that others often give him compliments and praise him for being a competent and friendly person. When others say such nice things to him, he is simply unable to believe them. He also cannot imagine why his girlfriend is committed to him and wants to stay with him. Growing up, he reports intense physical and verbal abuse by his parents, mainly his father, who was an alcoholic. The father often called both Michael and his sister names and referred to them as "filthy," completely independent of the children's actual behavior.

(5) Social isolation/alienation People with this schema feel alienated from others and have a feeling of not belonging with anyone. Moreover, they typically feel like they are completely different from everybody else. In social groups they do not feel like they belong, even though others might regard them as quite well integrated. They often report that they were literally isolated in their childhood, for example because they didn't speak the dialect of the region, were not sent to the kindergarten with all the other children, or weren't part of any youth organizations such as sports clubs. Often there seems to be some discrepancy between the child's social and family background and their achievements in later life. A typical example is a person growing up in a poor family with a low level of education, but managing to become the first and only educated family member. These

people feel that they belong nowhere—neither to their family, nor to other educated people due to their different social background. In such cases, this schema can also be combined with defectiveness/shame, particularly when the own social background is perceived as inferior.

Case example: social isolation

David, a 48-year-old technician, completely lacks feelings of belonging. This applies to all kinds of formal or informal groups alike; he actually reports never feeling any sense of belonging in any group throughout his whole life. In his childhood, his family moved to a very little village when he was 9 years old. Since this village was far away from his birthplace, initially he hardly understood the dialect of the other kids. He never managed to become truly close to other children, and since his parents were very occupied by their new jobs and their own personal problems, they hardly offered him any support. Being different from his classmates, he was not integrated into the sports club or the local music groups. He remembers feeling very lonely and excluded when he didn't participate in local activities and festivities.

1.1.2　Schemas in the "impaired autonomy and achievement" domain

In this domain, problems with autonomy and achievement potential are at the fore. People with these schemas perceive themselves as dependent, feel insecure, and suffer from a lack of self-determination. They are afraid that autonomous decisions might damage important relationships and they expect to fail in demanding situations. People with the schema "vulnerability to harm and illness" may even be afraid that challenging and changing their fate through autonomous decisions will lead to harm to themselves and others.

These schemas can be acquired by social learning through models, for example from parent figures who constantly warned against danger or illnesses, or who suffered from an obsessive–compulsive disorder (**OCD**) such as contamination anxiety (schema "vulnerability to harm and illness"). Similarly, the schema "dependency/incompetency" may develop when parents are not confident that their child has age-appropriate skills to cope with normal developmental challenges. However, schemas of this domain can also develop when a child is confronted with demands which are too high, when they have to become autonomous too early and do not receive enough support to achieve it. Thus patients with childhood neglect, who felt extremely overstressed as children, may develop dependent behavior patterns in order to ensure that somebody will provide them the support they lacked earlier in life, and thus do not learn a healthy autonomy.

(6) Dependency/incompetency Patients with this schema often feel helpless and unable to manage their daily life without the help of others. This schema is typically held by patients with a dependent personality disorder. Some people with this schema report experiences of being confronted with excessive demands in their childhood. These are often (implicit) social demands, such as feelings of responsibility for a sick parent. Since they felt chronically overstressed, they could not develop a sense of competence and healthy coping mechanisms. Other patients with this schema, however, report that their parents actually did not ask enough of them. Instead of helping their children to adequately develop their autonomy during adolescence, they refused to let go and continued to help them with everyday tasks, without giving them any responsibilities.

It may take some time in therapy before this schema becomes apparent, as patients often demonstrate very good cooperation in the therapeutic relationship. After some time, the therapist will feel a lack of adequate progress despite the good cooperation. When a patient starts therapy in an extraordinarily friendly manner and reacts enthusiastically to each of the therapist's suggestions, but a lack of progress is made, the therapist should consider dependent patterns. This might especially be the case when the patient has already been through several therapies with limited success.

Case example: dependency/incompetency

Mary, a 23-year-old student, comes across as very shy and helpless. Her mother still cares for her a lot, particularly by taking over the execution of boring or annoying tasks. She always calls Mary to remind her of deadlines for her studies. Mary has been used to this overly caring behavior all her life. When she was a child and an adolescent, she did not have any chores to attend to, unlike her classmates. The idea of taking over the full responsibility for her life discourages and scares her. She would actually like to look for a job to earn some money, but feels unable to do so. She reports high levels of insecurity when talking with potential bosses and lacks the confidence in her own skills to start working.

(7) Vulnerability to harm and illness   This schema is characterized by an exaggerated anxiety about tragic events, catastrophes, and illnesses which due to their nature could strike unexpectedly at any time. This schema is seen particularly frequently in hypochondriac or generalized anxiety disorder patients. Patients with this schema often report their mothers' or grandmothers' overcautiousness, frequent worry, warnings against severe illnesses and other of life's dangers, and requests for extreme carefulness and caution during childhood. This cautious guardian may have instructed the child to obey very strict rules regarding hygiene, such as never eating unwashed fruit or always washing their hands after visits to the supermarket in order to avoid sicknesses. This schema can also be found in patients who actually were the victim of severe and uncontrollable events in their lives, such as natural disasters or severe illnesses.

Case example: vulnerability to harm and illness

Connie, a 31-year-old physician, is unsure whether she should try to have children or not. She loves the idea of having two children, but she becomes horrified when she considers just how many traumatic and catastrophic events could happen to a child. Connie knows she might not get pregnant easily in the first place; if she did, the pregnancy could be difficult; the child could suffer from horrible diseases, it could die or suffer horrendous damage in an accident, and so on. However, Connie does not suffer from any heritable disease, and she has no risk factors for a difficult pregnancy, and thus there is no actual reason for her to be worried to such an extent.

The therapist asks her to recall any childhood events related to her pervasive feelings of insecurity and constant worry. Connie spontaneously starts talking about her maternal grandmother. Granny always got very upset when little Connie did things autonomously. The grandmother complained about her inability to fall asleep when Connie was out, even when Connie was 17. She nearly died from anxiety when Connie went to summer camp at 12. Connie's mother was always very close with her grandmother, and mostly shared the grandmother's concerns.

(8) Enmeshment/undeveloped self People suffering from this schema have a weak sense of their own identity. They hardly feel able to make everyday decisions without the need for reassurance from some other—often their mother. Without this special person, they lack the ability to form opinions. This may go as far as an inability to feel like an "individual" altogether. Patients report very close, often also very emotional relationships with the person with whom they are enmeshed. People with enmeshment schema may be very intelligent and well educated, but this does not help or in any way enable them to recognize their own feelings or make their own decisions. Frequently "enmeshed people" do not suffer directly from this schema, because the enmeshed relationship can be experienced as mostly positive. However, secondary problems may arise due to the impairment of autonomy and social functioning, or it could happen that the patient's spouse or partner becomes frustrated with the enmeshment. Often this schema is also related to obsessive–compulsive symptoms.

Case example: enmeshment/undeveloped self

Tina, a 25-year-old secretary, reports occasional aggressive compulsions towards her boyfriend. Their relationship is very close—they spend every waking minute together, either chatting or watching TV—but neither of them has any hobbies or friends of their own. In spite of this close relationship, sexual interaction is rare, mainly due to a lack of interest on her part. During the first psychotherapy sessions, Tina reports intense feelings of insecurity related to nearly every domain of her life. However, while the therapist sees this insecurity and the lack of hobbies and interests as being part of Tina's problems, Tina herself regards her life as "perfect," except for the compulsions. In particular, she is very enthusiastic about her "wonderful parents." She has a very close relationship with them, too, which she evaluates as 100% positive. She calls her mother several times a day, asking for her advice on virtually any aspect of everyday life, no matter how small, and claims to be happy to discuss any problems with her parents, including her lack of sexual desire.

(9) Failure This schema is characterized by feelings of being a complete failure and of being less talented and intelligent than everybody else. People with this schema believe they will never be successful in any domain of their life. They tend to have frequently experienced very negative feedback in school or in their families, often including global devaluations of their personae. People engaged in a perfectionist, achievement-oriented activity in their childhood and youth (such as playing classical music, competitive sports, etc.) sometimes develop this schema as well. Demanding and stressful situations, including examinations, are very problematic for such people. This schema sometimes functions like a self-fulfilling prophecy: since people with this schema are so afraid of demanding situations, they may avoid them altogether, resulting in poor preparation and—in a vicious circle—in actual bad results when such situations are unavoidable.

Case example: failure

Toby is a 24-year-old university student who comes to therapy because of depressive symptoms and extreme exam anxiety. With regard to his intelligence and interest in his subject, there is nothing disabling him from being successful, however he often stays in bed all day and postpones doing his homework, and his avoidant behavior patterns are prominent. He is convinced that he will never be able to finish his studies, as he regards himself as a complete failure. This feeling of failure has persisted over the last few years, although he was able to achieve good marks at school and during the first year of university. Toby talks a lot about his brother, who is 2 years older. The brother is very talented and has always excelled in any activity he participates in. Toby has always experienced feelings of being less smart than and inferior to his brother. Furthermore, Toby was on a swimming team as a child and teen and participated in local competitions. His coach was very ambitious, and whenever Toby came second, the coach displayed his disappointment at Toby's failure to win.

1.1.3   Schema in the "impaired limits" domain

People with schemas of this domain have difficulty accepting normal limits. It is hard for them to remain calm and not cross the line, and they often lack the self-discipline to manage their day-to-day lives, studies, or jobs appropriately. People with the schema "entitlement/grandiosity" mainly feel entitled and tend to self-aggrandize. The schema "lack of self-control/self-discipline" is principally associated with impaired discipline and delay of gratification. Just like those of the domain "impaired autonomy and achievement," these schemas can be learned by direct modeling and social learning. Often patients were spoiled as children, or their parents were themselves spoiled in their childhoods and/or had problems accepting normal limits. However, these schemas can also develop when parents are too strict, when they inflict too much discipline, and when limits are too narrow. In such situations, these schemas develop as a kind of a rebellion against limits and discipline in general.

(10) Entitlement/grandiosity   People with this schema regard themselves as very special. They feel that they don't have to care about usual rules or conventions, and they hate to be limited or restricted. This schema is typically associated with narcissistic personality traits. Patients with this schema strive for power and control, and they interact with others in a very competitive way. They often report that an important figure, such as their father, was a narcissistic role model or a powerful overachiever, thus modeling this schema. It is often the case that controlling and powerful interpersonal behavior was directly reinforced in the patient's childhood. Perhaps the father reinforced the son when the latter controlled his peers, or the parents told their children to feel special because they belonged to a very special family.

Case example: entitlement/grandiosity

Allan is a 48-year-old team leader who first sought psychological consultation due to being bullied in his workplace. With regard to therapy goals, he says: "I have no idea at all how those morons at work can be taught to behave." Towards the therapist he acts in a controlling and bossy manner. According to his self-report, he often devalues his coworkers and behaves insolently at work. When the therapist addresses this behavior, he proudly comments that "It's certainly important to come prepared if you have to deal with me."

(11) Lack of self-control/self-discipline   People suffering from this schema typically have problems with self-control and with the ability to delay gratification. They often give up boring things and don't have enough patience for tasks requiring discipline and perseverance. Others often perceive such patients as lazy, caring only about their own well-being and not working hard enough to fulfill their obligations. The biographic roots of this schema are often similar to "entitlement/grandiosity." However, "lack of self-control/self-discipline" can also be found in individuals who suffered some form of abuse in their childhood. In families that neglect or abuse their children, the kids typically lack the guidance necessary to learn sufficient self-discipline.

Case example: lack of self-control/self-discipline

Steven, a 46-year-old, calls himself a "freelance artist." In reality he relies on social welfare and benefits to make ends meet, but he regularly talks about artistic and musical projects he is currently working on. The only real work he does on his projects is to maintain a very glamorous presence on the Internet. He came to therapy due to depression and a lack of perspective. However, when the therapist tries to identify clear goals with and for him so that he can actually start changing his life for better, he becomes unwilling or unable to make decisions regarding personal goals. Whenever a certain goal becomes more materialized and clearer, he does not want to invest the time and energy to make it a reality.

1.1.4 Schemas in the "other-directedness" domain

People with schemas of this domain typically put the needs, wishes, and desires of others before their own. In consequence, most of their efforts are directed towards meeting the needs of others. However, the ways in which they attempt this differ with the type of schema they possess. Individuals with a strong "subjugation" schema always try to adapt their behavior in a way which best accommodates the ideas and needs of others. In the schema "self-sacrifice," on the other hand, the focus is more on an extreme feeling of responsibility for solving everyone else's problems; people with this schema typically feel that it is their job to make everybody feel good. Those with the schema "approval-seeking" have as a sole purpose pleasing others; thus all their actions and efforts reflect that desire, rather than their own wishes. With regard to the biographical background and development during childhood, these schemas are often secondary. The primary schemas are often those from the domain "disconnection and rejection". I.e., schemas in the domain "other-directedness" may have developed to cope with schemas of disconnection and rejection. Patients may, for example, report that an important parent figure, often the father, was an alcoholic and used to behave aggressively when intoxicated. Thus they felt threatened and developed the schema "mistrust/abuse." To avoid confrontation with the drunken father, they may have learned to behave submissively in such situations. This "secondary" submissive behavior then resulted in a subjugation schema. Often they also had subjugating models, for example when the mother did not stop the father's behavior or did not leave the aggressive father all together, but rather subjugated herself to his aggression.

(12) Subjugation   People with this schema generally allow others to have an upper hand in interpersonal relationships. They mold and adapt their behavior according to the desires and ideas of others, sometimes even when those desires are not explicitly stated but only deduced or guessed. For individuals with this schema, it can be very difficult to get in tune with their own needs, even with the therapist's efforts to help them discover these. During their childhood, patients often experienced dangerous family situations, with one parent subjugating to the other one. Perhaps the mother was very submissive when the father was violent or aggressive, or perhaps any expression of needs and desires was severely punished. Susan (see the start of this section) presents a typical example of this schema.

(13) Self-sacrifice   Patients with this schema constantly focus on fulfilling the needs of others. This schema differs from "subjugation" however insofar as the main goal is not primarily to adapt and succumb to the ideas of others, but rather to discover the needs of others or situational requirements as quickly as possible and attend to those needs. So it is more active and voluntary. Typically such individuals experience feelings of guilt whenever they focus on their own needs. There are high rates of this schema among people working in fields related to providing care and help. In everyday life it can often be observed that time-consuming and effort-requiring jobs or tasks, which are not associated with much financial gain or respect, are often repeatedly performed by the same people. For example, often a person will be a member of the parent–teacher association (**PTA**) first in their child's kindergarten and then later in their primary and secondary schools—even though they may have decided a hundred times not to agree to be elected again. When the PTA holds elections, people with this schema feel so guilty if they do not accept nominations that before they know it they are again reelected. Seen in this light, this schema can frequently be spotted in a number of healthy individuals, often without much clinical repercussion, provided that the person's support system is healthy enough.

Case example: self-sacrifice

Helen is a 35-year-old nurse who has a very good reputation in the clinic she works at, because she is always willing to do extra tasks, and usually does them extremely well. She is a quality-assurance representative at her clinic, she often provides cover for sick colleagues, and she always does a perfect job. Alongside this involvement at work, she is also very involved in her private life as a member of the PTA and similar groups. Helen first seeks psychotherapeutic treatment for a burn-out syndrome. She seems to be extremely overstressed and overwhelmed by her existing high levels of work and personal engagements. However, when the therapist asks her, "Why on earth would you care about *all* these things?" she looks truly surprised and says, "Well, it's not a big deal, is it?"

(14) Approval-seeking People with this schema find it extremely important to make a good impression on others. They spend a lot of time and energy on improving their looks, their social status, their behavior, and so on. The goal, however, is not to become the best (narcissistic self-aggrandizing), but to receive the approval and appreciation of others. Such individuals often find it hard to tune in to their own needs and desires, as the opinions of others and the need for status and approval are always in the foreground.

Case example: approval-seeking

Sarah, a 32-year-old lawyer, seems to be a very satisfied and happy person. She has many friends and interesting hobbies and is married to a very successful man. She comes to therapy because she begins to perceive herself (and her whole life) as "fake." She reports feelings of being an uninteresting and insufficient person. She describes her active and interesting lifestyle as follows: "I always feel under pressure to be part of all the coolest groups and activities and juggle many balls at once, so that I can at least pretend to be interesting and lovable, although I don't feel that way myself at all."

1.1.5 Schemas in the "hypervigilance and inhibition" domain

People with these schemas avoid the experience as well as the expression of spontaneous emotions and needs. People with the schema "emotional inhibition" devalue inner experiences such as emotions, spontaneous fun, and childlike needs as stupid, unnecessary, or immature. The schema "negativity/pessimism" corresponds with a very negative view of the world; people with this schema are always preoccupied with the negative side of things. Those with the schema "unrelenting standards" constantly feel high pressure to achieve; however, they do not feel satisfied even when they achieve a lot, as their standards are extremely high. The "punitiveness" schema incorporates moral codes and attitudes that are very punitive whenever a mistake is made, regardless of whether the mistake was on purpose or accidental.

These schemas may have been acquired by reinforcement and social modeling, for example when parent figures mocked the spontaneous expression of feelings, thus teaching their children to be ashamed of being emotional. This can also take place indirectly, for example when parents reinforce only achievement and success, and devalue or ignore other important aspects of life such as fun and spontaneity.

Some patients with these schemas report mainly negative experiences regarding intense emotions in their childhood. They started to avoid intense emotional experiences in order to protect themselves against these aversive stimuli. This may relate to the emotions of others rather than their own, for example when members of their family used to argue in a very aggressive and emotional way. Caregivers' moral and achievement standards, and when and how they punished or showed disappointment and anger, contribute to the "unrelenting standards" and "punitiveness" schemas.

(15) Negativity/pessimism   Patients with this schema constantly focus on the negative or problematic side in every situation. They are always anxious that things will not turn out all right, and expect problems everywhere. They often report that this schema has been modeled by parents or other significant figures, who themselves were also extremely pessimistic and always held a very negative view about pretty much everything. This schema can be extremely frustrating for others, because affected individuals slips right back into the negative world view over and over again, no matter how hard others try to help them to see things in a more positive light.

Case example: negativity/pessimism

Eric, a 46-year-old math teacher, has been asked by his wife to see her therapist for couple's therapy. His wife tries to experience more positive activities in her life with the help of her therapist but she keeps mentioning her husband's negative attitude in life, which makes it hard for her to become more positive. Eric confirms that emotionally he is quite a negatively charged person. However, he argues that there are many reasons why it is appropriate to regard the world as a bad place and life itself as a conglomeration of sorrows and problems. He believes that it would be completely unrealistic to have a positive view of life. The therapist asks him about his current job situation. He talks at length about problems with colleagues, bad arrangements within his team, and so on. His wife interrupts him and points out that he is actually working in the exact field he always intended, and that his career has been very successful so far.

(16) Emotional inhibition   Patients with this schema find it unpleasant or ridiculous to show spontaneous feelings. Emotions are regarded as unimportant and unnecessary. Often such individuals recall childhood memories of parent figures mocking them for being enraged or upset. Subsequently the sufferers learned to perceive their emotions as ridiculous and childish, and to devalue them all together. In some cases, people acquired this schema because they felt that the emotions expressed by family members were too difficult to deal with and too intense. Perhaps family members dealt with interfamilial conflicts in an extremely emotional way, or used to complain and talk heatedly about other members of the family with the child. In such cases, the child experienced emotions as threatening and overwhelming. In the treatment of this schema, it is important to establish whether the individual perceives emotions as ridiculous or as threatening.

Case example: emotional inhibition

Peter, a 36-year-old architect, first comes to therapy with a diagnosis of dysthymia. He comes across as an even-tempered man; however, he displays only limited joyful or funny affect. When the therapist tries to joke with him, he hardly even cracks a smile. The therapist senses anger in Peter when he starts talking about his brother, with whom he has a very complicated relationship. However, when the therapist tries to explore these angry feelings more deeply, the patient denies feeling any emotions at all. The therapist inquires about early experiences of emotional expressiveness in his family and Peter reports that his father was emotionally inexpressive and hardly showed any feelings at all. His mother, on the other hand, was an overly emotional person, who often appeared overwhelmed by her feelings. She frequently argued with Peter's brother when both he and Peter were still children. These arguments made her very upset, to the point that she often cried. Peter's job was to soothe her and calm her down, since she used to come to his room drenched in tears after such conflicts. He experienced these situations as emotionally exhausting and since then he has hated intense emotions.

(17) Unrelenting standards People with this schema feel permanently under pressure to achieve and to meet their ambitious goals. They usually strive to be the best at everything they do. They find it very difficult to allow themselves to spend time doing fun and spontaneous activities, and almost impossible to value activities which are not related to achievement. Such individuals are typically perfectionist and rigid. They usually do not question their own high standards, but rather view them as natural, even when those standards are quite clearly not achievable or have negative consequences.

Case example: unrelenting standards

Nick is a 44-year-old physician who seeks psychotherapy for the treatment of his depressive symptoms. His depressive episode began after he was appointed as a director of a newly founded department; it was his responsibility to develop the department and his goal to make it successful. In the first sessions, the therapist addresses Nick's own expectations and goals. Nick explains that he has to run all scheduled projects by himself and to do everything perfectly, efficiently, and without major delays. On a rather abstract level, he realizes that his expectations are simply not realistic, because the workload is much too high and he is unable to work more than 16 hours a day. However, on a more concrete level, it is impossible for him to compromise and minimize the overly high and frankly unrealistic standards he has set himself. At the beginning of therapy, he finds it unthinkable to reduce even one of his professional goals or projects in order to make his life more bearable.

(18) Punitiveness Patients with this schema are convinced that people deserve punishment when they make mistakes. They are usually merciless and very impatient with both themselves and others. They typically report similar models from their childhood.

Case example: punitiveness

Tom, a 52-year-old, is not motivated to start therapy, but his GP urged him to do so after noticing how much he was complaining about his neighbors. Tom is the caretaker of a large house and is always focusing on the mistakes of others. He constantly complains that his neighbors do not comply with the household rules: they make too much noise and so forth. Tom seems to be very engaged in changing the behavior of his neighbors by arguing with them about the smallest of things. Not surprisingly, all of his relationships with the people in his social surroundings are negative. Tom shares with the GP his memory of his parents—they were also very bitter and they did not teach (or even allow) their son to enjoy life. Not unlike Tom, they were very punitive and accused others a lot.

1.2   The Focus on Needs

The focus on human needs is a central idea in schema therapy. Human needs (and the frustrations resulting from their not being met) are seen as the main factor in explaining the genesis of psychological problems. We assume that maladaptive schemas develop when childhood needs are not met adequately. For example, the schemas social isolation/alienation and abandonment/instability develop when the needs for social contact with peers and for stable relationship-forming, respectively, are not met in childhood. This assumption is supported by the increasing number of studies showing high correlations between traumatic or emotionally stressful childhood experiences and psychological problems later in life.

Apart from being the root of the problems, the focus on needs also plays an important part in subsequent therapy. Maladaptive schemas hinder people from recognizing, experiencing, and fulfilling their own needs. One main goal of schema therapy is to help patients tune in to their own needs and be able to identify them more clearly; the other is to help them meet those needs more adequately and appropriately, and to emotionally process the needs that were not met during childhood—and will never be met, since the patient is now an adult. The analysis of both current and past problematic situations focuses on the questions: Which needs of the patient are currently not fulfilled or have not been fulfilled in a given situation? How can patients improve their ability to fulfill these needs? It is important to note that nobody is able to fulfill all their needs in all situations and without any limits—this would neither be realistic nor functional. Psychologically healthy people are able to find a healthy balance between their own needs and the needs of others, as well as to estimate situational requirements. This includes knowing your own limits, therefore the need for realistic limits has to be fulfilled.

Placing human needs in focus is also an essential idea in other humanistic therapies. Conversely, it is very likely that every therapist refers in some way to a patient's needs. The difference in schema therapy, however, is that the patient's needs are addressed in a very explicit fashion and so an explicit reference to the patient's needs is integrated in all schema-therapy interventions. For example, imagery rescripting exercises (see Section 6.3.2) always follow the needs of the patient figure in the imagined traumatic situation, and chair dialogues (see Section 8.3.1) are used to defend the needs and the rights of the patient.

Young et al. (2003) defined five groups of basic human needs. Each schema domain is thought to be heuristically related to one of these groups (see Table 1.2). Like the list of maladaptive schemas, this list of human needs has been developed in everyday clinical work, and as such it is not derived from experimental research. It can be viewed rather as a clinical

Table 1.2　The relationship between schema domains and basic needs

Schema domain	Related basic needs
Disconnection and rejection	Safe attachment, acceptance, care
Impaired autonomy and achievement	Autonomy, competence, sense of identity
Impaired limits	Realistic limits, self-control
Other-directedness	Free expression of needs and emotions
Hypervigilance and inhibition	Spontaneity, playfulness

taxonomy with large overlaps with other theories of human needs, such as the approaches of Rogers (1961) and Grawe (2006).

As mentioned earlier, dysfunctional schemas develop when childhood needs are not appropriately met. Unlike other models (for example, Grawe, 2006), schema therapy introduces the assumption that there is a need for limits and discipline. If this need is not met, schemas such as lack of self-control/self-discipline and entitlement/grandiosity develop. This has not been empirically tested, but from an educational or parental point of view such a need is easily understood as important. Thus one can see that maladaptive schemas can either develop when needs are frustrated, particularly the needs for interpersonal closeness and safe attachment, or when children are spoiled.

In the course of therapy, the focus on needs is weaved into many interventions. An important part of psychoeducation is the discussion about how unmet needs in the patient's childhood laid the basis for his current problems. Later in life, schemas that are caused by unmet early childhood needs maintain the deprivation of the patient, since they usually prevent the patient from meeting their current needs, too. As a form of structured intervention, homework exercises or behavioral pattern-breaking techniques are prescribed, as they are thought to help the patient find ways of meeting their personal needs appropriately.

Case example: focus on needs in susan

Susan (see Section 1.1) had agreed with her therapist to start setting clearer limits on her ex-boyfriend and to discuss this issue in group therapy. However, she repeatedly failed to raise her hand in the group therapy sessions in order to talk about it. As a consequence, the therapist addressed this issue again in an individual session and highlighted how this avoidant pattern maintained frustrated needs in the patient. "Susan, I can perfectly understand how avoidance became the most important coping strategy during your childhood. When you were a child, the only way to survive was to avoid conflicts and stressful situations in your family. However, if you don't start reducing your avoidance today, I'm afraid that you will never learn to fulfill your very important need for setting your own limits. In the group therapy, you can easily learn how to talk about your own needs and your own concerns. You know the other patients very well and you know that nobody will harm you in the group. Moreover, I will make sure that you will not get harmed again. I am completely convinced that the other group members will understand your problem very well. It might be a very positive experience for you to feel the support of the other patients."

1.3   Schema Coping

One schema can express itself in people with very different behavioral problems. The term "schema coping" describes how people deal with their schemas and how schemas become obvious in their interpersonal patterns. The schema coping concept is closely related to the psychodynamic concept of defense mechanisms. In schema therapy, we heuristically define three different categories of coping style:

Three coping styles

The coping style *surrender* means that a person acts as if the schema were true and surrenders into the subsequent behavior patterns.

When a person uses the coping style of *avoidance*, social situations and/or emotions are put aside by social withdrawal, substance abuse, and other avoidant behaviors.

Overcompensation means behaving in a very dominant and self-confident way, as if the opposite of the schema were true.

1.3.1   Surrender

With a surrendering coping style, a patient experiences schema-associated feelings very intensely and surrenders as it were to the "messages" of the schema, thus accepting them. In a surrendering coping mode, the patient behaves as if the schema was true and there was no other choice but to tolerate bad treatment by others. Typical examples of this coping style are the subjugating patterns of patients with a subjugation schema and the frequent phenomenon whereby patients with severe sexual childhood abuse experiences tend to accept abuse in intimate relationships later in life as well.

Case example: surrender

Susan sometimes receives phone calls from her violent ex-boyfriend and then typically visits him and engages in a sexual activity, although she actually does not desire or wish for it. However, she suffers horribly from the lack of love and attention she believes she receives from everyone. When she engages in a sexual activity with her ex-boyfriend, she feels no arousal; however, she does experience at least a minimal amount of interpersonal warmth and affection. Nobody else is interested in her, anyway . . . Furthermore, she can hardly imagine expressing her own needs towards somebody else. She feels very anxious to do so but she is convinced that nobody would be interested in her needs.

1.3.2   Avoidance

We talk about avoidant schema coping when people avoid activation of the schemas or the emotions associated with them in order to protect themselves. The associated behavior patterns that are typical here are social withdrawal and avoidance or lack of emotional contact with others. In the therapeutic relationship, this coping style is activated when the therapist feels a lack of connection and contact with the patient. Beyond behavioral avoidance in the narrower sense, other behavior patterns can also be regarded as emotional avoidance and are thus considered to be related to this coping style. These include in particular substance abuse to avoid experience of and dealing with emotions. Sometimes patients keep themselves continuously occupied in order to maintain a constant level of stimulation, which helps them to avoid their current feelings. This might take the form of computer games, workaholism, television and the Internet, or overeating. When patients report the use of such activities to reduce feelings of anxiety and so on, we speak about an avoidant schema coping.

Case example: avoidance of a mistrust/abuse schema

Sabina, a 27-year-old borderline patient who was sexually abused as a child, says that she can hardly interact with men at all. Sometimes friends convince her to go to a party or a similar event which provides opportunities for interaction with men. When a man approaches her in such a situation, she feels panic and experiences being driven into a corner. Her initial instinct is to run away. Such emotions are typical for a mistrust/abuse schema. Often she copes with such situations by consuming a lot of alcohol. This mutes her feelings of desperation, although she still does not feel really safe, even when she is drunk. After the alcohol consumption, she is highly stimulated and feels less threatened. When under the influence, she sometimes engages in spontaneous sexual activities with men whom she has only just met. In these sexual contacts, she usually lacks any sort of feeling or emotion. So far she has never had sex in her adult life without having consumed alcohol. Sabina feels very ashamed about the alcohol abuse and the related sexual affairs. However, without alcohol she would hardly be able to relax. Even when she truly intends not to drink anything and stay sober at a party, she tends to consume alcohol after all, due to her unbearable emotions in these situations—if she doesn't simply cancel her attendance at the last minute.

1.3.3   Overcompensation

With the schema coping style of overcompensation, people act as if the opposite of the schema was true. People with a failure scheme, for example, might show off and talk excessively about their achievements. Somebody with a mistrust/abuse schema might behave in an overly self-centered and aggressive manner. Sometimes people with a mistrust/abuse schema who are overcompensating even abuse others in order to avoid abuse or threat against themselves. People who overcompensate for a subjugation schema may insist that others subjugate themselves to them and accept their ideas without discussion. In the therapy situation, overcompensation can be easily identified in the therapeutic relationship when the therapist feels dominated, driven into a corner, or even threatened by a patient. Patients with narcissistic overcompensation, for example, typically devalue their therapist, provoking them by questioning their experience and qualifications, and so on. In contrast, people with an obsessive-controlling overcompensation mode might correct their therapist in a very detailed and rigid way. In both cases, the therapist feels controlled and devalued.

Case example: overcompensation

Nicole, a 25-year-old patient with borderline and antisocial personality disorder, experienced horrible sexual and physical violence during her childhood. From the age of 15, she took different illegal drugs, worked as a prostitute, and even became a perpetrator in violent offenses. In the therapeutic relationship, Nicole is mostly enraged and angry, behaving aggressively and attacking the therapist verbally. The therapist validates and stops Nicole's aggressive mode and starts exploring the feelings behind her wall of aggression. Nicole then starts talking about her feelings of being threatened by others and about her lack of trust. She believes that she will not be supported by others, even if she openly displays a need for it. Since she has never felt supported by anybody, she is not able to feel supported by her therapists and other medical staff either, although she is cognitively aware that these people are here to help her.

Unlike the actual schemas, schema coping can be detected and identified quite easily. Patients who come across as submissive and dependent, without focusing on their own needs, probably surrenders a lot when they feel the schema-associated emotions very strongly. Patients in whom the therapist senses a lack of any emotions and/or with whom they fail to establish an interpersonal rapport are probably in an avoidant coping mode. Overcompensation can be identified when the therapist (or other people of significance in the patient's life) feels dominated or threatened.

1.4   The Schema Mode Model

One particular schema can be connected to a range of different behavioral and experiential patterns, as has already been partly described in Section 1.3. For example, a patient with a strong failure schema may sometimes feel sad, desperate, and helpless due to the smallest mistake he makes. On the other hand, however, he may at other times be in an overcompensation mode, trying to demonstrate his own achievements in a potentially exaggerated manner and denying any mistakes. Further, such a patient may sometimes also avoid situations related to achievement altogether in order to avoid the possibility of failure and its associated feelings.

Patients with personality disorders typically show specific schema-related behavioral patterns which interact negatively with therapy progress (just as they interact negatively with other life domains). A good example is the high social avoidance levels in patients with avoidant personality traits. Such patients usually only attend a few sessions with the therapist, maintaining a very limited interpersonal contact, since their avoidant coping style is very strong and is continuously activated in the therapy session.

In a similar way, patients with narcissistic overcompensation may constantly dominate others, both in the therapy session and in other life situations. In such cases, therapists have to take an active stand and play their role in therapy. However, in other patients, mainly patients with BPD, the situation is different—they do not show one enduring coping mode, but instead frequently change between different schema-associated states. Again, frequent changes of the emotional state may cause problems in therapy, because these changes are associated with changes in the patient's opinions and plans, as well as in their subsequent modes. While they may be very optimistic about changing a given problem behavior in one moment, they may feel absolutely incapable of doing so the next.

Case example: persistence of one coping state

Phillip, a 45-year-old computer programmer with narcissistic features, seeks psychotherapeutic treatment to reduce his social anxiety. He reports being very afraid of people. He actually hates interpersonal contact, since he continuously feels extremely insecure and devalued by others. The background to these feelings is quite unsurprising, as it stems from childhood trauma: when he was a child, he suffered from severe neurodermitis and was therefore bullied for several years by his classmates. He developed severe feelings of shame and still feels very easily ashamed and devalued today, even though the dermatitis remitted long ago.

Although Phillip talks about his anxiety, he comes across as a very dominant person. It can thus be deduced that he is in an overcompensating state. He speaks constantly, to the point that the therapist is hardly able to interrupt him. He talks about his prior treatments and therapies in a professional manner, as if he was discussing another patient and the therapist was a colleague. When the therapist makes a comment, he immediately interrupts and corrects her. He seems out of touch with himself, his social anxiety, and his therapist. After half an hour, the therapist feels dominated and frustrated. It seems to be impossible to talk with this patient in a normal way, so long as the overcompensating pattern is present. Although Phillip reports a severe defectiveness/shame schema, the therapist cannot perceive it in his behavior, nor sense such feelings in him.

In such cases it is an important principle in schema therapy to confront the patient empathically with his overcompensation very soon, and to work with this pattern to begin with.

Case example: frequent schema mode changes

Betty, a 39-year-old patient with BPD, has been in treatment for 15 months so far and has managed to build up a very close therapeutic relationship with her therapist. Today the therapist is a bit late for the session, and the patient is waiting in front of the therapist's office in a room without any chairs. When entering the room, the therapist notices some anger in Betty. The therapist addresses this anger, and Betty says, "It's all the same to you whether there's a chair in front of your ugly room or not, because *you* never need it!" When the therapist directly addresses her anger, Betty doesn't admit to it and calls herself "ungrateful," because she knows that the therapist is very engaged and she thinks that it's horrible to treat her in an ungrateful way and believes that she should not be angry at her. The therapist, however, disagrees, and validates Betty's right to become angry when her therapist does not arrive on time. Betty would not be an evil person for getting angry at her therapist. Betty, who feels quite safe in the therapeutic

> relationship already, starts crying and says that she felt very lonely
> when she had to wait on her own in the unfurnished room.

The *schema mode concept* was developed to explain and describe such phenomena. A "schema mode" is defined as a current emotional state which is associated with a given schema. Schema modes can either change frequently or be very persistent. In patients with many different schemas and intense schema modes, it is often much easier to address these modes than to refer to the schemas behind them. Schema modes are divided into modes associated with mostly negative emotions and modes used to cope with these emotions.

1.4.1   Child modes

Child modes are associated with intense negative emotions such as rage, sadness, and abandonment. They resemble the concept of the "inner child," which is used in many therapies (such as transactional analysis). A patient with a mistrust/abuse schema, for example, may feel threatened and at the mercy of others when they are in the abused child mode.

1.4.2   Dysfunctional parent modes

The other category of highly emotional modes is the so-called dysfunctional parent modes. Conceptually, these modes overlap with the notion of (perpetrator) introjects in psychodynamic theory. In schema therapy, they are viewed as internalizations of dysfunctional parental responses to the child. In dysfunctional parent modes, people keep putting pressure on themselves or hate themselves. Patients with a mistrust/abuse schema, for example, davalue and hate themselves when they are in the punitive parent mode.

1.4.3   Dysfunctional coping modes

Coping modes are related to avoidant, surrendering, or overcompensating schema coping. In avoidant coping modes, people avoid emotions and other inner experiences, or avoid social contact altogether. In overcompensating coping modes, people stimulate or aggrandize themselves in order to experience the opposite of the actual schema-associated emotions. Phillip shows a strong overcompensating mode, for example, while Betty switches between different modes.

1.4.4 Healthy modes

Healthy modes are the modes of the healthy adult and the the happy child. In the healthy adult mode, patients are able to view their life and their self in a realistic way. They are able to fulfill their obligations, but at the same time can care for their own needs and well-being. This mode has conceptual overlap with the psychodynamic concept of "healthy ego functioning." The mode of the happy child is particularly related to fun, joy, and play.

> Schemas are conceptually close to *traits*, while schema modes depict the schema-associated *states*. Schema modes are divided into the categories of
>
> 1. child modes,
>
> 2. dysfunctional parent modes,
>
> 3. dysfunctional coping modes and
>
> 4. the healthy modes of the healthy adult and the happy child.

Modes can be much more easily recognized and addressed than can schemas. Therefore, they are central to the treatment of difficult patients. In schema therapy using the schema mode concept, all therapeutic techniques are always adapted to the current emotional mode of the patient. It makes little sense to work on a mode that is not sufficiently activated, since new information will not affect it. Working on the current mode helps the patient to recognize and change both the schema mode and the actual schemas.

Case example: Phillip—confronting the overcompensation mode

The therapist first observes Phillip's overcompensatory mode for about half an hour and then directly addresses it: "Phillip, I understand that you suffer a lot from your social anxiety. However, interestingly, I feel that right now, in our session, these fears don't seem to be present at all. Even when we directly address them, you seem to come across as very distant and dominant. This is in quite a contrast to the anxieties you report. I guess that you are exhibiting some kind of overcompensation. Do you happen to be familiar with the term 'overcompensation'? When you overcompensate, you behave as if the opposite of your problems were true. Over-compensation is meant to show others that you are cool, in control of the situation, and not anxious at all. What do you think about this possibility?"

Case example: Betty—different reactions to different modes

In the situation with Betty, the therapist focuses on validating the anger of the patient. Since the therapist knows Betty quite well already, she is aware of Betty's inability to allow herself to be angry with other people (demanding, guilt-inducing, and punitive parent mode). Therefore, the therapist tries to stop the punitive parent mode: "Betty, you do absolutely have the right to become angry when you have to wait unexpectedly in a dark corridor without any chairs! Your punitive parent mode is incorrect when telling you that you must not be angry with me!" Thus the patient learns to limit this mode herself in other domains of her life by internalizing the model of the therapist. Finally, during the course of the session, the therapist mainly focuses on feelings of sadness, which are related to the mode of the vulnerable child. A central idea of the schema-therapy model states that patients have to learn to accept emotional support (and learn to form safe attachments) in order to heal their schemas. On the level of therapeutic techniques, an imagery exercise focusing on the aban-donment feeling would be suitable. Alternatively, a chair dialogue focusing on expressing anger and limiting the punitive parent mode could also be suitable here.

The mode model offers a direct link to the current problems of the patient and to their interaction within the therapy session. It links different modes with problems and symptoms of the patient. In the following chapters, we will explain how patients' problems can be conceptualized within a mode case concept, and which intervention strategies are appropriate for which modes.

1.5   FAQ

(1) Why does schema therapy distinguish exactly 18 schemas? Couldn't there be 15 or 20?

The number and structure of the schemas is heuristic and has been derived from clinical observation. We actually do not have clear empirical support for the presence of exactly 18 schemas. Some authors and researchers did not find one or two of the 18 schemas, while others added one or two more. Taken as a whole, psychometric research in schema questionnaires shows an acceptable fit between the factor structure and the 18-mode concept (Oei & Baranoff, 2007). However, this cannot be found in all translations of the questionnaire. Thus it is possible that other factor structures could have a better empirical fit.

(2) What is the difference between schemas and basic assumptions?

The schema concept is broader than the concept of basic assumptions. While basic assumptions include primarily (conscious) cognitive aspects, schemas also include emotional, interpersonal, and other behavioral facets, as well as unconscious or implicit information.

(3) There seem to be hierarchical relations between different schemas. For example, there is a schema called "subjugation," but subjugation is also part of submissive schema coping. How do these different facets relate to each other?

The schema concept implies that all schemas exist more or less at the same level. However, some schemas seem to be more "primary" in nature, mainly those from the domain disconnection and rejection. Others, such as those in the domain other-directedness, are typically more "secondary" coping patterns. These relations have not been explicitly addressed yet. However, in the mode model, parent and child modes can be regarded as primary modes, while coping modes are secondary patterns used to cope with the emotional pain connected with the parent and child modes. Thus the relationships between different schema modes are more clearly defined than the relations between different schemas.

(4) What's the exact difference between schemas and modes? Punishment can be a schema, but there is also a punitive parent mode. Is the differentiation necessary?

In some cases the two concepts of schemas and schema modes cannot be very easily separated. The main difference is that the mode model is always focused on different schema states (resembling the ego-state concept); these can be either intense emotional states associated with a schema or schema coping patterns, which are less emotional in nature. This differentiation is less important in the schema model, since schemas describe broad traits rather than particular states.

(5) What about positive schemas? Do they also exist?

The schema concept was first created in experimental psychology in order to describe information processing in psychologically healthy individuals. All people develop schemas during their childhood: representations of the world, the self, other people, social relationships, and so on. When children are raised by caring parents, they have a high probability of developing a self-schema of themselves as worthy, lovable persons and schemas of others as basically friendly and reliable (within realistic limits).

However, the concepts of schema therapy focus mainly on negative or dysfunctional schemas and modes, although in the mode concept the healthy modes of the healthy adult and the happy child are defined too—though they are less differentiated than all the negative and dysfunctional schemas and modes. However it is important to note that the mode concept can be integrated with many other approaches. Therapists may include positive schemas or modes depending on their preferred clinical approach. Within the schema-therapy approach as presented here, work on defining and testing positive schemas has just begun (Lockwood & Perris, private correspondence).

2

The Mode Concept

In their first version of the schema mode model, Young et al. (2003) defined 10 different schema modes. Further schema modes were established and described with the development and amplification of the mode approach by the groups of Arnoud Arntz and David Bernstein (at Maastricht University in The Netherlands). They broadened the mode concept to cover other frequent personality disorder diagnoses. Most of the currently identified schema modes can be assessed via self-report with the Schema Mode Inventory (**SMI**: Lobbestael et al., 2010). However, much like the original schema model, the schema mode model can be regarded as a heuristic approach, being open for further development and extension. In this chapter we present 18 schema modes (overview in Table 2.1; detailed description in Table 2.2). Of these, 14 are assessed using the SMI (Lobbestael et al., 2010), while the rest are described by Bernstein et al. (2007). In day-to-day clinical work, there are also variations in the schema modes, as well as combinations of different modes.

2.1 Overview of Schema Modes

We generally define three different types of dysfunctional schema mode (overview in Table 2.1): dysfunctional child modes, dysfunctional parent modes, and coping modes; the latter are divided into modes related to the coping styles of surrender, avoidance, and overcompensation. The modes of the happy child and the healthy adult are healthy, functional aspects of

Schema Therapy in Practice: An Introductory Guide to the Schema Mode Approach,
First Edition. Arnoud Arntz and Gitta Jacob.
© 2013 John Wiley & Sons, Ltd. Published 2013 by John Wiley & Sons, Ltd.

Table 2.1   Mode categories—overview

Dysfunctional child modes
Lonely, abandoned/abused, humiliated/inferior, dependent child modes
Angry, obstinate, enraged, impulsive, undisciplined child modes
Dysfunctional parent modes
Punitive parent mode
Demanding parent mode
Dysfunctional coping modes

Surrender	Compliant surrender mode
Avoidance	Detached protector mode
	Avoidant protector mode
	Angry protector mode
	Detached self-soothing mode
Overcompensation	Self-aggrandizer mode
	Attention-seeking mode
	Perfectionistic overcontroller mode
	Paranoid overcontroller mode
	Bully and attack mode
	Conning and manipulative mode
	Predator mode

Functional, healthy modes
Happy child mode
Healthy adult mode

the patient. To diagnose and understand a patient's current mode, it is usually helpful to understand the general type of a mode first, and then to explore its more specific aspects. In Table 2.2, the different modes are described in more detail.

Table 2.2   Schema modes

	Dysfunctional child modes
Vulnerability	*Lonely child*
	Feels like a lonely child. Due to the fact that the most important emotional needs of the child have generally not been met, the patient usually feels emotionally empty, alone, socially unaccepted, undeserving of love, unloved, and unlovable.

Abandoned and abused child

Feels the enormous emotional pain and fear of abandonment and/or abuse. Has the affect of a lost child: sad, frightened, vulnerable, defenseless, hopeless, needy, victimized, worthless, and lost. Patients appear fragile and childlike. They feel helpless and utterly alone, and are obsessed with finding a parent figure that will take care of them.

Humiliated/inferior child

A subform of the abandoned and abused child mode: experiences less abandonment feelings, but instead feels humiliation and inferiority related to childhood experiences within and outside the family.

Dependent child

Feels incapable and overwhelmed by adult responsibilities. Shows strong regressive tendencies and wants to be taken care of. Related to a lack of development of autonomy and self-reliance, often caused by authoritarian upbringing.

Anger   *Angry child*

Feels intensely angry, enraged, infuriated, frustrated, or impatient, because the core emotional (or physical) needs of the vulnerable child are not being met. Rebels against maltreatment and vents suppressed anger in inappropriate ways. May make demands that seem entitled or spoiled and which alienate others.

Obstinate child

A subform of the angry child: feels angry, but doesn't display anger openly, instead passively resisting unreasonable requests or violation of autonomy. Others may experience the patient as stubborn or pigheaded.

Enraged child

Experiences intense feelings of rage that result in uncontrolled aggression, such as hurting people or damaging objects. The displayed aggression is out of control, and aims to destroy or exterminate the aggressor, sometimes literally. The patient may display the affect of an enraged or uncontrollable child, acting out or screaming at an (alleged) perpetrator.

Lack of discipline   *Impulsive child*

Act on desires or impulses in a selfish or uncontrolled manner to get their own way, without regard to possible consequences for the self or others. Often has difficulty delaying short-time gratification and may appear "spoiled." May be driven by protest against lack of need gratification.

Undisciplined child

Cannot force themselves to finish routine or boring tasks, becoming frustrated quickly and soon giving up.

Dysfunctional parent modes

Punishment   *Punitive parent*

This is the internalizing voice of the parent or other upbringers, criticizing and punishing patients, who become angry with themselves and feel that they deserve punishment for feeling and/or displaying normal needs which were punished when expressed in childhood. The tone of this mode is harsh, critical, and unforgiving. Signs and symptoms include self-loathing, self-criticism, self-denial, self-injury, suicidal fantasies, and self-destructive behavior.

Criticism   *Demanding parent*

Continually pushes and pressures the child to meet excessively high standards. Feels that the only acceptable way to be is to be perfect and an overachiever, to keep everything in order, to strive for high status, to be humble, to put other's needs before one's own, or to be efficient or avoid wasting time. The person feels that it is wrong to express feelings or to be spontaneous.

Dysfunctional coping modes

Surrender   *Compliant surrender*

Acts in a passive, subservient, submissive, reassurance-seeking, or self-deprecating way towards others out of fear of conflict or rejection. Passively accepts abuse, or simply does not take steps to get healthy needs met. Selects partners or engages in other behavior that directly maintains the self-defeating schema-driven pattern.

Avoidance   *Detached protector*

Withdraws psychologically from the pain of the schemas by means of emotional detachment. The patient shuts off all emotions, disconnects from others and rejects their help, and functions in an almost robotic manner. Signs and symptoms include depersonalization, emptiness, boredom, substance abuse, bingeing, self-injury, psychosomatic complaints, and "blankness."

Avoidant protector
In this mode, behavioral avoidance is in the foreground.
Avoids social situations, particularly of a challenging
nature, and conflicts. May avoid emotions in general,
intense sensations, or in any way arousing activities
altogether.

Angry protector
Use a "wall of anger" to protect themselves from others
who are perceived as threatening and to keep others at a
safe distance through displays of irritation or anger. Some
people with this mode mainly vocalize and display
complaints in order to put a distance between themselves
and others.

Detached self-soother
Shut off their emotions by engaging in activities that will
somehow soothe, stimulate, or distract them from feeling
altogether. These behaviors are usually undertaken in an
addictive or compulsive way, and can include workaholism,
gambling, dangerous sports, promiscuous sex, or drug
abuse. Another group of patients compulsively engages in
solitary interests that are more self-soothing than self-
stimulating, such as playing computer games, overeating,
watching television, or fantasizing.

Overcompensation   *Self-aggrandizer*
Behave in a competitive, grandiose, denigrating, abusive, or
status-seeking way in order to get and maintain whatever
they want. Almost completely self-absorbed, and show little
empathy for the needs or feelings of others. Demonstrate
superiority and expects to be treated as special. Do not
believe they should have to follow the rules that apply to
everyone else. Crave admiration and frequently brag or
behave in a self-aggrandizing manner in order to inflate
their sense of self.

Attention-seeker
Try to get other people's attention and approval by
extravagant, inappropriate, and exaggerated behavior.
Usually compensate for underlying loneliness or lack of
recognition.

Overcontroller
Attempt to protect themselves from a perceived or real
threat by focusing attention, ruminating, and exercising
extreme control. Two subforms can be distinguished:

Perfectionistic overcontroller
Focus on perfectionism to attain control and prevent misfortune and criticism.
Paranoid overcontroller
Focus on vigilance, scanning other people for signs of malevolence, and controls others' behavior out of suspicion.
Bully and attack
Use threads, aggression, and intimidation to get something they want, or to protect themselves from perceived or real harm.
Conning and manipulative
Con, lie, or manipulate in a manner designed to achieve a specific goal, which involves either victimizing others or escaping punishment. This mode is often seen in criminal offenders, but is also seen in some narcissistic individuals, who use deceit and manipulation to get what they want.
Predator
Focus on eliminating a threat, rival, obstacle, or enemy in a cold, ruthless, and calculating manner. In contrast to the bully and attack mode, which involves "hot" aggression, the predator mode involves cold, ruthless aggression. This mode is almost exclusively seen in individuals who are psychopathic.
Functional, healthy modes
Happy child
Feel at peace because core emotional needs are currently met. Feel loved, contented, connected, satisfied, fulfilled, protected, praised, worthwhile, nurtured, guided, understood, validated, self-confident, competent, appropriately autonomous or self-reliant, safe, resilient, strong, in control, adaptable, optimistic, and spontaneous.
Healthy adult
This mode performs appropriate adult functions such as working, parenting, and taking responsibility. Pursues pleasurable adult activities such as sex, intellectual, esthetical, and cultural interests, health maintenance, and athletic activities.

2.1.1 *Dysfunctional child modes*

Child modes are present when a patient experiences intense, negative, stressful, or overwhelming feelings which are inadequate to the current situation. These feelings may constitute anxiety, desperation, hopelessness, loneliness, abandonment, or a deep sense of threat. However, "hot" feelings such as anger or rage can also be part of child modes. When patients are asked how old they feel when they are in such states, they typically report feeling "like a child." Some patients may have a rather clear sense of their "felt age," while others may not. Typical answers are "very young, like a baby," "kindergarten age," or sometimes even "early teens" (12 or 13 years old).

Child modes are further categorized into the vulnerable child modes on the one hand, which are characterized by feeling sadness, desperation, and abandonment, and the enraged or impulsive child modes on the other, defined by emotions such as rage, anger, lack of discipline, and obstinacy. Every mode can be named using the main affect related to it, such as "Lonely Lara," "Desperate, Abused Maria," or "Pigheaded Tom."

> To find out whether patients are currently in a child mode, ask them how old they feel. In a child mode, the perceived age of the individual is significantly decreased.

2.1.2 *Dysfunctional parent modes*

Like child modes, dysfunctional parent modes are also concerned with negative feelings. However, in contrast with the child modes, parent modes are characterized by high pressure and self-hate or self-reproach. Whereas child modes are related to primary needs and emotions, these modes are secondary. Schema therapy assumes they are internalizations of parental moral attitudes and behaviors. When in dysfunctional parent modes, patients put extreme and exaggerated pressure on themselves. Dysfunctional parent modes constitute a dysfunctional conse-quence (= superego), with too-punitive moral values represented by the punitive parent mode, and too-high ideals represented by the demand-ing parent. When cognitions or emotions related to the self are largely characterized by guilt, self-hate and self-devaluation, this is indicative of a *punitive* parent mode. Patients with strong punitive parent modes may have ideas such as "I am bad," "I am a horrible person," "I am a monster," and "I am rubbish."

Demanding parent modes, however, are instead characterized by having high requirements and putting high pressure on oneself—however, such modes do not necessarily consist of profound self-hate. Patients with a demanding parent mode may have ideas such as, "Unless I successfully finish all my tasks, I do not deserve a break," "If I do not manage to get this job done as expected, I will surely lose my job," or "I should get the highest grade, otherwise it is a failure." Note that the demands of a demanding parent mode can relate to different aspects of achievement or behavior. It is important to understand which domain of life the demands of the demanding parent mode are related to. Sometimes demands focus mainly on the field of (professional) achievement, but they may also focus on the patient's behavior in relationships with other people.

Demanding parent modes with a focus on achievement   Patients with this type of demanding parent mode mainly experience pressure and feelings of failure when they do not manage to meet their own expectations regarding professional or educational achievements. Their aims are to do everything in the correct and perfect way and to be better than others. To them, high achievement is a number-one priority. In terms of their background, such patients often report having been surrounded by overdemanding parent figures, such as parents who themselves were very much oriented towards achievement, strict teachers, or overambitious trainers. In some cases, the parents were not necessarily very demanding towards the child, but rather indirectly influenced the child by modeling extreme striving for achievement in their own behavior. Such parents typically had very high standards for themselves.

Punitive (guilt-inducing) parent modes with a focus on emotions and social behavior   In this type of punitive parent mode, demands relate mainly to the behavior of the patient in interpersonal relationships and situations. Typically such patients are convinced that they have to make self-sacrifices for the sake of others, and that they always have to care for the well-being and the needs of others. They feel like they are not allowed to fulfill their own needs if this will in any way compromise the interests of others. When a patient with this kind of punitive parent mode puts their own needs above the needs of others or sets limits to the demands of another person, they typically experience feelings of being very egoistical and of guilt. With respect to the familial background, such patients often recollect their mothers (or other close people) being and looking visibly upset when they failed to behave in a certain way. Often these mothers were depressive or in some other way chronically ill and the child was put in the position of the mother's caretaker. The concept of *parentification* is often related to these patterns—patients felt responsible for the well-being of their parents as a child, or even had to be emotional "substitutes" for the mother's partner, who did not care or was absent. Patients with this type of punitive parent mode often say things like, "It's impossible for me to tell my partner that I do not want to do something, because it will make him unhappy," or "It is extremely important to me that everybody around me feels good." It was the often nonverbal response of the parent that induced a feeling of guilt in the child.

Individuals with jobs in the social-work field, such as nurses, therapists, and social workers, often have this kind of guilt-inducing parent mode. To some extent, this mode is functional and may even be a prerequisite for these jobs, because it leads to high professional engagement and in the best case to very effective help for other people. However, it becomes dysfunctional when people are overinvolved or reach burn-out. Similarly, sometimes people with this mode do not dare to confront clients with important but unpleasant issues, because they do not want to hurt them; or they take over a high level of responsibility for their clients, instead of helping their clients to become more responsible for themselves. Altogether, this mode becomes dysfunctional when the person is not able to set adequate limits on others or becomes overstressed.

To identify the background of a parent mode, it is often helpful to ask the patient whose voice they feel they are hearing and with whose voice they are speaking themselves. Frequently patients spontaneously say that they recognize the voice as that of their mother, father, grandmother, judo trainer, classmate, pastor, and so on.

Dysfunctional parent modes are characterized by feelings of self-hate, guilt, or being a failure, as well as by administration of exaggerated pressure on oneself. The demanding parent mode can be related primarily to achievement; the punitive parent mode to moral values, often related to relationships. To find out the familial background of this mode, you may ask the patient whose voice they are using and hearing.

2.1.3   Dysfunctional coping modes

Unlike dysfunctional parent and child modes, coping modes are usually not characterized by intense emotions. The concept of coping modes is used to describe states in which patients overcompensate for, avoid, or surrender to the emotions connected to parent and child modes. These modes can be identified by the related affect, which is typically less negative and less intense than in other modes. In the short term, from a moment-to-moment perspective, patients feel a sense of relief from their coping modes, because they are detached from negative feelings or stimulated by thrilling or calming activities. However, in the long term, coping modes create problems and stress too, due to their negative effect on the self and others. In the compliant surrender coping mode, patients may feel the emotions and demands connected to the parent and child modes more strongly than in the other coping mode types, since they do not avoid or overcompensate for them. When patients in a coping mode are asked how old they feel, they typically do not report child ages, but rather their real age. Nevertheless, we view coping modes as survival strategies developed in childhood to deal with difficult (overwhelming) situations. As such, they were at that time useful.

> In a coping mode, patients do not suffer as much emotionally as in parent or child modes. However, in the long term the coping mode becomes problematic anyway. The "felt age" in a coping mode is usually the actual age of the patient.

Surrendering coping mode   In the compliant surrender coping mode, the patient completely subjugates themselves to the needs and wishes of others. This includes accepting abuse or maltreatment from other people and making self-sacrifices for the needs of others. Patients may accept the tasks of others, and find it impossible to set limits on others' demands. In this mode, people may also show dependent behavioral patterns.

Case example: compliant surrender mode

Evelyn is a 52-year-old secretary with a diagnosis of OCD and dependent personality traits, who is currently enrolled in inpatient treatment for exposure of her OCD. In terms of her current relationship, she reports aggression and overstepping of limits on the part of her current partner. She accepts being treated like this as she is afraid of him. She always tries to behave in a way which pleases her partner (dressing as he likes, fitting her plans with his schedule, doing everything he suggests, etc.). Her therapist questions this surrendering pattern, but Evelyn insists that she does not have any other choice. Her OCD symptoms often put a spoke in the surrendering wheel—due to OCD, she is sometimes not able to have her partner stay for the night, to leave the house to meet him, and so on. Her surrendering pattern is conceptualized as compliant surrender mode, while the OCD symptoms have the effect of setting some limits.

Avoidant coping modes   The main function of avoidant coping modes is, as the name suggests, an avoidance of emotions related to either dysfunctional schemas or dysfunctional parent and child modes. On the one hand, emotions or emotional triggers can generally be avoided in a narrower sense, via typical means such as social withdrawal, alcohol or other substance use in social situations, lack of interpersonal contact in the therapy situation, and so on (avoidant or detached protector mode). Some patients soothe themselves excessively in order to avoid emotions, either with calming activities such as (binge) eating, watching TV, or fantasizing (detached self-soother mode), or with more stimulating activities such as thrilling computer games, stimulating drug use, and so on (self-stimulating mode). On the other hand, patients may be more active, but act in certain ways so as to avoid "real" interpersonal contact in social situations. This may be the case when a patient engages in excessive complaining in therapy but does not seem to be strongly impaired in other situations. Other patients seem to be angry in such a way that the anger mainly puts distance between the therapist and themselves but is not related to "real" emotions (angry protector mode).

Case example: detached protector mode

Jane, a 28-year-old patient, seeks treatment for her BPD. In the first session, she comes across as very friendly and agreeable. She smiles a lot and is able to provide reports about herself and her biography. She seems to be well-educated and polite, she takes good care of herself, and at first one would never assume that she suffered from a serious psychological disorder. However, during the course of the therapy it becomes clear how much Jane is emotionally triggered even by very small things. When she makes a very little mistake at work, at a sheltered workshop, she experiences extreme tension, anxiety, and rage, which she can regulate only by social withdrawal and through alcohol and medication abuse. Her competent facade, which is conceptualized as a detached protector mode, she labels her "small-talk facade."

Case example: angry protector mode

Caroline is a 48-year-old patient whose biographical background includes a violent father, abusive peers, a number of miscarriages, and the death of her second husband due to cancer. Since she became a widow 2 years ago, she has been asking for treatment in different psychosomatic clinics, mainly complaining about pain problems. During the last 10 years she has seen various physicians from various medical specializations, who have not found any physical reasons for her ever-changing complaints. Several therapists and physicians have tried to suggest a psychosomatic model of her problems to her, but she keeps focusing on her physical pain and reacts quite angrily to these suggestions. She claims that her pain will never change and will remain the same for all of her life. She is angry at all the physicians and therapists who have been unable to find a medical problem.

However, the physiotherapist and the occupational therapist notice her being much more relaxed, and even having fun sometimes, when she does things of positive valence, such as dancing or painting. When her individual therapist addresses this contrast in their session, she starts complaining about her pain again and becomes angry at the therapist, who in her view "suggests that she's not really suffering." The therapist feels pushed away through her anger expression. This strong focus on pain, which turns into anger when being addressed in therapy, is conceptualized as a complaining and angry protector mode.

Overcompensating coping modes   When people are in an overcompensating coping mode, other people feel dominated, attacked, powerless, or in some other way controlled by them. This is typical for narcissistic patterns, where a patient constantly shows off and degrades the therapist by correcting him, questioning his competency, or making suggestions regarding reading material and so on.

Another version of overcompensation is a planned aggressive behavior used to dominate others. In forensic patients, this type of over-compensation is related to delinquency or to aggressive or cunning behaviors intended to cheat or threaten others.

A compliant surrender coping mode is present when patients comply with others' demands and surrenders to others' wishes at the expense of their own needs. These patients disconnect with their own needs.

Avoidant coping is characterized by avoidance in the narrower sense, and includes avoidant behavior patterns and avoidance of emotions and of connection to other people.

Overcompensating coping modes are present when a patient behaves as if the opposite of the vulnerable child mode was true.

2.2   Case Conceptualization with the Mode Model

At the beginning of treatment, a case concept is developed, which contains the problems and symptoms of the patients, their interpersonal patterns, their problematic emotions, and related biographical information.

Case example: Phillip's mode model

The therapist develops a mode model with Phillip (see Section 1.4) during the first phase of treatment (see Figure 2.1). Feelings of anxiety, insecurity, and shame, which are rooted in Phillip's childhood experiences with his classmates, are related to the

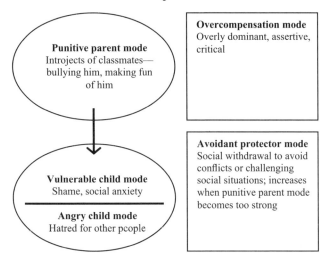

Figure 2.1   Phillip's mode model

vulnerable child mode of "Little Phillip." His hatred for people and social situations is conceptualized as an angry child mode. The former classmates who bullied Phillip and made him feel ashamed are related to the punitive parent mode. Phillip's dominant interaction pattern in the therapy situation (and in other life situations) is characterized as a narcissistic overcompensation mode. Apart from this narcissistic pattern, Phillip's most important coping strategy is avoidance. He has frequently ended interpersonal relationships and friendships and often does not show up for social events, due to anxiety over being criticized or rejected. Meanwhile, he became socially isolated, which in a vicious circle has increased both his social fears and his depressive symptoms. His avoidant behavior is conceptualized as an avoidant/detached protector mode.

Schemas and schema modes can be assessed using self-rating inventories (Bamelis et al., 2011; Lobbestael et al., 2010). However, self-report questionnaires are never a sufficient source of information, since they do not include qualitative information about the particular meaning of a particular mode for the individual patient in question. Moreover, people might not be aware of, or might be unwilling to openly report, mode manifestations. Apart from questionnaire data, we always need information regarding (1) important problems and symptoms of the patient, (2) the patient's biographical information, (3) the patient's interaction patterns, and (4) the patient's expectations from and goals for therapy.

2.2.1 Important problems and symptoms of the patient

First of all, the problems and symptoms which are of highest subjective concern for the patient must be mirrored in the mode model. These might include actual disorder symptoms, relationship problems, general life problems, dysfunctional interaction patterns, and so on. The relationships between different problems and symptoms as reported by the patient are relevant as well.

Intense depressive or anxious feelings are typically part of the vulnerable child mode. When a patient reports numbing anxiety or desperation through the use of alcohol or Internet gambling, we connect the feelings of anxiety and desperation to the vulnerable child mode, and the use of alcohol or Internet gambling to the detached or self-soothing coping mode.

To set up the mode model efficiently in the first phase of therapy, the therapist must ask for the information you need directly: "You just told me that one of your main goals in therapy is to become more self-confident at your job. You often do not manage to show your actual competence, because you avoid challenging situations. Are you aware which feelings are related to this problem? How do you feel when you have an opportunity to show your competence and you don't do it? What do you usually do in such situations instead?"

Some symptoms are typically related to one particular mode. This applies for example to substance abuse, dissociation, and pathological gambling, which are typically related to an avoidant or avoidant/stimulating coping mode. Similarly, intense sadness and/or anxiety is always connected with a vulnerable child mode.

However, sometimes one and the same symptom can be related to different modes in different patients (or even to different modes in the same patient). Many patients with BPD, for example, report self-injuring (cutting) behavior as a means of self-punishment. In such cases, the symptom is related to the punitive parent mode. However, other BPD patients use self-injuring behavior to finish a dissociative state, which is usually part of a detached protector mode; in such cases the symptom of self-injury will serve the function of allowing the patient to escape from the detached protector mode when such a mode becomes too much for the patient. Still other patients report that self-injuring behavior helps them to distance themselves from the negative emotions connected with the parent and child modes. Such patients typically report that they use self-injury when they feel particularly down, because their self-injuring rituals (which may be connected to particular music, candlelight, etc.) help them to stop the unpleasant feelings; in these cases, the self-injuring behavior is actually a part of the detached protector mode.

To make things even more complicated, sometimes the same patient experiences one particular symptom in different situations with different functions. In this case the symptom has to be related to different modes in the patient. For example, a patient may report self-injuring behavior in several of the above-mentioned contexts. Similarly, patients with severe eating disorders and binge attacks sometimes describe such attacks as a means of self-punishment, because they are connected with self-devaluation ("Then I say to myself, fat pig, eat yourself to death") or with pain (when they eat until their stomach hurts). In these cases, binge-eating can be part of the punitive parent mode. However, patients reporting this problem might under other circumstances eat too much because they feel empty and lonely, in order to soothe themselves. In that case, eating or overeating would additionally be a part of the self-soothing coping mode. The symptom is then related to several modes in the mode model. Whenever such a symptom is addressed in therapy, the therapist and patient must first find out to which mode the problem is most closely connected in the acute situation.

> Some symptoms are very typical of a particular mode; for example, dissociation is always related to an avoidant coping mode. However, other symptoms may belong to different modes depending on the individual patient and/or the particular problematic situation; these relationships must be explored and comprehended by the therapist and the patient.

2.2.2   The patient's biographical information

The patient's biographical information is the second important source of information for the individual mode model. On the one hand, the therapist must directly ask patients for connections between their symptoms and their biography. They must ask patients whether current emotions are in their view associated with childhood and youth, whether they experienced models with similar problem behaviors during childhood, and so on. Patients with a strong demanding parent mode, for example, often report very high pressure for achievement from parents or teachers; in some cases, however, parents may only have modeled the mode via their own extreme ambitions, without putting direct pressure on the child. Some patients can spontaneously explain how their self-devaluing schemas have developed through their lives.

On the other hand, therapists must develop their own hypotheses as well regarding the biographical background of schema modes based on the patient's reports, and discuss these hypotheses with the patient. When the patient reports frequent moves between very remote places during their childhood, for example, the repeated experience of new social surroundings was probably a stress factor. This may have laid the ground for a social isolation schema, particularly when the patient felt isolated in the new places. However, some patients and their families may have coped very well with this stressor, in which case no isolation schema will have developed. Thus, alternative hypotheses have to be discussed openly with the patient. Similarly, a patient's report indicating a very close connection with his or her parents (for example, a 30-year-old patient who visits his parents every weekend and has daily phonecalls with his mother) may hint at enmeshment, a dependent child mode, or a dysfunctional parent mode which questions the autonomy of the patient.

In addition to self-report and open discussion, diagnostic imagery exercises are also conducted to help further understand the biographical origins of current emotional problems and dysfunctional patterns. In these exercises, patients are asked to experience a current problem situation in their imagination, and then associate memories and pictures from earlier phases of their life, most often from their childhood, with it. These exercises often add important information to the case conceptualization.

Case example: use of biographical information— self-report

Catherine, a 23-year-old BPD patient, can hardly eat anything, since food triggers intense disgust, nausea, and self-hatred. When she eats something, she feels like she is a profoundly "bad" person. In her childhood, Catherine says that her foster mother often unjustly accused her of having stolen food, and her foster parents then punished her by excluding her from family meals and prohibiting her from eating. Self-hatred related to food is therefore connected with the punitive parent mode, which says things like, "You are such a bad person that you don't even deserve to eat."

Case example: use of biographical information— imagery exercise

Maria is a 42-year-old psychologist who is a member of a very strict sect. She became depressive after an elder female friend from the sect broke off their relationship because Maria had criticized the community. Although Maria feels that her critique was absolutely justified, she does feel upset about the situation, saying that "I am not OK the way I am," and she is now afraid of being abandoned. The intensity of this reaction is surprising at first glance, since Maria is very happy with her husband and family and actually does not depend on the relationship with the elder friend. In an imagery exercise, in which current feelings are linked to her childhood, Maria experiences a situation with her mother. Her mother punished little Maria by depriving her of love whenever Maria contradicted or criticized her. These emotions and the connected punitive parent mode have now been triggered again by the reaction of the elder (maternal-figure) friend.

2.2.3 *The patient's interaction patterns*

The third important source of information is the actual behavior of the patient in the social situation of therapy. To deepen their observations, the therapist should also directly discuss the patient's interactions with other people with the patient. When the therapist sees the patient as behaving very submissively in the therapeutic relationship, the therapist should highlight this in the initial sessions, at the same time as the mode model is being set up. "I can see that you are very considerate and polite with me.

Sometimes it even seems to be quite submissive. Do you know what I'm talking about? [If the patient does not immediately understand the therapist, this should be illustrated with an example.] Is it possible that you behave this way in other relationships as well?" The therapist should assume that interpersonal patterns and modes appearing in the therapeutic relationship might be present in other relationships as well.

Case example: using his interaction with the therapist in Phillip's mode model

The therapist observes very dominant and narcissistic behavior patterns in Phillip during the therapy session. Phillip speaks a lot about his feelings of anxiety, helplessness, and helpless anger when he talks about his interactions with other people. The therapist confronts Phillip with her observations and suggests building his behavioral pattern in the therapy sessions into the case concept as an overcompensation mode. During this discussion, Phillip remembers being told he was dominant and narcissistic by other people, but says he never completely understood what they meant. In particular, several of his ex-girlfriends have accused him of being arrogant and overly dominant. The therapist demonstrates Phillip's behaviors to him by showing him a video of one of their therapy sessions. From this observer perspective, Phillip confirms the overcompensating character of his behavior and agrees to include it in the mode model as an overcompensating coping mode.

Case example: using information from the therapeutic relationship in Maria's mode model

Maria is always very friendly and agreeable in the therapeutic relationship. At the beginning of each session, she asks the therapist how she's doing, in such a way as if they were close friends and Maria was more interested in the well-being of the therapist than in her own. The therapist reflects on her impressions with Maria and they discuss whether this overly other-directed interaction is

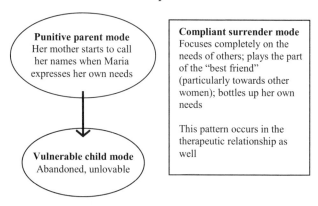

Figure 2.2 Maria's mode model

related to a compliant surrender coping mode. With this mode, the patient relates herself in a self-sacrificing and altruistic way to other women, like she had to relate towards her mother as a child. Maria absolutely agrees with this suggestion.

In this case, it is important to notice that this behavior is strongly reinforced by the social environment, as other people feel good in her presence and like her very much. It is important for Maria to start differentiating between when this behavior pattern is adequate and functional and when it becomes a dysfunctional compliant surrender coping mode, since it obviously puts a block on her ability to care for her own needs. Maria's mode model is depicted in Figure 2.2.

2.2.4 Excursus: differentiating between different modes related to anger

The expression of anger or rage plays an important role in some modes, particularly the angry or enraged child mode, the angry protector mode, and the bully and attack mode. Sometimes it is not easy to label the problematic behavior of a patient clearly as one of these modes, because they may be jointly activated. For example, the bully and attack mode is often triggered when patients are angry because their needs have not been met.

However, there are some basic guidelines on how to differentiate between these modes. The angry child mode is the main candidate for a label when the anger or rage seems to be rather uncontrolled and childish, when it is clearly triggered by a situation which you can understand would make somebody angry and can empathize with (even though you find the level of anger exaggerated), and when the patient reports feeling like a child or an adolescent when the mode is activated. In this mode, the patient protests against their needs not being met by the other person. Patients are angry at the other person, not because they want to create a distance, but because they are fighting for repair of the relationship.

In angry coping modes (angry protector mode, bully and attack mode), on the other hand, the expression of anger usually seems to have more of a coping function than an actual emotional function. Thus, the anger is secondary, and not a primary emotion. Accordingly, therapists do not usually feel any close interpersonal contact with the patient when an angry coping mode is triggered. They usually feel attacked or dominated instead. The patient tries to keep the therapist at a distance. The coping function might be to dominate somebody else or to distract oneself from negative emotions. In some cases, these modes are not clearly triggered by a specific situation but are chronic and do not show the course of an impulsive affect of rage. Typically the patient does not report feeling like a child.

The differentiation between bully and attack and angry protector mode can normally be made through the countertransference experience of the therapist. An angry protector mode is present when the therapist mainly feels that the patient "uses" anger to keep the therapist at a distance, or to keep the patient's own (negative) emotions at a distance. When the mode comes across in a very dominant way—when the therapist feels controlled or threatened—the bully and attack mode is active. Sometimes the angry coping mode of a patient seems to lie in between the angry protector and the bully and attack modes. This should be described accordingly in the mode model. Since the main strategies in treating these two modes (confront, validate, discuss function, set limits) are basically the same, it is better to define the mode as a mix of both than to complicate the patient's mode model by distinguishing modes that always come together.

2.3 Specific Mode Models for Different Personality Disorders

The schema mode model is a general model that can be applied to different disorders or problems. However, in terms of research studies of specific disorders, specific models have been developed for different disorders, particularly for personality disorders (overview in Bamelis et al., 2011; Lobbestael et al., 2007, 2008). These specific mode models depict prototypes of the modes we see in patients with the respective disorders.

Young et al. (2003) defined the first specific mode models for borderline and narcissistic personality disorder. The treatment for BPD based on Young's model has been made into a manual by Arntz & van Genderen (2009). Initial studies investigating the effectiveness of schema therapy in BPD (Farrell et al., 2009; Giesen-Bloo et al., 2006; Nadort et al., 2009) have been conducted using this treatment manual. Since these studies have shown very good effects of schema therapy in BPD, further specific mode models for other personality disorders have also been developed.

All these models are meant to be prototypes. However, an individual case sometimes can't be sufficiently described by a prototypical model. Due to the complexity and high comorbidity in patients with personality disorders, a prototypical mode model often has to be extended in certain individuals. This means that the mode model has to fit with the individual problems and patterns of the respective patient. To achieve this fit, the therapist discusses the mode model with the patient and connects the typical patterns of the individual patient to the different modes of the mode model. Eventually, comorbidity or problems beyond the main personality disorder diagnosis are included via an additional mode, or via linking of specific problems to a given mode.

Each schema therapy based on the mode model starts with the development and formulation of an individual mode model. This model includes the main problems and symptoms of the patient in a systematic and logical manner. It is helpful if both the patient and the therapist agree on the model. If they don't agree, it is agreed that there is a difference of opinions and that later in treatment the model will be discussed again. For example, quite a few patients with BPD don't initially recognize the punitive parent mode, but they usually start to acknowledge it after some months of therapy. Similarly, vulnerable child modes are often hidden from the patient's awareness at the start of therapy in cases with strong overcompensation modes (Bamelis et al., 2011; Young et al., 2003). In this section, the specific mode models that have been developed in our research studies so far are described.

2.3.1   Borderline personality disorder

The following four dysfunctional schema modes are central to the mode model of BPD, which is very thoroughly described in Arntz & van Genderen (2009):

- The *abandoned, abused child mode*, which is characterized by intense feelings of abandonment and threat, typically connected with the fear of being abused and/or abandoned again.
- The *angry impulsive child mode*, which reflects the anger concerning the patient's unfair treatment as a child. Often this mode is accompanied by an undisciplined or impulsive child mode, reflecting the tendency to fulfill needs without control, regardless of consequences.
- The *punitive parent mode*, the main dysfunctional parent mode, which extremely devalues the patient. It captures the typical self-hatred so often found in such patients.
- The *detached protector mode*, the main coping mode, which has the function of protecting the patient from emotions related to the child and parent modes. It is typically related to behavioral problems such as social withdrawal, avoidance, substance abuse, abuse of (sedative) medication, binge-eating sessions, and so on.

Case example: borderline personality disorder

Jane (see Section 2.1.3 and Figure 2.3) typically has her "facade" up when she meets other people. This facade is part of her detached protector mode. The vulnerable child mode ("Little Jane") gives her intense feelings of shame and threat, which are triggered very easily by stressful social situations. In this mode Jane feels unloved, alone, and rejected. However, in many of these situations she also experiences helpless anger, seeing other people as having the power which triggers these negative emotions and makes her feel bad ("Angry Little Jane"). The social situations triggering these modes are usually minor events, such as a colleague saying hello in a tone perceived by Jane as unfriendly or insincere. Jane's punitive parent mode can sound like a number of different people who were problematic in Jane's childhood. Her father was an alcoholic who behaved aggressively and threateningly when drunk. Her

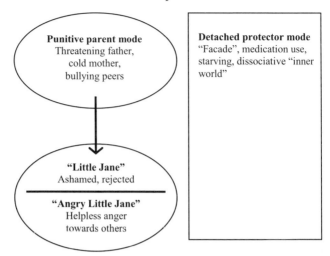

Figure 2.3 Jane's mode model

mother, who was overstressed by the family situation, was cold and critical in her relationship with Little Jane. Moreover, in high school Jane was bullied for being overweight by members of her peer group. All these people formed Jane's punitive parent mode.

The "facade" in social situations is not the only feature of Jane's detached protector mode. She also uses neuroleptic medication to stop herself from having any feelings and to enable herself to "switch off." She starves herself—on the one hand due to her punitive parent mode, which criticizes her weight (anorexic patterns can thus be related to the punitive parent mode), and on the other hand in order to stop having any feelings, since fasting leads to a flattening of emotions. When this function is the main reason for anorexic behavior, fasting can be regarded as part of the detached protector mode as well. Adding to this, Jane withdraws herself in stressful situations and enters a perfect inner world full of fantasies. This daydream-like pattern has a strong dissociative character and is also related to the detached protector mode, because it helps Jane to cope with her emotions.

2.3.2 Narcissistic personality disorder

The main modes of the narcissistic personality disorder are as follows:

- A *lonely vulnerable child* mode, often characterized by feelings of inferiority or humiliation.
- An extremely *demanding parent mode*.
- The *enraged child mode*. When the vulnerable child mode threatens to be activated, patients can get into a narcissistic rage, and may lose control over their aggression.
- The *self-aggrandizer mode*, the most prominent of the coping modes, which contains both idealization of the self and devaluation of others. In this mode, narcissistic patients overcompensate their feelings of failure and inferiority.
- The *detached self-stimulating or self-soothing mode*, in which patients stimulate themselves through gambling, substance use (particularly stimulating substances, such as cocaine), excessive consumption of pornographic products, excessive sexual activities, and so on. Excessive workaholism can be part of this mode, too.

Case example: narcissistic personality disorder

Michael's main complaints in outpatient psychotherapy are his impulsive and addictive behavioral patterns. He spends most of his time playing computer games and using Internet porn sites—behaviors which have already caused him professional and financial problems. He frequently orders prostitutes in a way which has become addictive as well. Michael's career plan is to become a successful music producer; currently, however, he only occasionally helps out in a local party band, with very limited success. He complains about not being adequately appreciated by other people. Others seem unable to recognize his talent and his potential; he does not get the respect and admiration he believes he deserves.

As a child, his parents were very successful company owners. Both parents worked a lot and regarded their only son as their successor and the future boss of their company. However, due to unfortunate circumstances and inheritance disputes, he has not become influential in the company after all. This has made him feel like a failure. Since his parents left the company some years ago, his financial situation had gotten much worse. While his family was rather rich during his childhood, Michael himself lost a lot of money through his addictive behaviors and now has a lot of debts. His family is no longer willing to support him financially and pay his expenses. Michael is very upset about this rejection and repeatedly gets into furious arguments with his family. The therapist asks him about any negative feelings related to his financial situation, but Michael avoids this issue and reacts with irritation to the therapist's questions. When the therapist addresses Michael's professional failure, he reacts with rage and attacks the therapist verbally.

In Michael's mode model (Figure 2.4), addictive behaviors (computer gambling, use of pornography, compulsive ordering of prostitutes) are related to the self-stimulating mode. The narcissistic self-aggrandizer mode is connected both with his unrealistically high expectations regarding the success of his music career and with his devaluation of others for not regarding him as "special." His idea that his family should pay for his addictive and undisciplined behavioral problems is related to the narcissistic self-aggrandizer

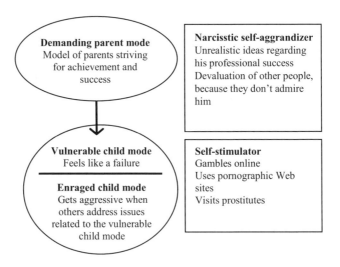

Figure 2.4   Michael's mode model

mode as well. High demands, as modeled by his parents during his childhood, are conceptualized as a demanding parent mode. Although Michael does not currently report intense negative feelings (apart from feelings of failure, which are however at least partly justified), the therapist nevertheless assumes the existence of a vulnerable child mode. If somebody evokes feelings related to failure in him, which he fails to control through his coping modes, instead of the vulnerable child mode, an enraged child mode gets activated and attacks that other person. If Michael were to stop his overcompensatory coping behaviors, and limit the acting-out of his enraged child mode, he would probably get in contact with feelings other than failure, such as shame or abandonment. This will be discussed with Michael in the further course of his therapy.

2.3.3   Histrionic personality disorder

The following modes are typical in people with a histrionic personality disorder:

- A *vulnerable child mode.*
- An *impulsive/undisciplined child mode.*
- The overcompensatory *attention-seeking mode*, which includes typical histrionic behavior patterns such as dramatization and over exaggeration, as well as or overly sexualized behaviors.

Case example: histrionic personality disorder

Elisa, a 46-year-old laboratory assistant, seeks help from the psychotherapist for her interpersonal problems, anxiety, feelings of insecurity, and what she calls "her helper syndrome." Her problem descriptions are kind of vague, and do not make her main problems any clearer. On the one hand, the patient presents herself as extremely impaired. She bursts into tears in the very first sessions, but the related affect seems to be somehow unreal and decreases quickly. On the other hand, she also presents herself as a

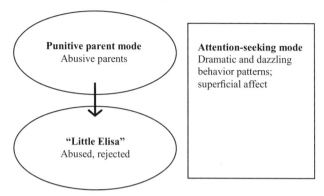

Figure 2.5 Elisa's mode model

very competent person, although she does so in a similarly dramatic and loud manner. She talks almost to the point of being unstoppable about her "helper syndrome," by which she means that "It always ends up being me who does everybody else's jobs." The interpersonal contact with Elisa is characterized by quick changes of the superficial affect, her dramatic but inconsistent problem descriptions, and her generally loud and dominant behavior. With regard to her childhood, she reports severe trauma at the hands of her seemingly sadistic parents; when talking about these experiences, her emotions seem to become a bit more real.

Elisa's mode model is depicted in Figure 2.5. Her traumatic experiences and related anxiety are connected with her vulnerable, abused childhood, even though these affects cannot be clearly experienced within the initial therapy sessions. Her abusive experiences with her parents are related to the punitive parent mode. Her dramatic interpersonal style is connected with the attention-seeking coping mode.

2.3.4   Avoidant personality disorder

The main modes of the avoidant personality disorder are the following:

- A *lonely, vulnerable child mode.*
- A *punitive parent mode*, which particularly induces feelings of guilt.

- An *avoidant protector mode*, which helps patients to distance themselves from inner needs, feelings, and thoughts.
- The *compliant surrender* mode, which relates to the typical submissive behavior patterns of these patients, where they subjugate to the needs and ideas of others.

2.3.5   Dependent personality disorder

People with dependent personality disorder typically show the following modes:

- A strong *abandoned/abused child mode.*
- The *dependent child mode*, which reflects the feeling of being unable to cope with everyday life all by oneself.
- The *punitive parent mode*, which typically induces feelings of guilt when patients put their own needs first, as in people with avoidant personality disorder. But it also gets activated if patients make their own decisions or try to develop autonomy ("You don't know how to do that").
- The *compliant surrender mode*, which is the main coping mode in the dependent personality disorder.

Case example: combined dependent and avoidant personality disorder

Nadine is 21 years old and comes to therapy due to her extreme social anxiety. She feels insecure, inferior, and helpless in nearly all social contexts. She has had to quit professional training and several jobs after only a few months each. Currently she is unemployed and she mainly stays at home. She always tries to sense the needs of others in interpersonal relationships, because subjugating herself to other people seems to be the only way for her to feel accepted and acknowledged. However, in cases of conflicts or problems, for example at work, she feels helplessly overstressed, cannot stand the situation, and usually stays at home in order to avoid further episodes. One important problem is her inability to ask for advice when she feels insecure at work, even though her bosses have always been very friendly to her. She feels like a failure when she does not manage to do everything perfectly all by herself, which is of course impossible.

In therapy, Nadine is very friendly, polite, and attentive. She has a very reliable and considerate boyfriend. She cannot articulate her own needs or desires in her relationship, however. For example, she always tries to find out what her boyfriend wants to do in their free time, without considering her own likes and dislikes. When he asks her for suggestions, she feels insecure and cannot give an answer, although she is aware that other people are often annoyed by her oversubmissiveness.

As a child, her father was hot-tempered and drank too much. Until their divorce when Nadine was 10 years old, her mother always submitted to her father and did not protect Nadine from her father's aggression. After the divorce, her mother became very depressive and hopeless; Nadine was frightened that her mother would not manage to survive this difficult situation, so she always tried to make her feel good in any way she could. Already as a little child, she felt responsible for the well-being of her mother. Whenever Nadine had fun with her friends, knowing that her mother was feeling down made her feel horribly guilty. This parentification and early responsibility for her mother's needs is probably the root of Nadine's current submissive inter-personal pattern and her inability to identify and accept her own needs.

In Nadine's mode model (Figure 2.6), feelings of insecurity, inferiority, and dependency are related to the vulnerable child

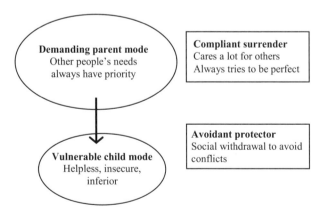

Figure 2.6 Nadine's mode model

mode. The critical parent mode contains introjects of both the punitive aggressive father and the emotionally very demanding mother, whose needs and well-being were always in the foreground. Note that it is not relevant whether the mother actively asked the child to care for her or whether this was mainly an internal drive of Nadine's. With regard to coping modes, the patient's constant efforts to care for the needs of others and her perfectionism are conceptualized as a compliant surrender mode. Avoidant behavior patterns—that is, social withdrawal in stressful situations—are related to an avoidant protector mode.

2.3.6   *Obsessive–compulsive personality disorder*

In obsessive–compulsive personality disorder, the following modes are typical:

- The *lonely child mode*, usually not acknowledged at the beginning of therapy.
- A *demanding* and/or *punitive parent mode.*
- The *perfectionistic overcontroller mode*, which aims to avoid mistakes and accidents, and subsequent feelings of guilt about these mistakes. This is an overcompensatory mode, which may also be related to workaholism.
- The *self-aggrandizer mode*, which is a narcissistic coping mode. This is related to the patient's feeling that their perfectionism makes them morally superior to other people. Others are seen as less reliable and less thorough than themselves.

Case example: obsessive–compulsive personality disorder

Peter, a 40-year-old teacher, suffers from chronic depression. He only ever pursues a few positive activities, although he does have hobbies and friends. He seems to waste his energy on irrelevant things instead. Thus he is often not successful at his daily chores or at finishing tasks for which he has plenty of time. To compensate for this, he excessively (but without any success) alters his to-do lists. Although these to-do lists contain lots of meaningful activities and tasks, he often ends up in front of the TV, drinking half a liter of wine each night. He clearly understands that this behavior is dysfunctional; however, he would not actually like to give up such leisure-time practices.

As a child he grew up in a rather poor family, which was unable to afford "luxuries." Thus he learned to be very cautious and to save up. Today he is still parsimonious, even though he earns enough money and has enough time for pleasurable activities. To compensate for its low material status, his family was very close, perhaps even enmeshed. Accordingly, when he expressed a need for more autonomy during adolescence, his parents were very disappointed ("Are you not happy with us?"). In his adult relationships he experiences problems in articulating his own needs and desires, feeling guilty easily and wondering whether his partner will accept his ideas. He has had several intimate relationships, but so far all his girlfriends have felt him be "too complicated and too mean with money." He is currently single, which probably causes an increase in depressive symptoms, since there is no one to try to get him away from the TV or computer screen in his leisure time.

In Peter's mode model (Figure 2.7), feelings of guilt and isolation are related to the vulnerable child mode. A critical parent mode contains the nonacceptance of his own material desires and need for both attachment and autonomy. His obsession with details and his exaggerated parsimoniousness belong to a perfectionistic overcontroller coping mode. His intense TV and alcohol consumption is conceptualized as a self-stimulation mode.

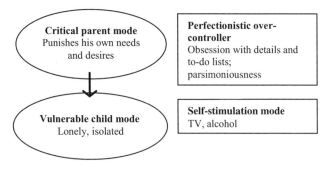

Figure 2.7   Peter's mode model

2.3.7   *Paranoid personality disorder*

In people with a paranoid personality disorder, the following modes are typical:

- An *abandoned/abused vulnerable child mode*, usually not acknowledged at the beginning of therapy.
- An *enraged child mode*.
- A *punitive parent mode*.
- The *paranoid overcontroller mode*, which mirrors paranoid experiences and behaviors.
- An additional *avoidant protector coping mode*, which reflects the social avoidance and alcohol problems typical of people with this personality disorder.

Case example: paranoid personality disorder

Eric, a 54-year-old house painter, is urged by his wife to consult his GP about his alcohol consumption. He comes across as disapproving and constantly seems to be at least latently aggressive. His wife reports frequent conflicts with neighbors, especially when Eric has been drinking. Meanwhile, he is involved in several lawsuits, which he started over minor conflicts with several neighbors. He is convinced that everybody thinks badly of him and tries to harm him, even if the person in question behaves completely neutrally.

Eric grew up in a very violent family. His father, an alcoholic, abused him verbally and physically, until he left the family when Eric was 5 years old. Eric lived in several orphanages and foster homes during his childhood and youth, where he experienced even more abuse. Alcohol problems and conflicts with neutrally natured people are a long-standing problem in his life. He has no friends because he mistrusts everybody. His mistrust is linked with the aggression sensed by the GP.

With regard to his mode model (Figure 2.8), his experiences of childhood abuse are reflected by a strong punitive parent mode.

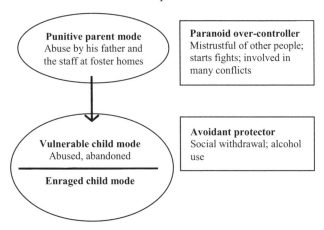

Figure 2.8   Eric's mode model

The vulnerable child mode contains mistrust, threat, and abandonment, since he experienced both abuse and abandonment as a child. His mistrustful and aggressive attitude towards others (including his tendency to start lawsuits) is conceptualized as a paranoid overcontroller mode. Social isolation and alcohol use can be understood as an avoidant protector mode.

2.3.8   Forensic patients

The mode model for forensic patients is suitable for patients with different cluster-B personality disorders. However, it does not actually depict a specific psychiatric disorder, but rather mirrors the patterns related to delinquent behaviors, since the main goal of all forensic treatments is to understand and reduce such behaviors. The following modes have been identified for forensic patients:

- *Vulnerable* and *enraged child modes* (similar to other personality disorders).
- *Dysfunctional parent modes* (similar to other personality disorders).

- The *bully and attack mode*, a specific forensic overcompensation coping mode, in which patients act aggressively in a planned manner in order to accomplish their needs or meet their interests.
- The overcompensatory *conning mode*, which contains lying and cheating behavior patterns. In this mode, the patient tries to make others believe that they behave well, as expected by other people—be it hospital or prison staff, or any cheated person in general. However, patients in this mode are not honest—they lie or hide important information in order to avoid sanctions or to get needs met (for example, to get money).
- The *predator mode*, in which patients severely hurt or even kill somebody in a cold and premeditated way in order to pursue own interests or get rid of someone they don't like.

Forensic patients typically also show severe personality disorders, often antisocial and/or BPD. Therefore, in the individual case concept, the mode model of the respective personality disorders have to be integrated with the forensic modes.

Case example: forensic patient

Nicole, 31-years-old, fulfills the criteria for a borderline and anti-social personality disorder. She has been involved in the drug and criminal scene for many years; she has worked as a prostitute since the age of 12 and has been involved in drug-dealing and aggressive conflicts with her pimps. During her childhood she experienced extreme physical and sexual violence—both her parents were criminal drug addicts themselves.

She has all modes of BPD, including a very vulnerable, abandoned, and abused child mode, a strong enraged child mode, and a punitive–abusive parent mode. She takes drugs in order to cope with her job as a prostitute and with her boyfriend, who is sexually abusive. Thus drug use is conceptualized as a detached protector mode. Her main offenses have been physical or verbal violence, both in the context of fights with pimps, and in personal conflicts.

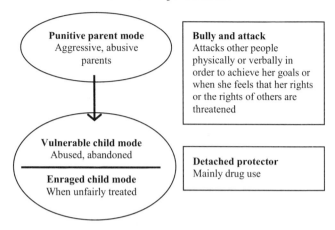

Figure 2.9 Nicole's mode model

She blackmails people and gets into fights, sometimes even using weapons. This part of her is conceptualized as a bully and attack mode (Figure 2.9).

2.3.9   Chronic axis-I disorders

Personality disorders can be conceptualized and treated well using the schema mode model. However, the mode model can also be used for patients with other chronic psychological conditions, such as chronic axis-I disorders. Arntz (2008) hypothesized that many patients with eating disorders are characterized by the following modes: (1) vulnerable child mode (the patient needs love, recognition, and autonomy; but feels rejected, abused, and criticized); (2) demanding and/or punitive parent mode (internalized parental criticism/high standards; often related to eating or body shape, but certainly not restricted to these areas); (3) detached protector mode (the patient uses overeating or starvation to push away difficult feelings); and (4) overcontroller mode (patients try to overcontrol food intake and body shape; but also their parents' care and power—but this doesn't lead to real care and autonomy, instead eliciting worry and controlling behavior from the parents, so that a power struggle over control and autonomy starts).

Here are some quotes from "Ana", a so-called pro-anorexia Web site,[1] with the modes we can easily associate with them within parentheses:

- *"I believe that I am the most mean, worthless, and useless person that ever existed."* (punitive parent)
- *"Never eat without guilt."* (punitive parent)
- *"I believe in control, the only thing that has power enough to create order in the chaos that is called 'my life'."* (overcontroller mode)

Another area for which schema therapy has been proposed is chronic depression (e.g. recurrent depression, dysthymia, depression that doesn't recover: Renner et al., 2012). However, an approach based on a schema mode model is not known to the present authors. Nevertheless, one can speculate that modes that are prevalent in cluster-C personality disorders (Bamelis et al., 2011) are probably also prominent in chronic depression (abandoned child and other vulnerable child modes; punitive/demanding parent; detached protector). Experiential avoidance has been suggested to play an important role in the maintenance of chronic depression (e.g. Hayes et al., 2005) and one can easily see the conceptual overlap with the detached protector coping mode. From a study on risk factors for bipolar disorder and some theorizing, one can hypothesize a schema mode model of bipolar disorder, in which a self-aggrandizer coping mode (perhaps in addition to a self-soother mode), a demanding parent mode, and both an undisciplined child mode and a vulnerable child mode play a prominent role (Hawke et al., 2011).

Some considerations on conceptualizing OCD patients within the schema mode model can be found in Gross et al. (2012). OCD patients typically show a vulnerable child mode, a highly demanding parent mode, and a detached protector and an overcontroller coping mode. OCD symptoms can be related to different modes: when patients try to be perfect and meet high standards by means of controlling behavior, OCD symptoms are mainly related to the demanding parent mode. However, OCD symptoms may also have the effect of reducing

---

[1] At the time of publication, the original Web site can no longer be retrieved. There are still many so-called "pro-ana" sites available online, however. Most list "10 thin commandments," of which "thou shalt not eat without punishment" is a common one. Norris et al. (2006) provide a qualitative analysis of such Web sites. See also Wikipedia: http://en.wikipedia.org/wiki/Pro-ana, accessed April 15, 2012.

unpleasant feelings (detached protector mode) or controlling other people (overcontroller mode).

Case example: mode model of a patient with OCD

Evelyn (see Section 2.1.3) is a 52-year-old secretary who retired 10 years ago due to her OCD. She has been suffering from severe compulsions and obsessions since the age of 20. Compulsions to wash and to control alternate over time; sometimes she suffers from both types of compulsion simultaneously. Both washing and controlling compulsions are mainly related to anxiety over being contaminated with diseases or with actual poison; controlling compulsions also relate to catastrophes such as a potential fire in her house.

As a child, Evelyn's living conditions were very unstable. Her father suffered from a bipolar disorder and was addicted to alcohol. Manic phases and alcohol intoxications sometimes led to unexpected outbursts of aggression. Thus Evelyn as a child was constantly frightened of such sudden outbursts, fearing harm for herself and for her mother. Her mother was often very unwell, which was another factor in making the family situation so stressful—Evelyn was frightened of her mother "not surviving all the problems." As a consequence, Evelyn was a very quiet and socially withdrawn child, since she wanted to avoid provoking either of her parents and thus inducing "dangerous" situations. Subsequently she was not able to develop a healthy style of social interaction; she did not learn how to approach other people without fear, or how to articulate her needs in interpersonal relationships. Not surprisingly in the light of her biographical information, Evelyn repeatedly has engaged in intimate relationships with dominant and aggressive alcoholics, to whom she has subjugated herself as her mother did to her father. Apart from therapists and other health care professionals, Evelyn does not have any contact with people whom she perceives as friendly and supportive of her.

In the therapy situation, Evelyn is very friendly, open, and grateful for every kind of support. Since she became sick with OCD, she has undergone a variety of inpatient and outpatient psychotherapy treatments. In each treatment, she was rather successful in reducing her obsessions and compulsions, but as soon as the therapy was over, she fully relapsed. Similarly, Evelyn is able to follow exposure therapy in the current treatment, including very unpleasant and difficult exercises such as touching things in the kitchen without using her usual washing rituals. During inpatient treatment, she even manages to cook meals for herself and other patients and to join in with the activities of the other patients on the ward. However, as soon as she enters her apartment, she relapses. During the therapy, Evelyn is strikingly unable to articulate her own thoughts and needs in the patient group, even when this has been prepared in detail in an individual therapy session.

With respect to the function of obsessions and compulsions in her everyday life, compulsions help Evelyn to put a distance between herself and others, mainly her current partner. When she has strong compulsions, she can tell him not to sleep in her apartment or in her bed; she does not allow him to sit on her sofa, and so on. Her partner is verbally and physically aggressive towards Evelyn, and she is not able to set limits to this behavior, nor to implement healthier interaction strategies. Compulsions quite naturally help her to put the violent partner at a distance. During exposure-therapy sessions, she typically suffers from intense feelings of sadness, desperation, and loneliness. She also reports that the death of people close to her, such as that of her sister last year, leads to an increase in her compulsions. Maybe, she says, she is unable to stand her feelings of sadness without the protection of the compulsions, particularly since she does not have other positive relationships in her life.

Evelyn's mode model (Figure 2.10) largely overlaps with that of the dependent and avoidant personality disorder, which she also has as a comorbid diagnosis. Feelings of loneliness and worth-lessness are related to the vulnerable child mode. Not being allowed to articulate her own needs is related to the deman-ding/punitive parent mode. Subjugating herself to others and putting her own needs aside are conceptualized as a compliant surrender mode. Compulsions, on the one hand, are connected with the detached protector mode, because she is able to reduce

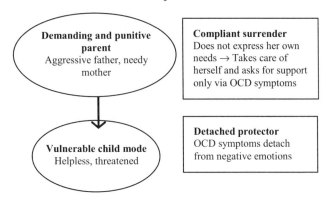

Figure 2.10   Evelyn's mode model

negative feelings via compulsions. In addition, compulsions help her to express her needs, mainly the need to not be treated violently by her partner, and they enable her to ask for support in the psychiatric health care system. Health professionals seem to be the only people in Evelyn's life with whom she feels safe.

When discussing mode models for patients with chronic axis-I disorders, we first of all aim to understand the additional personality pathology of the given patient. This means that their problems become conceptualized with the mode model for the relevant personality problem first; then the axis-I symptoms, such as obsessive–compulsive or depressive symptoms, are fitted in according to the function they serve in the individual patient.

For axis-I disorders, no specific mode models have been tested so far. Usually the model that fits best with the comorbid axis-II pathology is used as the basic model for the patient. Axis-I symptoms are then integrated into the model in a similar way as with problems in personality-disordered patients.

Note that some axis-I symptoms are typically related to a specific mode. Alcohol abuse, for example, most often has the function of enabling detachment from negative emotions and can therefore usually be regarded as being linked to a detached protector mode. However, other axis-I symptoms can be related to the mode model in quite different ways. Depressive symptoms may be part of a vulnerable child mode, so far as extreme forms of sadness are concerned. However, when patients show a high level of avoidance, depressive lack of drive might actually be part of an avoidant protector mode instead—or depression may be regarded as a consequence of avoidance, since the latter leads to a lack of reinforcement.

> An individual mode model can usually be conceptualized within a few sessions at the beginning of therapy. Many sources of information can be used, including self-report questionnaires and other self-reports, observations by the therapist in the therapy session, information from former therapists or family members, biographical information, and so on. Note that a mode model is always discussed with the patient (see Chapter 3).

2.3.10   Excursus: sexual problems in the mode model

Problems of a sexual nature or in intimate relationships in general often do not get enough attention in therapies, even though they may be very relevant to the patients. In the context of schema therapy, sexual behavior or sexual problems can be linked with different schema modes, depending on the function of the behavior or problem.

Vulnerable child modes   Intuitively, one would not link sexual behavior to child modes, since we usually think about sexual behavior as a part of adult life only. However, a problematic sexual behavioral pattern may be related to a vulnerable child mode. This is the case when patients begin sexual relationships not because they are sexually interested in somebody, but because it's their only strategy to experience some interpersonal warmth and closeness. Typically these patients say that they unwillingly put up with sex in order to experience some connection, attachment, and physical contact. Susan, for example (see Section 1.1), reports that she meets her ex-boyfriend not because she wants to have sex with him—on the contrary, she is disgusted by the sexual contact itself—but because the contact will be "in some way positive," and he is the only person who is sometimes nice to her and holds her in his arms. This is related to the vulnerable child mode ("Does everything to experience at least a bit of physical contact"). Fulfilling the sexual needs of her partner in spite of not desiring him, or being sexually gratified by him, is related to a compliant surrender coping mode.

Overcompensation   Rather frequently, problematic sexual behaviors are related to an overcompensatory coping mode. This is the case when patients aim to seduce others in order to feel strong and dominant themselves. For example, Nicole (see Section 2.3.8) reports, "I can seduce any man and afterwards I can drop him like a hot potato. I feel strong and powerful when I seduce them, though they are of no importance to me."

Avoidant coping modes   Avoidant coping modes may play a role when the problem consists of a lack of intimacy and sex. These patients may either avoid sexual interactions in order to avoid getting in touch with complicated feelings or—as part of their avoidant patterns—regard (intimate) connections as nonimportant.

   Another type of avoidant mode, namely the self-stimulation mode, is in the foreground when sex has the function of intense self-stimulation. This is the case when patients use sexual behaviors, such as use of prostitutes, use of pornographic materials, excessive masturbation, and so on, to stimulate themselves and distract themselves from boredom or from overcomplicated feelings they may be experiencing. These patients might engage in affairs because they love the related stimulation and excitement, even though it damages their primary relationship; or use a lot of pornographic materials or Internet sex chatrooms in order to avoid frustrating feelings, even though it impairs their functioning (for example, because they spend their working hours doing it, or they cannot afford it financially).

Punitive parent mode   Sexual problematic behavior is related to the punitive parent mode when patients punish themselves via their sexual practices. A typical example is a patient who frequently starts affairs which she herself finds disgusting and nasty, "Since I'm so dirty, and I don't deserve anything better anyway." Other patients may report very physically painful masochistic sexual behaviors despite clearly not having a masochistic preference. Instead, they accept such practices "Because I need to be treated badly and don't deserve anything else." These patients often make intense use of Internet chatrooms and forums to talk about their practices. The main difference from "normal" masochistic preference accentuation is that people with masochistic preference report sexual excitement connected with the masochism. Often masochistic behaviors or fantasies are even necessary for sexual arousal. In these people, masochistic fantasies were typically connected with sex and sexual arousal when they were still prepubescent.

> Not every deviant sexual behavior is necessarily pathological. However, problematic sexual behavior patterns can be related to all kinds of modes. The therapist should explore this issue with caution, but also openly and clearly.

Note that patients rarely report the discussed sexual problems or problematic behavior patterns spontaneously, since there are often feelings of shame associated with their sexual behaviors. Moreover, it is still a taboo to talk about deviant or problematic sexual behaviors. This is particularly true when the behavior in question is not socially appreciated, such as with prostitution or masochistic online dating. However, it is sometimes impossible to understand a patient's problems sufficiently without knowing about sexual issues such as actual sexual behavior and also potential excessive porn usage or excessive sexual fantasies. Thus it is important that the therapist breaks through the taboo and explores these issues.

To help the patient in this discussion, it is useful to normalize things during the exploration. "You just said that you watch a lot of videos and gamble a lot online. Often people with such habits also watch a lot of pornographic material and surf pornographic Web sites. It is common that they do not talk about it however, even though the behavior itself is actually quite common. As you may know, 'sex' is often said to be the most searched term on Google . . . Do you do that as well?", "You just mentioned briefly that you sometimes get to know new people online. Many patients have told me about people they got to know that way, and that they often quickly became sexual partners. Sometimes patients only get to know others online in order to engage in sexual relations with them. Does this seem similar to the friendships which you mentioned?"

Directly asking for such information is first of all important to completing the case conceptualization. It also offers a model to the patient for talking about taboo issues which might be a big problem in their life. In addition, sexually problematic behaviors may be risky or dangerous. Patients might not only put their primary relationships on the line, but be in actual danger, either from sexually transmitted diseases or from issues related to prostitution, sexual violence, and so on. For all these reasons, the therapist should always pay at least some attention to this issue.

2.4 FAQ

(1) How do you know that a mode model is complete?

You cannot 100% precisely define when a schema mode model is actually "saturated." It is most important to include the main problems, all important symptoms, and any strange or problematic interpersonal behaviors of the patient. It's vital that all the problems presented by the patient as reasons to come into therapy be represented in the mode model. If patients mention too many problems (for example, say that they have extreme problems in all areas of life, though their functioning actually seems to be sufficient in certain areas) or complain unstoppably about a broad variety of things, this should be mentioned in the mode model as well (for example, as an attention-seeking mode). Don't forget to include problematic interpersonal behavior which you find conspicuous in the therapy session—even if the patient doesn't mention it or isn't aware of it. However, to keep a sensible balance, not every problem needs to be included in the mode model—a problem can be excluded if it does not have a clearly dysfunctional character. Usually the first draft of the mode model is finished within about one to five sessions. However, during the course of therapy we often get additional information that has to be later incorporated into the model as well.

(2) Is it possible to overlook important information at the beginning of therapy?

Often patients do not address taboo issues, even though knowing them would be important to understanding the patient and to completing the mode model. Therefore it's highly recommended to ask directly and empathically about such issues (see Section 2.3.10). According to our experiences, the following issues often do not get enough attention, because they are not reported spontaneously: rage, shame, sexuality, drug and medication abuse, eating problems, (Internet) porn usage, and grandiose fantasies. Of course, watching porn videos is not automatically pathological; it is relevant to the patient's mode model only when it creates problems, for example when excessive porn usage impairs personal functioning or hinders relationships.

Patients with strong overcompensating modes usually don't experience and don't acknowledge vulnerable child modes. It is actually the main function of overcompensating modes to keep vulnerable child modes out of their awareness. As long as they are strong, the patient might disagree about hypothesizing a vulnerable child mode in the model.

(3) How do we connect problems or symptoms and modes?

Basically, the connection between the symptoms, problems, or interaction patterns of a patient and a specific mode is made according to the affect related to the problem. The main questions are always, "How does the patient feel?" and, "How does the therapist feel?" Intense negative feelings are related to child modes; pressure and self-hatred are related to parent modes; the absence of emotions, or sometimes the presence of inadequately positive emotions, is related to coping modes. Asking about the feelings of the therapist is particularly relevant to identifying overcompensatory modes, which may be present when a therapist feels threatened, dominated, or controlled by the patient. Often therapists can use their own feelings to infer modes that the patient is not yet aware of.

(4) When can we start to set up the mode model? How long does it take to finish it?

In schema therapy, the therapist pays attention to the patient's modes from the very first session. Often information from the first session will enable you to draft a first preliminary model. After an average of five sessions, most relevant information will have been communicated and combined, and the mode model can be discussed with the patient. Note that the mode model is always a "work in progress" during the whole of therapy; any information can be included at any time. For example, shifts in symptoms or symptomatic changes can often be understood as different variations of the same mode—Jane (see Section 2.1.3) managed to reduce her medication use and dissociative experiences at some point in therapy, for example, but at the same time she began a strong diet which actually fulfilled criteria of anorexic symptoms; anorexia had in her the same function as medication use, since starving generally decreased all emotional experiences and thus helped her to detach. Thus dissociation and medication use as part of the detached protector mode were more or less replaced by anorexic behavior.

(5) How exactly should the mode concept be discussed with the patient?

This topic is discussed at length in Chapter 3.

(6) How directly can you ask about modes or related problems and symptoms? Particularly with regard to shameful issues, shouldn't you wait until patients feel comfortable enough in the therapy to mention them themselves?

You should ask very directly for this kind of information. It's also helpful to ask directly about shame-related issues such as substance use or sexual abnormalities, which are often important to understanding the patient and their modes, but which tend not be reported because patients are too ashamed. You should explain the basic ideas of the mode concept to the patient very early in therapy (see Chapter 3) and highlight the importance of talking about taboo issues. This helps the patient to understand questions regarding complicated issues. According to our experience, patients do not necessarily report shameful issues by themselves over time; they may actually feel even more ashamed about hiding important information for so long . . .

(7) How do you react when a patient does not report any negative feelings at all?

We assume that a patient would not seek therapy without having any problems. Even when they are not willing to talk about negative emotions in the sense of vulnerable child modes in the first sessions, we still know that they came to therapy with complaints such as depressive or anxiety symptoms. Thus we use at least this information for the conceptualization of emotional modes and discuss this directly with the patient: "When I just explained the concept of vulnerable child modes, you said that you don't experience vulnerable emotions a lot. However, you made an appointment because you want help with your social anxiety. Can you tell me a bit more about this anxiety, as we can probably link it with the vulnerable child mode?"

Sometimes, however, patients do indeed fail to report any negative emotions at all—for example, narcissistic patients who have been sent to therapy by somebody else, typically their spouse. In these cases, we also assume the importance of negative emotions "beneath the narcissistic coping," and explore the layers of the patient accordingly. Some patients still will not report any negative feelings, except perhaps for feelings related to those conflicts which resulted in the spouse sending the patient to therapy. In such cases it might be necessary to first work with the coping mode very thoroughly (see Chapter 5) before the patient becomes able to relate to their negative feelings (assuming that they stay in therapy long enough . . .).

Case example: a patient who does not report any negative feelings at the beginning of therapy

Mark, the 48-year-old vice-principal of a secondary school, comes into outpatient psychotherapy because his principal wants him to retire even though Mark himself is clearly willing to continue working. Apart from the "strange retirement idea" of his principal, he "does not have any problems at all." The therapist is struck by Mark's aggressive and dominating interaction pattern. The highly intelligent patient talks about his colleagues and particularly about his boss in a very devaluing way. He pronounces the excellence of his own work in contrast to the "stupidity" of his colleagues. Obviously the patient is very isolated at his workplace, although he does not complain about it ("Do you think I am interested in being close to those idiots?"). The therapist conceptualizes the interpersonal pattern of the patient as a very pronounced narcissistic self-aggrandizing coping mode, and starts exploring some of the patient's other relationships in order to get some idea of how badly this mode affects other areas of his life. Most seem to have suffered from this mode as well. The patient reports that his wife left him 2 years ago with "strange reproaches"; moreover, his friendships also came to an end, initiated either by Mark or by his now ex-friends. The patient talks in a very devaluing way about most of his old friends. In the first sessions of the therapy, the therapist firmly confronts the patient with his overcompensatory mode, which is—after some discussion—labeled as "Superman". Some chair dialogues between "Superman" and other parts of the patient are conducted, although the patient is at first rather resistant to doing any emotion-related work. However, within these chair dialogues, step by step the loneliness and helplessness of the patient regarding his desolate social situation becomes clearer. He gradually becomes able to talk about emotions.

(8) Do positive modes exist as well?

The schema mode model contains the healthy adult and the happy child mode as positive modes, which are related to functional and joyful behaviors and experiences. However, the schema mode model is basically a very open model, and further positive modes or modes containing the patient's important resources can easily be integrated.

(9) Can coping modes be regarded as important resources too?

Clearly coping modes can be very functional at certain times. In the patient's past, typically during childhood, the coping may often have been a true "survival" strategy. Some degree of coping mechanism is important in every healthy human being. These issues are discussed in the context of working with coping modes in Chapter 5.

(10) How can we differentiate between different modes connected with anger?

Several modes are associated with the expression of anger: the angry and enraged child mode, the bully and attack mode, and the angry protector mode. Sometimes it is difficult and complex to differentiate between these modes, for example in patients whose bully and attack mode is usually triggered by the angry child mode. However, it is possible to differentiate between different qualities of anger: angry or enraged child modes are present when the anger of the patient seems to be intense and more like the anger of a child; when the patient is clearly unable to control the anger; and when the anger expression has the quality of an impulsive outburst. In contrast, in the bully and attack mode the patient uses the expression of anger in a controlled way to intimidate others. This differentiation should be discussed directly with the patient.

When, however, a patient is in an angry protector mode, the therapist mostly feels distanced by the anger; the therapist's impression may be that the anger helps the patient to avoid other negative feelings apart from the anger itself, or to avoid closer contact with the therapist. Through countertransference, the therapist may have the impression of the anger standing between therapist and patient, almost like a thick wall. Anger expression is in these cases typically not very intense, but rather persistent.

(11) How can we differentiate the healthy adult mode from the detached protector mode?

This differentiation can indeed sometimes be difficult, since patients can appear rather "sensible" in both modes. A focus on needs is helpful. In the healthy adult mode, the patient can perceive and express emotions and needs and act upon them in an adequate way. In the detached protector mode, however, patients do not clearly feel current emotions and needs and cannot relate adequately to them, even if they superficially show healthy adult behaviors.

(12) How can the demanding parent mode be differentiated from the perfectionist overcontroller in very perfectionist patients?

This differentiation is sometimes not easy, since high demands are important in both modes. The main factor is the affect related to the different modes. When patients constantly worry because they feel extreme pressure and demands, this will mostly be related to the demanding parent mode. When constant work and perfectionism helps patients to distance themselves from negative feelings, or prevents demanding/punitive parent modes from being activated—which would make the patient feel bad and a failure (vulnerable child mode)—this can be regarded as an overcompensatory mode instead. Thus, the perfectionistic overcompensator prevents the vulnerable child mode from being activated by demonstrating its opposite. In the latter case, the therapist typically gets the impression of the patient being in a rat race and at risk of decompensating if the rat race were to stop.

(13) How does the schema concept fit with the schema mode concept? Can we differentiate schemas and schema modes?

In many cases, schemas are very clearly related to schema modes. For example, schema-related emotions associated with domain-I schemas are nearly always related to vulnerable child modes and dysfunctional parent modes, much like two sides of a coin. Some coping modes overlap with specific schemas, such as the compliant surrender mode and the schema subjugation or self-aggrandizer mode with the grandiosity schema. In such cases, schemas may also be mentioned in the mode concept if this is regarded as helpful by the therapist and the patient. However, the therapist might also choose to work with the schema modes only in order to make things easier.

(14) Do we still need the schema concept now we have the schema mode concept?

In many cases, the schema mode concept is simpler than the schema concept. Certain states and problems of the patient can usually be quite clearly related to one mode, according to the main affect. When we use the schema concept only, however, things can sometimes become more complicated, since one behavior may be connected to different schemas, or it may not be clear whether a certain pattern is a schema by itself (for example, a subjugation schema) or is related to schema coping (for example, surrendering coping of an abandonment schema).

Sometimes, however, it is the other way round, and the schema concept describes the patient's situation in simpler terms than the schema mode concept. This is particularly true in patients with the vulnerability to harm and illness or enmeshment schema as their main (maybe even only) schema. These patients often talk about overly cautious, protective, or enmeshed parent figures, which do not really fit with the idea of punitive or demanding parents. If they do not show other emotional problems in addition to these schemas, the use of the schema mode concept does not simplify the model compared to the original schema model.

3

Communicating the Mode Concept to the Patient

During the first phase of schema therapy, the individual mode model and its implications for the treatment are thoroughly discussed with the patient. This procedure is similar to a CBT treatment. Therapy also starts with a detailed behavior and problem analysis, which is openly discussed with the patient.

Case example: discussing the mode concept with Phillip

Phillip, after our first two sessions I would like to discuss with you my ideas about you and your problems. In schema therapy we assume that all individuals have a number of different parts or layers to them. Psychological problems are often associated with conflicts between different parts of oneself. It is important to keep that in mind in order to gain a better understanding of your problems. When I talk about different parts, I do not wish to imply that you are schizophrenic or suffering from a multiple personality disorder. Instead, this refers to the fact that everybody can feel and behave quite differently in different situations.

In many individual psychological problems, one part of the person feels very vulnerable or weak. Many patients tell us that they feel as

---

Schema Therapy in Practice: An Introductory Guide to the Schema Mode Approach, First Edition. Arnoud Arntz and Gitta Jacob.
© 2013 John Wiley & Sons, Ltd. Published 2013 by John Wiley & Sons, Ltd.

if they were little children inside. We often call this the 'inner child' or the 'little self' of the person. I think that you have such a side too. This is the part of you that is particularly present when you feel anxious, and is emotionally related to your childhood and adolescence, when you suffered from bullying by your peer group. What do you think about this idea? [Therapist waits for feedback.] What could we call this part of you? Maybe 'Ashamed Little Phillip'? [Therapist waits for feedback.]

Another part of you becomes very angry when you feel you have been treated unfairly. This happens quite easily, even when, from an outside perspective, not very much has happened. [Therapist waits for feedback.] What could we call this side of you? 'Enraged Phillip?' [Therapist waits for feedback.]

Another part of you probably came about as a direct consequence of the bullying by your classmates. People who experience abuse or bullying typically have a side of themselves which devalues them and regards them as worthless or ridiculous. You told me that you often feel extremely ugly, although you know on a cognitive level that you look absolutely fine. What do you think about this idea of an inner critical, punitive part of yourself? [Therapist waits for feedback.]

The therapist paints the vulnerable child mode and the punitive mode (see Figure 2.1), which in Phillip is represented by the punitive and bullying peer group, into circles on the left-hand side of a sheet of paper or on a flipchart. She then continues:

When you have to live with the severe emotional stress that these child or punitive parts stir in you, you need some kind of coping behavior. One way of coping with stressful emotions is to suppress them. It is my impression that this is what you do when you show this behavioral pattern, which I called overcompensation in our first meeting. Do you remember this? [Therapist waits for feedback.] Can you understand that this overcompensation might be a coping strategy to deal with the pain caused by the parent and punitive child modes? [Therapist waits for feedback.] What could we call this coping part of you? Maybe the 'Big Boss'? Or simply the 'Overcompensator'? [Therapist waits for feedback.]

However, you also told me that you withdraw from many relationships or situations when you feel overstressed by them. We would call this an avoidant behavior and we should add an avoidant protector coping mode to our mode model. [Therapist waits for feedback.] Of course, you do not consist of problematic modes alone. There is also a healthy part in you, which helps you to live in a healthy way. Let us call this your 'healthy adult mode.'

In most cases it is useful to start the discussion of the mode model with the vulnerable child modes, followed by the punitive- or demanding parent modes. This order validates the negative emotions of the patient first, even if the patient has not been able to express them in therapy yet. This validation is typically a good basis for the next step, which is to confront the patient with the coping modes. This confrontation is often not very comfortable, either for the patient or for the therapist, since it may require discussing quite openly parts of the patient which are neither very positive nor very functional. It is often easier for patients to accept these parts of the mode model when their psychological suffering has been extensively validated beforehand. Finally, the healthy adult mode is discussed, which is validating for the patient, as it acknowledges that they also have a functional side.

> At the start of schema therapy, the mode model is discussed in detail with the patient. First, we introduce vulnerable child modes and dysfunctional parent modes, followed by coping modes and the healthy adult mode. If the views of the patient and the therapist differ with respect to their understanding of modes, they have to be discussed and clarified.

It is vital in the discussion of the mode model that the therapist keeps track and touches upon all important modes in the patient. On the other hand, it is important not to force a model on the patient. Therefore you have to get open and honest feedback from the patient with respect to all aspects of the patient's mode model. Furthermore, when the therapist and the patient differ in their view of the patient's problems, an open discussion is necessary to reach a solution that is satisfying for both sides. According to our experiences, patients often accept the idea of vulnerable child and dysfunctional parent modes quite easily, but it is more difficult to reach agreement with regard to coping modes. One solution is to agree on what modes you disagree about, and agree that you will return to the issue later in treatment.

With respect to parent modes, it is important to keep in mind that at the beginning of therapy, patients may be unable to identify the biographical background of their parent modes, particularly if their parents were the most complicated people in their childhood. This is often related to the issue of loyalty. Patients may feel guilty for defining their parents as the sources of their psychological problems. This is especially problematic if one or both of the patient's parents suffered from depression or took a victim role, and nonverbally induced feelings of guilt in the child. Patients may cling on to the idea of their being responsible for the development of their problems instead of their parents, and even feel responsible for their parents' problems. In such cases it is important to stress that the dysfunctional parent modes in the mode model are usually not perfect mirrors of the real parents of the patient. Instead they capture the so-called "introjects" or "stamps" which developed in the patient due to experiences with their parents. Sometimes it is helpful to state at the beginning of therapy that patients put pressure upon themselve or devalue themselves, without trying to define the cause of these stamps right away. Discussing the responsibility of the patients' actual parents for the development of their current problems may be done later in therapy. Finally, it is important to keep in mind that so-called dysfunctional parent modes might also have been triggered and developed under the influence of classmates, dysfunctional authorities, or other people, rather than the actual parents.

With respect to coping modes, patients and therapists may have quite different evaluations, particularly at the beginning of therapy. This is particularly true for overcompensating coping modes. When the patient rejects the interpretation of certain behavioral patterns as a coping mode, even though the therapist is very convinced of this interpretation, therapists should always be open for discussion, in which they should clearly explain their own viewpoint. Of course, this discussion should not have a completely predetermined conclusion. Sometimes particular behavior patterns of a patient, which give a very dysfunctional impression in the therapy context, may be much more functional in other life situations (for example, professional situations). This is particularly true for patients working in fields characterized by high levels of overcompensation, such as business or medicine. Perhaps dominant or aggressive behavior patterns, which seem to be very inadequate in therapy sessions and in other situations, are functional at the patient's workplace. Such modes remain dysfunctional if used in situations where they are not adaptive, however.

Case example: discussing the coping mode with Phillip

You say that you can follow my explanations regarding child and parent modes. However, you disagree that you have any narcissistic and overcompensatory part in yourself. What are your ideas regarding your dominant interaction patterns, which are so conspicuous to me? [Phillip continues to explain that his dominating interaction pattern is completely normal. If he didn't behave so dominantly, nobody would ever pay attention to him at all.]

Phillip, that sounds very interesting to me. Actually, it is not contradictory to my own interpretation, because I also think that overcompensation is quite an effective way to get attention. I also guess that it was important for you to develop this pattern in your past exactly for this reason. However, please let me explain in more detail why I still think that although this pattern is functional, it is nonetheless overcompensatory: first, it is extremely hard for me to interrupt you when you talk this way. I tend to feel very controlled by you and you don't seem to accept that I should be allowed to explain my opinions as well. Do you understand what I mean? Have other people told you that you are overly dominant and controlling? [Phillip confirms this. His former wife often accused him of being arrogant and dominating; however, he does not miss the chance to claim he could also accuse her of being guilty of several things.] Phillip, I do not doubt that your marriage was very complicated, and probably both of you had a part in it. I do not want to suggest that your overcompensation mode is responsible for all the problems you have ever had with everybody. Still, I find it interesting that other people have given you similar feedback about your dominant behavior patterns. How do you propose to explain this? [Phillip explains that he does not understand this feedback and that he has no explanation for it.] Phillip, I think perhaps you don't fully understand what people mean when they say you behave in this way. Would it be interesting to you to discuss this in further detail here in therapy? I could also get a video recording of our sessions and we could watch them together. Then I could explain to you more clearly what I find conspicuous about this pattern. Sometimes it may be quite hard for you to take on another perspective, but watching yourself behaving this way may help you to understand what it is that others are talking about. What do you think about this?

When the patient rejects part of the first mode model, this is not necessarily purely "defensiveness." When the first mode concept is created, the therapist develops many hypotheses regarding the relationship between the patient's current problems and symptoms on the one hand and the patient's biography on the other. This is important and the therapist should not hesitate to share these ideas with the patient; however, some of these ideas may be erroneous. Therefore, the complete model has to be discussed in detail with the patient. According to our experiences, psychotherapists frequently reach erroneous conclusions about patients' intimate relationships, for example. So the therapist may find it conspicuous that a patient has had several relationships with much older or much younger partners. However, if these relationships used to work well and the patient was truly fine with them, this may not be relevant for the mode model at all. Therefore, when creating the mode model, it is vital that the therapist repeatedly asks for the patient's feedback to avoid misunderstandings.

The patient's feedback and perspective on the mode model is vital. We want the patient to become involved with the mode model, so that they can clearly sense the personal meaning of different modes for themselves. As with every explanatory model in therapy, the schema mode model is more helpful the more the patient identifies emotionally with it. Therefore we ask patients to characterize each mode from their own perspective and to explain more about their development and background to the therapist. For example, it is very welcome when patients start talking about punitive and critical experiences during their childhood once the therapist has introduced the punitive parent mode. Such information should get the whole attention of the therapist, and the therapist should include it in the mode model, for example in the form of notes related to the different modes. The thorough discussion of the different modes and their biographic background may also help in collecting information for later interventions, such as chair dialogues or imagery rescripting exercises.

3.1   Treatment Planning with the Mode Model

After discussing the mode model of the patient, and creating a joint perspective, the main features of the treatment approach following from this mode model should also be discussed. This includes the information that soothing and strengthening vulnerable child modes is an essential goal of the therapy; that it will be important to help the angry child mode to express its anger in inappropriate ways; and that punitive parent modes should be reduced in therapy in order to reduce their influence in the patient's life. Dysfunctional coping modes should become more flexible during the course of therapy, and the therapy should help the patient to learn more flexible options regarding inter-action patterns and other healthy choices: the strengthening of the healthy adult mode. The interventions related to these different goals should be briefly characterized.

The first discussion of the mode model and related treatment ideas is also a good time to reflect on the functionality or reinforcement balance of the modes. Patients with intensely spoiled or undisciplined child modes, whose lack of discipline is compensated for by parents or partners, may not find it very rewarding to work on these modes and take more responsibility for their lives or enhance their capacity for delay of gratification. This might be related to a higher level of stress and thus a loss of reinforcement. Such issues should be openly discussed with the patient as early as possible. However, note that they are sometimes not clear at the very beginning of therapy. Often they emerge as therapy progresses, when patients do not seem motivated to change their dys-functional modes, since they would lose too much positive reinforcement. When this becomes clear, the therapist should not hesitate to openly address it with the patient.

3.2   FAQ

(1) Is it possible to present a complete model of their functioning to patients after only a few sessions?

According to our experience, it is possible to introduce the first mode model for a patient after a very limited number of sessions—say, three to five. Of course, this model will not include all relevant details right away. However, if you concentrate on the exploration and explanation of modes, you will probably manage to detect the most important, with their main features and central biographical background issues.

(2) This model seems to be rather suggestive—don't we impose something upon patients which may not have anything to do with them?

The process of conceptualizing and discussing the mode concept is indeed very structured, and the therapist actively suggests explanations regarding the connections between the patient's problems and modes. Therefore it is particularly important to discuss every detail with the patient and to always get the patient's feedback. It would not be meaningful just to present the mode model to the patient without thoroughly discussing it first.

(3) What can you do when a coping mode is so strong at the beginning of therapy that the patient more or less refuses to reflect on the mode model—for example, due to very controlling or narcissistic patterns?

This can be a problem in patients with very intense complaints (angry-protector mode or attention-seeking mode), in very narcissistic patients who devalue the therapist for creating the mode model, or in overly dramatic patients with a strong attention-seeking mode. Sometimes it is helpful to insist on the discussion of the mode model, as demonstrated in the case example above. The question of whether the patient has ever received similar feedback from others (complains a lot; behaves like a narcissist; shows dramatic behavior) can help to focus the patient's attention on the mode model; people with extreme overcompensation or complaining angry-protector modes will typically have already been criticized for these behaviors by others before they ever reach therapy. This may help them to see the relevance of the therapist's opinions. It can also be helpful to mirror and demonstrate a coping mode in a patient by playing it as therapist—like a brief roleplay. This can be particularly helpful in patients with very angry or aggressive coping modes. However, in some cases patients are nearly completely "stuck" in their coping mode and cannot identify at all with the idea of different parts of themselves. In such cases, you should regard the work with this coping mode as a first important step in therapy. The discussion of the complete mode model may be postponed until patients are better able to reflect upon their coping mode(s) and to see their own patterns more from an external perspective. This approach is explained in more detail in Chapter 5.

II
TREATMENT

4

Treatment Overview

As a first step in treatment, the mode concept is discussed with the patient.
The patient's mode model summarizes the main problems, symptoms, and
interaction patterns and should be reasonable and plausible for both the
patient and the therapist. In the treatment that follows, each type of mode
is linked with specific treatment goals (see Figure 4.1). The combination of
treatment elements and the relative importance of different treatment
techniques, as well as the balance between interventions treating specific
symptoms and interventions treating personality symptoms, have to be
adapted to the individual case.

4.1   Treatment Goals for Individual Modes

4.1.1   Vulnerable child modes

The basic goal of schema therapy with regard to vulnerable child modes is
to help patients to care better for their own needs. They should develop a
stronger focus on their own needs. They should establish or strengthen
activities which fulfill important emotional and social requirements. A
main task of the therapist in treating vulnerable child modes is validating,
soothing, and helping to process abuse and other negative experiences.
Thus the therapist offers a model for caring for vulnerable child parts (and
for self-care in general).

Schema Therapy in Practice: An Introductory Guide to the Schema Mode Approach,
First Edition. Arnoud Arntz and Gitta Jacob.

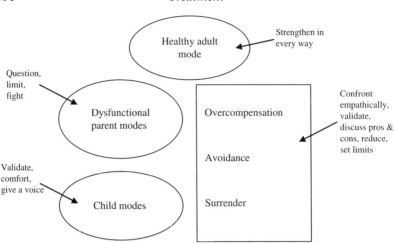

Figure 4.1 Treatment overview

4.1.2 Angry/enraged child modes

These modes should be aired in therapy. Patients are encouraged to experience and articulate anger. Anger comes up when their own needs are hurt; it is therefore regarded as an important feeling. The associated needs are validated and accepted. However, the patient has to learn more adequate ways of communicating these needs.

4.1.3 Impulsive/undisciplined child modes

As with angry child modes, the general needs behind impulsive or undisciplined child modes should be validated and accepted. However, these modes express needs in an exaggerated way. Thus it may be important to set limits to these modes and to help the patient find more realistic expectations regarding the needs associated with these modes. Furthermore, a patient with these modes should be taught discipline and frustration tolerance.

4.1.4 Dysfunctional parent modes

The main goal with these modes is to weaken them. Dysfunctional parent modes should be questioned, limited, or even fought. The therapist must help the patient reduce the extremely high standards and self-devaluations associated with these modes.

4.1.5   Dysfunctional coping modes

Patients should first be empathically confronted with these modes. The reasons these parts were important for the patient during childhood, and how protective they were at that time, should be discussed. At the same time, the negative consequences of these modes must be addressed. The influence of these modes has to be reduced in order to enable the patient to react more flexibly and more adequately to stressful situations. When dysfunctional coping modes constrain the course of the therapy, clear limits must be set.

4.1.6   Happy child mode and healthy adult mode

These modes should generally be strengthened and reinforced in therapy, and their intensity and frequency of activation increased.

4.2   Treatment Techniques

Schema therapy combines cognitive, emotion-focused, and behavioral interventions.

4.2.1   Cognitive interventions

Cognitive interventions (Figure 4.2) are used to test the validity and "truth" of schemas or modes by means of pro-and-con discussions. With cognitive

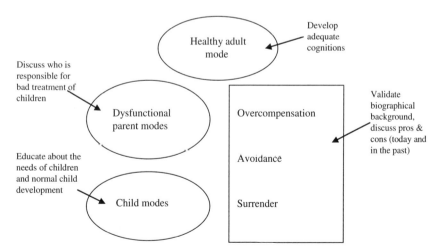

Figure 4.2   Cognitive treatment interventions

reframing techniques, different "proofs of a schema or schema mode" are explained in turn. All cognitive interventions can be used. For example, a therapist might discuss with a patient why the woman at the supermarket cash desk did not say "hello" that morning. The patient might spontaneously interpret this in connection with a particular schema, and regard it as an indicator of rejection. Cognitive techniques may help this patient to get another perspective and adopt more functional interpretations. Similarly, schema-congruent errors in reasoning and the pros and cons of coping strategies are discussed. Psychoeducation plays an important role, too. Patients are informed about the normal needs of children, normal emotions, normal behavior patterns, and the differences between a healthy and normal childhood development and their own childhood.

> Cognitive interventions include all CBT methods, such as reframing, discussion of errors in reasoning, and the use of pro-and-con lists.

Child modes   An important cognitive technique is psychoeducation about the normal needs of human beings. People with severe personality disorders in particular often have no clear and realistic idea of how they should actually have been treated as a child (even though many of these patients know quite well how children should be treated as far as other people—or their own children—are concerned).

Dysfunctional parent modes   The main focus of cognitive interventions is on the discussion of guilt and the adequacy of parental behaviors in the patient's childhood. Patients often feel that the way they were treated as a child was their own fault. Such misinterpretations have to be reattributed using cognitive treatment techniques. An important technique is to take an external perspective: "Would you still regard the child as responsible and guilty for the bad treatment if it was someone else, or if you were to imagine your own child in your place?". Some patients say that they had a very complicated temperament or were in some way difficult as a child. Even if this is true, the patient should be told that the parents were wrong to have blamed the child for its temperament (the child didn't choose its temperament) and that the parents were responsible for adequately adapting their care to the child's temperament. Important topics that often need to be addressed with cognitive methods include: (1) when you are actually responsible, as distinct from "bad luck" (bad luck is a concept that is usually not incorporated in dysfunctional parent modes); (2) the fundamental right to make mistakes, and the necessity of making mistakes in order to learn new things; (3) the fundamental needs and rights of children (you may refer to the UN Declaration of the Rights of the Child: http://www.un.org/cyberschoolbus/humanrights/resources/child.asp).

Coping modes The important protective function of coping modes during childhood is first validated. The pros and cons of coping modes are then discussed, with regards to both the childhood situation and the current situation of the patient. Steps for reducing coping modes are explored, first within the therapeutic situation, then in the patient's life outside therapy.

Cognitive work is embedded in emotion-focused interventions. For example, the adequacy of guilt can be addressed in chair dialogues between dysfunctional parent modes and the healthy adult mode. More explicit cognitive interventions in schema therapy include schema diaries or schema flash cards (Chapter 6), and pro-and-con lists for coping styles or schemas (Chapter 5).

4.2.2   Emotion-focused interventions

Emotion-focused interventions (Figure 4.3) are supposed to help the patient express sadness and rage. Experiencing and processing these emotions helps patients to focus more on their own needs and their own goals. They thus experience themselves as more important and finally as more positive and more valuable. Problematic emotions can be actively changed using emotion-focused techniques.

The main emotion-focused techniques in schema therapy are imagery exercises and so-called "chair work."

Imagery exercises In imagery exercises, schemas or modes are activated by deepening current emotions and connecting them with biographical memories. The main intervention technique for (traumatic) childhood memories is "imagery rescripting." In an imagery rescripting exercise, traumatic or difficult situations are changed in the imagination in such a way that the needs of the traumatized or badly treated child are fulfilled.

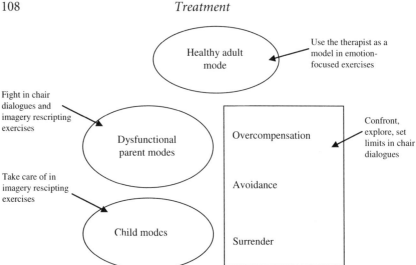

Figure 4.3   Emotion-focused interventions

This might mean stopping a violent or abusive perpetrator, taking the child out of the situation, and caring for it, for example. The use of imagery exercises is not restricted to the treatment of childhood memories. Imagery exercises can also be used to rescript later-life trauma or to prepare the patient for future situations (for a broad introduction, see Hackman et al., 2011). Imagery exercises are explained in more detail in Chapter 6.

> Imagery rescripting exercises and other emotion-focused inter-ventions support patients in experiencing feelings related to the fulfillment of needs, such as rage against punitive parent modes, or empathy with vulnerable child modes.

Chair work   In chair-work exercises (overview in Kellogg, 2004), dia-logues are conducted between different modes or between a schema and a healthy side of the patient. The different parts of a patient are represented by different chairs. Chair work helps patients to express emotions related to their different modes. Patients are supported in accessing angry or enraged feelings by the chair seating the enraged child mode, or in developing an adequate and helpful emotional-cognitive-behavioral response against highly demanding punitive parent modes by the chair seating the healthy adult mode. Chair dialogues are particularly helpful when the patient feels ambivalent or when inner conflicts need to be clarified. An overview and more detailed explanation of chair work can be found in Chapter 8.

With regard to the mode model (see Figure 4.3), imagery rescripting exercises are most important in the treatment of vulnerable child modes. Dysfunctional parent modes can also be a target for imagery exercises, in which images of dysfunctional parent modes (= the perpetrators in the image) are stopped or destroyed. Dysfunctional parent modes can also be reduced or fought in chair dialogues. Chair dialogues can also be used to set limits on very dominating coping modes, particularly overcompensatory coping modes. This intervention helps with validating, understanding, and confronting dysfunctional coping modes.

4.2.3   Behavioral interventions

In behavioral pattern-breaking and the treatment of symptoms, basically all behavioral therapy techniques can be used. This includes roleplays, homework assignments, exposure techniques, skills training, and relaxation exercises.

Behavioral interventions can be combined with specific schema-therapy interventions, such as schema flash cards or other memory aids. These mainly connect a symptom or a behavioral problem with the related schema mode. CBT treatment techniques such as social skills training, reduction of perfectionism, increase of positive activities, establishment of regular exercises, and a clearer expression of the patient's own needs are frequently employed.

With regard to the mode model (Figure 4.4), important behavioral techniques for child modes include the training of social skills which help the patient to experience healthy interpersonal closeness and intensify relationships with helpful and supportive people. Patients should learn to fight against dysfunctional parent modes on a behavioral level, by for example reducing perfectionism, accepting their own mistakes and errors, and engaging in activities in which they can experience personal success (instead of always trying to meet overly high standards without success). Behavioral interventions are mainly supposed to establish behavioral

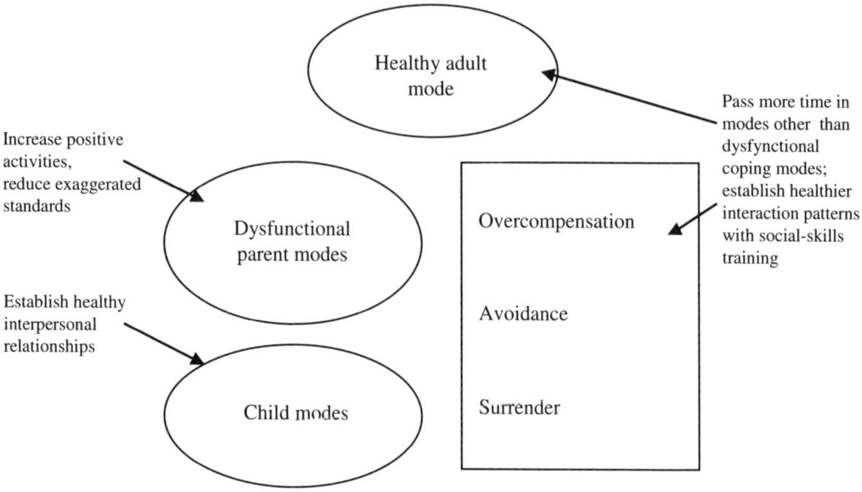

Figure 4.4   Behavioral interventions

patterns associated with non-coping modes—that is, patients should start to spend less time in dysfunctional coping modes. This is typically connected with the implementation of healthy adult interactions and activities, including social or leisure-time activities and sports.

4.3   The Therapeutic Relationship

In the therapeutic relationship, therapists match their interactions to the schemas and modes of the patient (Figure 4.5). For example, emotionally very depressed patients are treated with particular warm-heartedness and emotional care. Patients with strong dependency, however, are encouraged to act more autonomously. The therapist discusses with them whether it is helpful or not to fulfill their dependent interaction patterns—not with the goal of annoying or frustrating them, but in order to help them accomplish more autonomy.

4.3.1   *Empathic confrontation*

An important technique is "empathic confrontation," in which patients are very clearly confronted with their interpersonal patterns in the therapeutic relationship. This confrontation is "empathic" because the therapist

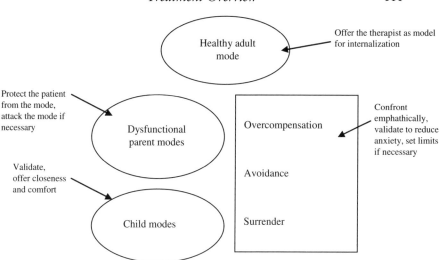

Figure 4.5 The therapeutic relationship

explains and validates the biographic background of the patient's interaction patterns and interprets them as a (dysfunctional) way of caring for the patient's needs. Patients are then supposed to learn more healthy ways of articulating their needs.

Case example: empathic confrontation with the coping mode in the therapy session

Phillip (see Section 1.4) often displays an overcompensatory mode in the therapy session. He talks a lot in this mode and shows off his abilities and experiences. When this mode is present in the session, it is impossible to address his anxiety in a constructive way. The therapist addresses this interaction pattern in the second session: "Phillip, I'd like to give you some feedback on how I experience you right now in our session. I can hardly sense your anxiety, because you talk very smartly about a lot of different things. I hardly contribute anything to our conservation, because it's really hard to interrupt you. I have the impression that it's very important for you to be the boss here in this room. When I think of your childhood and how you suffered from bullying, I assume that this kind of overcompensation probably protected you against feelings of helplessness and abandonment. What do you think?"

Phillip agrees with regard to the overcompensatory and persistent character of this pattern. The therapist thoroughly explains the biographical background of overcompensation and they discuss how this applies to Phillip. During the discussion, the therapist tries to stay in close interpersonal contact with Phillip; when Phillip starts flipping back into the overcompensatory mode, the therapist immediately stops him and addresses the mode-flipping. After a couple of minutes, the therapist starts to address the more dysfunctional aspects of this pattern: "It's paradoxical in a way. While this pattern was very important and protective for you when you were a child, and helped you to feel in control of the situation, it meanwhile became an important part of your problem. If you are always in this mode, it's impossible for you to experience true and positive human contact with me. It's certainly the same with other relationships, right? This may actually increase your feelings of abandonment. Do you agree?"

4.3.2   Limited reparenting

The therapeutic relationship in schema therapy is conceptualized as "limited reparenting." The therapist meets—though to a limited degree—those needs of the patients which have not been met by their parents or by other important parental figures during their childhood and adolescence. For example, for patients with BPD it is very important, particularly at the beginning of therapy, that the therapist enters the traumatic scene in imagery rescripting exercises as a model for the healthy adult mode. Therapists have to accept that patients with severe emotional disorders such as BPD need them as a personal attachment figure, at least in the first phase of the therapy. To become a caring parent figure, therapists have to present themselves as a "real person" in therapy. This makes a big difference to the classical neutral therapeutic relationship in the psychoanalytic setting. It is also different from the relationship model of cognitive therapies, in which the therapist plays a Socratic role, rather than a warm and caring one. Reparenting mainly addresses the vulnerable child mode of the patient. This should be made clear to the patient, and of course professional limits have to be strictly regarded.

4.3.3   Limit-setting

Parental care includes setting limits. Limit-setting is frequently necessary in patients treated with schema therapy. For example, therapists have to set limits on spoiled, undisciplined, or other inadequate behavior patterns. As with all other interventions, the therapist should explain this aspect of the therapeutic relationship, if necessary. It is important that the patient understands why the therapist is setting limits.

> "Limited reparenting" in the therapeutic relationship means that the therapist is warm and cares for the patient. However, the therapist also has to set limits on the patient's dysfunctional behaviors, just as healthy parents would do for their child.

With regard to different modes, the therapist has to consider the following in the therapeutic relationship.

4.3.4   Child modes

When a patient is in a vulnerable child mode, they need validation, comfort, and soothing. This applies to spontaneous switches into the vulnerable child mode—the therapist must react very warmly and caringly—and within emotion-focused techniques: in imagery rescripting exercises, the therapist should soothe the inner child of the patient and take care of it; in chair dialogues, the therapist should talk to the vulnerable child chair in a warm and caring way.

4.3.5   Dysfunctional parent modes

Patients have to be protected against their dysfunctional parent modes in the therapeutic relationship. Again, this applies to both emotion-focused interventions and spontaneous situations: the therapist should actively support the patient in fighting the dysfunctional parent mode during imagery exercises or chair dialogues, and when it arises spontaneously.

Case example: standing up to the punitive parent mode in the therapy session

Nicole (see Section 1.3.3) had planned to go to a job interview, but she avoided it at the very last moment. She devalues herself for her avoidant behavior and calls herself a horrible failure. The therapist replies: "Nicole, it is a pity that you didn't go to the job interview. However, these self-devaluations and this self-hatred you're feeling belong to your punitive parent mode. The punitive parent shouldn't have a voice here, because it makes you feel even worse and this will not help you to find better ways of handling similar situations in the future."

4.3.6 Coping modes

An important task for the therapist with regard to dysfunctional coping modes is empathic confrontation. The confrontation has to be balanced with a generally very validating and caring therapeutic attitude. When a patient experiences the therapeutic relationship as safe and caring, strong coping is no longer necessary, and patients will be much better able to stop their coping modes. However, with very dominating overcompensation modes it may also be necessary for the therapist to set clear limits, if possible in a playful way. If the therapist is too strict and firm in setting limits, the patient may feel that the therapist fears losing control or is starting a power struggle.

Case example: clear limit-setting for overcompensation modes

At the beginning of therapy, Nicole is constantly in her bully and attack mode. It is hardly possible for the therapist to establish real contact with her. After a couple of sessions, the therapist sets clear limits: "Nicole, please stop talking for a moment. It is important for me to contribute to our communication, too. I want to make sure that this treatment will help you; therefore, I will have to interrupt you sometimes and stop this mode. I'd like to have more of a joint discussion between the two of us instead. Is this OK with you?"

4.4 FAQ

(1) To what extent should the treatment plan be discussed with the patient, particularly emotion-focused interventions and the therapeutic relationship?

Basically, schema therapists are very transparent. This includes discussing the therapeutic relationship and emotion-focused interventions openly with the patient.

(2) When does the actual schema therapy (emotion-focused techniques, limited reparenting, and so on) start?

In many cases, a psychological treatment is carried out as schema therapy from the very beginning. In such cases, the problems and symptoms of the patient should be conceptualized, explained, and treated using the mode model from the commencement of therapy. Ideally, the first three sessions will contain at least one diagnostic imagery exercise and the first (possibly preliminary) discussion of the patient's mode model.

Sometimes a therapist will decide to suggest a switch to schema therapy in a later phase of therapy. This might for example be helpful when a patient was at first treated with CBT and a personality pathology became obvious following symptom reduction, calling for a change in treatment strategy. This approach (CBT first, schema therapy as a second phase) is essentially possible; however, it should be openly discussed with the patient as well.

(3) How are schema-therapy elements implemented on a practical level?

Just as in CBT, the therapist develops a case concept along with the patient. The treatment plan is jointly set up according to the main therapy goals of the patient and the professional opinion of the therapist. The therapist and patient then follow their treatment plan. As in CBT, it is important to find a balance between the treatment plan and the current issues the patient would like to address in the session. Typically, current issues are related to the mode model and treated with those schema-therapy techniques that have been defined in the treatment plan.

5

Overcoming Coping Modes

The main goals in working with coping modes are to confront the patient with the mode, to help them to identify the mode, to help them understand its main functions and how it developed, and to reduce the mode's use and replace it with healthier coping. For many patients it is important that they understand they developed an overcompensatory or avoidant coping mode in reaction to a difficult environment during their childhood. When such issues are discussed, the pros and cons of the mode in their current life should be discussed as well. While coping modes are typically experienced as in some way adaptive during childhood or adolescence, they are often related to serious interpersonal problems in adult life. In the long term, the patient should learn to reduce their coping mode and to spend more time in the healthy adult mode.

5.1   The Therapeutic Relationship

When a coping mode is present, the therapist should be very friendly and caring. The coping mode is a defense mechanism, and a friendly reaction from the therapist can help the patient to calm down, eventually reducing the defense. The patient should feel as safe as possible with the therapist and should be encouraged to open up as much as possible. This is in line with the general psychotherapeutic idea that an empathic therapeutic relationship helps to reduce defense and to access problematic feelings.

However, it can sometimes also be important to clearly point out a coping mode, to interrupt it, and to confront the patient with its interpersonal effect. In schema therapy, "empathic confrontation" means to

Schema Therapy in Practice: An Introductory Guide to the Schema Mode Approach, First Edition. Arnoud Arntz and Gitta Jacob.
© 2013 John Wiley & Sons, Ltd. Published 2013 by John Wiley & Sons, Ltd.

combine clear confrontation with care. The therapist is very interested in the well-being of the patient, never wanting to threaten the patient, but wants to help them to meet their own needs better in daily life: "I feel that you are often very distant and don't really feel your emotions and your needs, although you talk about very stressful emotional experiences. My impression is that you protect yourself with this detachment. I would be very interested to learn why you needed this protection earlier in your life and why this still seems to be necessary for you." This cautious and friendly confrontation is usually very helpful in patients with strong avoidant coping modes—that is, patients who only have very superficial contact with the therapist or who are always very quiet and withdrawn.

5.1.1   Overcompensation mode

When a patient displays a strong overcompensation mode, it may be necessary to explicitly name and limit this mode in the therapeutic relationship. In such cases, the therapist has to set limits, even if this means stopping being friendly and caring for some moments. Setting limits can be part of schema-therapy reparenting, just as it is a part of being a parent to set limits to one's children. Note that in most cases of strong overcompensation it is necessary to set limits repeatedly. Just as with children, it is usually not sufficient to set limits on intense overcompensation just once.

Case example: setting a limit on Nicole's bully and attack mode

When Nicole is in her bully and attack mode, she talks very badly about different people in her life, calls them bad names ("failures and old junkies"), has a loud and high tone of voice, and rants and raves. The therapist feels controlled by her and does not sense any emotional contact with her. It is hard for the therapist even to simply interrupt Nicole and speak up for themselves. This situation is typical of a strong overcompensation mode. It is necessary that the therapist steps in and sets limits: "Nicole, please listen to me for a couple of minutes. [The therapist waits for the patient to react. Nicole briefly stops speaking and watches the therapist mistrustfully.] Nicole, I want to explain to you how I feel with you. You are very talkative, you are very eloquent, and you typically dominate situations. I sense that you are angry about many things and that you have problems with many people around you. [Nicole starts to interrupt the therapist.] No, Nicole, please give me a couple of minutes to talk too! If I don't stop you, the whole session will be filled with your rage attacks at other people. I will not really get to know you and I will not learn anything about the negative emotions you're suffering when you're alone, which should get a place in therapy. I don't want to continue like this, because I am really interested in you and I really want to help you. However, as I want to learn more about you and I want you to get to know me, I also need some space in our relationship, even when I do not act as quickly and as assertively as you do."

By setting a limit, the therapist interrupts the coping mode. Furthermore, the therapist models within the therapeutic relationship that both people have the right to care for their own needs in any interpersonal relationship. Thus, the patient can experience a healthy model for addressing and meeting her own needs in relationships. It is also important to reduce this mode because while in it the patient is incapable of emotional learning.

5.2   Cognitive Techniques

On the cognitive level, it is important to identify a coping mode, to label it, and to help the patient recognize it in everyday life. The biographical development of the mode should be discussed, as well as its functions in the patient's life both during childhood and today. Finally, the pros and cons of the mode in the patient's current life situation have to be discussed. The patient should learn to identify the mode and to understand its effects on other people. It is also important to learn alternative behavioral patterns (see Section 5.4).

5.2.1   *Identify and label the mode*

When patients attend a specific (study) therapy or a group therapy for a particular disorder, the typical modes of the respective disorder are usually named in a predefined way. For example, in a schema-therapy group for patients with BPD, the schema-therapy model of BPD will be used, with the terms "punitive parent mode," "abused/abandoned child mode," "detached protector mode," and so on. However, in individual therapies individual names may be given to each mode by the therapist and the patient. This can help the patient to identify more with the mode model. Typical names for a detached protector might for example be "wall," "rolling shutter," "facade," "mask," "the cool part of myself," and so on. A narcissistic overcompensation mode might be called a "stunner," "Superman," "super hero," and so on. It is important that the name of each mode mirrors the mode's main functions and is accepted by both the therapist and the patient.

When we discuss a mode, we also reflect on how the patient can identify it—that is, how they can detect that they are in the mode when outside of therapy. It can be helpful to observe modes in others in order to learn more about them. To support the patient in identifying the mode, the therapist should point out when it pops up in therapy: "I just noticed that your rolling shutter came down again. Did you notice it too? Do you know why?" Additionally, it can be helpful to discuss how the patient actually experiences the mode—physical sensations, feeling driven, feeling annoyed or bored, feeling nothing, and so on. This part of cognitive work is supposed to help the patient learn to perceive their own (coping) modes.

5.2.2   *The biographical background of the coping mode*

The therapist should exhaustively discuss with the patient how the coping mode has developed in their life. Important issues include—as with every other mode—the functions of the mode in the biography of the patient and models with similar modes in the family or in other people when the patient was a child (for some useful questions to ask when exploring this, see Box 5.1). With regard to social learning, patients often report that one parent displayed (or still displays) a similar coping mode to themselves. Vicarious learning can be a very powerful mechanism for acquiring coping modes. Perhaps the mother was very avoidant and overly compliant with the father when he was choleric or aggressive. Thus the patient (the daughter) learned that there was nothing to do for the father and that it was not possible to stop him. Patients with strong narcissistic over-compensation, on the other hand, often had role models, such as their father, who themselves had a very black-and-white perspective on social relationships. In their view, one was either the top dog or the underdog, and it was always important to be the top dog. In some cases the patient as a

---

Box 5.1 Possible questions to use when exploring a coping mode

"How long have you had this mode?"

"Why was this mode important for you when you were a child?"

"What were the advantages of this mode during your childhood?"

"How did others react when you were in this mode? How did they react when you behaved differently?"

"Did anybody in your social surrounding have a similar coping mode?"

"You told me that your mother often behaved quite similarly—is it possible that you learned this pattern from her?"

---

child may have been a "victim" of this mode and been assigned the role of the underdog. However, some patients seemingly just assimilate the world view of the narcissistic model without ever being placed in the opposite role.

Furthermore, coping modes typically had important functions when the patient was a child or adolescent. We usually assume that the coping mode was in some way more adaptive when the patient was a child than today. For example, patients with a strong detached protector mode often learned to detach when they were still very young. "When my mother shouted so horribly at me, I always kind of froze. Then it was easier to stand the situation."

When the biographical origin of the mode is being explored, the adaptive value of the mode is stressed. The therapist should discuss with the patient how important it was for them as a child to be able to apply this coping strategy. When social learning played a role in the development of the mode, the therapist should explain the mechanisms of social learning: children usually learn interpersonal behaviors from models, both functional and dysfunctional.

5.2.3   *Discuss pros and cons*

On the level of cognitive interventions, the pros and cons of the coping mode should be discussed, and a detailed list of these developed.

Case example: pros and cons of a detached protector mode

Susie suffers from panic disorder and dissociative symptoms. However, her appearance and her social behaviors conflict with her symptom report. She comes across as very "cool" and confident, is talkative, makes small-talk with people, and does not seem to be particularly anxious. But both Susie and her therapist experience this behavior as superficial. Susie says that she could never show how she actually feels. This mode is conceptualized as a detached protector mode; Susie calls it her "facade." It helps her in many situations of her life. With the facade up, she feels prepared for all kinds of social interactions. However, the facade also inhibits contact with herself. She often does not know what she actually needs, she doesn't know what to do with herself, and she doesn't have any idea what to do for fun or for a leisure activity. Her contact with others is also reduced—she hardly talks about her feelings or other personal issues. In the therapy session, these pros and cons are summarized in a pro-and-con list (see Table 5.1).

Table 5.1   Pros and cons of Susie's detached protector mode

Pros of the facade	*Cons of the facade*
I come across as competent and confident	I don't feel my own feelings
Others don't realize that I have problems	I can't communicate my feelings to others
My functioning at work is mostly good	I always feel detached from others, even when I like them or when they like me
I don't come across like a "psycho"	I feel sad and lonely quite often
I feel quite safe	I can't reduce my social anxiety and insecurity, because I can't experience safe interpersonal closeness
I can avoid conflicts; I am not attacked by others	
It helps me to show the right appearance in my studies and at work	

Case example: pros and cons of Nicole's bully and attack mode

When Nicole is in her bully and attack mode, she prioritizes her own interests and the interests of her close friends, she intimidates others, and she is in control of every situation. However, it is hardly possible to get into positive contact with her and she often has serious conflicts with the police, shop staff, and other people whom she attacks in this mode. The pros and cons of this mode are listed in therapy (see Table 5.2).

This intervention has to be balanced between the structure given by the therapist and the personal meaning experienced by the patient. With regard to structure, it is essential that the therapist strictly follows the goal of collecting the pros and cons of the coping mode; they should not allow the patient to avoid this discussion (note that this frequently happens, particularly if the coping mode is strong and includes frequent switches of attention). However, it is also important to pay attention to the personal experiences, opinions, feelings, and comments of the patient. Only when the patient feels that their personal issues are the focus of the discussion will the pro and con list be personally relevant to them: "I am very happy that you are willing to discuss your bully and attack mode with

Table 5.2 Pros and cons of Nicole's bully and attack mode

Pros of the bully and attack mode	Cons of the bully and attack mode
Others respect me, as they are afraid of me	It's almost impossible for me to build up positive relationships
I am able to push through what I want	Others are afraid of me; that's why they don't like me
It feels great to be in control of the situation	I repeatedly get in trouble with the law, with the police, etc.
I feel strong; nobody can harm me	I can't have the experience of peaceful, safe, and friendly relationships
I make sure that abuse and hurt will never happen to me again	When somebody gets to know me in this mode, they might not take me seriously
I can protect other people who are weaker than me	I actually don't like this mode; my mother had the same mode and I always hated it

me. I would like to have a look at the pros and cons of this mode in your life. What are your spontaneous ideas about this?" Typically, patients first relate to the pros and positive functions of the mode. This is desirable, and the therapist should strongly support it, because the mode is thus validated from the outset: "You already mentioned some very important points. For example, this mode helps you to stay in control of situations and to push through what you want. Can you think about other pros of this mode?" Only after the pro side has been discussed in detail should the con side be cautiously approached. When the patient starts talking about disadvantages of the mode, these should be noted on a flipchart or a piece of paper; however, discussion of them should be postponed until the pros have been fully discussed. It is usually easier for a patient to look at a mode's negative side after they have validated its positives. From a psychodynamic point of view, validation weakens the defense and thus helps the patient talk more openly about difficult emotional or interpersonal issues: "We put together quite a long list of pros for this mode. At the beginning of our discussion you briefly mentioned that you dislike this mode, since it reminds you of your mother, who had the same mode. Do you see any other disadvantages of your bully and attack mode?"

Coping modes like this are typically very persistent patterns which developed early in the patient's life. The patient has been used to them for many years. It is important to take into account that a single discussion of a mode will never be sufficient. It will take some time before the patient gains stable insight regarding the dysfunctional nature of the mode in their adult life. Thus it is always very important to return to the pros and cons of coping modes throughout the course of therapy.

> The discussion of the pros and cons of a coping mode is an essential cognitive intervention. To validate the mode as much as possible, you should always start with its pros.

5.3 Emotional Techniques

In the treatment of coping modes, cognitive and behavioral methods are usually in the foreground. However, in some cases it is important to use emotion-focused methods too.

5.3.1 Two-chair techniques

Dialogues with two chairs often have the same goal as pro-and-con discussions of a coping mode. However, they can have a stronger emotional impact. Chair dialogues are often recommendable when patients are very afraid of discussing the pros and cons of the mode. Note that anxiety over discussing a mode can appear in different forms, which in schema therapy are related to different modes. Sometimes patients are able to directly express anxiety. In that case, the anxiety should be briefly validated and addressed as a vulnerable child mode.

Two chairs are set up for a two-chair dialogue between the coping mode and an external perspective. In this dialogue, the coping mode is "interviewed" about its development and its function in the patient's life.

Sometimes patients react to the suggestion of a two-chair dialogue with an increase of their coping mode. A narcissistic patient might increase their narcissistic patterns: "Oh, yes, I've already heard this. All therapists have the same idea: that's me being a horrible narcissist. Congratulations, it only took you one session to find out! So what's your expert recommendation for how to treat my super ego?" A patient with a strong detached protector mode, however, might react by increasing in-session dissociation and interpersonal avoidance. In such situations, it is particularly recommendable to use a two-chair dialogue, although it might take the therapist quite some effort to introduce it. This intervention can very effectively interrupt the coping mode and thus help the patient to actually start reflecting upon it.

> When it is particularly hard for a patient to talk about a dominant coping mode in the therapy session, the two-chair technique can be used to explore this mode.

In a two-chair exercise, the patient is asked to "completely get into the mode's perspective" and to talk to the therapist only from that perspective. The therapist addresses the patient with the name of the coping mode, as if they are only talking to that part of the patient. This technique stresses the importance of the mode, which is usually very validating and a good starting point for a more differentiated and critical discussion. Note that it is very important to highly appreciate the mode's functions and to reinforce the patient constantly for participating in this intervention.

Case example: two-chair dialogue to explore a coping mode

Therapist: Sabine, I would like to suggest an exercise which might sound a bit strange to you. I would really appreciate it if you would be willing to try it out with me.

Sabine: Yes?

T: We just started to talk about this "Wall" behind which you usually hide when you are with other people. The Wall is something very important to you and I would really like to learn more about it.

S: Hmm?

T: [Takes two chairs and places them opposite each other.] I would like to ask you to take a seat on one of these chairs and to completely take on the perspective of the Wall. I would like you to "become the Wall," so to speak, and I would like to talk with the Wall. Do you understand what I mean?

S: Yes, I think so.

T: That's great. [Sabine sits on the Wall's chair and the therapist sits on the other chair.] Do you mind if I actually call you "Wall" when I talk to you this way? Are you OK with that?

S: [Nods.]

T: Thanks. Then I would like to talk to the Wall about you. That means, the Wall and I talk about Sabine, and why she needs the Wall. Are you OK with that?

S: [Nods again.]

T: Perfect. Then let's start. [Takes a breath and starts addressing the Wall.] Hello, Wall. You are obviously very important for Sabine. How would you explain why Sabine needs you?

S: Well, since Sabine has me, she has some peace and quiet.

T: What do you mean, exactly? From who or what do you protect Sabine? Why does she need you to have some peace and quiet?

S: Others don't care about her. She won't be threatened or attacked and she doesn't feel so horrible.

T: Do I understand you right: you protect Sabine against attacks and threat from other people? And you protect her from negative emotions when she is in a social situation?

S: [Nods.] Yes, that's correct.

T: It sounds like you are really very important to Sabine. Do you happen to know when you started to play this role in Sabine's life?

S: Oh, that's very long ago. I can't remember if Sabine ever lived without me.

T: So you've protected Sabine against negative emotions and attacks since very early in her life?

S: Yes, exactly, and that was really essential!

T: Oh, yes, I can imagine! Sabine told me about her childhood and how threatening and aggressive her father used to be. Have you been important in dealing with her father as well?

S: Yes. Without me, she wouldn't have been able deal with her father.

T: I absolutely believe you. Do you still remember how you acted at that time to help Sabine?

S: When her father started to shout at her, I bounced up. Then Sabine felt protected and calm and could just wait until her father got tired of shouting at her.

T: I really understand how important you have been for Little Sabine. How did things continue with you and her?

S: Well, things didn't get much better for Sabine when she got older. Her classmates always bullied her, so it was very good for her to have me.

T: Yes, I can imagine. How about today?

S: Today I still take care of Sabine. Things like that will never happen to her again—she mustn't be hurt that way again.

T: Yes. That's understandable, too. From who or what do you protect Sabine today?

S: Well, I'm actually not completely sure whether I pro-
      tect her today. I'm simply present and make sure that
      nothing happens.
T: And how does Sabine feel when you're there?
S: Well, she feels safe, but sometimes she might feel a bit
      lonely, too.
T: Might she feel lonely because she has only a little
      contact with others? Perhaps you sometimes tend to
      overprotect her a bit?
S: Well, that might sometimes be the case.

In this exercise, the coping mode is confronted in a very validating way. This usually helps the patient to start thinking and talking about the negative sides of the coping mode as well. In a variation of the standard dialogue as described in the case example, the therapist can put another empty chair at the patient's side after validating the coping mode. The therapist then says that this chair belongs to "Little Sabine" and asks the Wall how Little Sabine feels right now. In the context of this intervention, patients are usually able to realize that the vulnerable child mode feels lonely because the coping mode blocks interpersonal closeness.

The therapist can end this exercise by asking the patient whether they'd be willing to try out a behavioral experiment and reduce the detached protector mode within the therapy situation. This question can be brought up during the chair dialogue, or it can be raised after the exercise, when the therapist and the patient are jointly reflecting upon it. The therapist reassures the patient that they will do everything to help the vulnerable child and that they will try very hard not to hurt it. They will also look out for the Wall in future therapy sessions; when it pops up, the therapist will try to ask the patient why that reaction was necessary at that time.

This type of two-chair technique can also be conducted with over-compensation modes such as a bully and attack mode or a narcissistic self-aggrandizer mode. In such cases, it is often very helpful to add a chair for the vulnerable child mode. This chair might stay empty, but the therapist can include it in the exercise by asking the patient how the vulnerable child feels about the overcompensation mode. The patient might even take a seat on this chair during the exercise, and talk about the feelings of the vulnerable child mode. The main goal of these dialogues is usually to confront the patient with the damaging interpersonal consequences of the overcompensation mode. Highlighting the loneliness of the vulnerable child mode can play an important part in this process. The following case example demonstrates this strategy. Note that it may take some time before it is possible to refer to the vulnerable child mode with patients with strong overcompensation.

Case example: two-chair dialogue with Phillip's narcissistic self-aggrandizer mode

Therapist: I would like to do a chair-dialogue exercise and talk with your overcompensation mode, which we called Super Philip. Is this OK?

Phillip: [Nods.]

T: Then I would ask you to switch completely into the perspective of the overcompensation mode when I talk to you. I will talk to you as Super Philip, and here [the therapist puts an empty chair at Phillip's side] is Little Phillip. OK?

P: [Nods.]

T: Super Philip, what's your most important job?

P: Well, that's quite clear, I'd say: to be superior, stay in control, and be invulnerable.

T: And what do you accomplish with that for Little Philip?

P: I guess I protect him.

T: And if you didn't protect him in that way, what would happen?

P: Well, if he shows vulnerability others might take advantage of that. I make sure that nobody will hurt him!

T: Hmm, yes, I can imagine. How do you think Little Phillip feels about you?

P: Well, I think he's glad to have me!

T: [Points to Little Phillip's chair.] Please take a seat on that chair and try to feel Little Phillip.

P: [Sits in Little Phillip's chair.]

T: Little Phillip, how do you feel when the over-compensation mode is in complete control of everybody?

P: Well, I feel quite lonely.

T: Yes, I can imagine. [The therapist addresses Super Phillip while the patient stays on Little Phillip's chair.) Super Philip, I think it's important to understand that Little Phillip does not automatically feel good when you're there, trying to dominate everybody. Little Phillip might feel quite lonely and rejected when others reject you because they don't want to be dominated. It's important to let Little Phillip experience close and warm contact with others. [Addressing Little Phillip:] How does that sound to you?

P: That sounds good!

Variation with toys or dolls Some patients seem to be completely "imprisoned" by their coping mode. The coping mode can't even be interrupted by the two-chair dialogue, because they simply won't participate in the exercise or they dissociate completely. Dissociation happens particularly in patients with a very strong detached protector mode, such as some patients with severe and chronic BPD. In such cases, the exercise can be introduced in a stepwise manner by using smaller materials than chairs to begin with. Such materials might include Playmobil or other figures, toy blocks, and so on. If a patient has been sitting in silence for several minutes and is obviously in a strong detached protector mode, the therapist might communicate their feelings about the situation by arranging some Playmobil figures on the table, the arrangement of the figures mirroring the patient's momentary schema mode activation: a child figure (representing the vulnerable child mode) sits or lies behind a larger standing figure (representing the present dissociation/detached protector mode), while the therapist, represented by a third figure, stands in front of the detached protector and cannot make contact with the little child behind it. The therapist explains the arrangement: "I would like to share with you what I am experiencing in our relationship just now. I understand that one part of you suffers horribly, is very needy, and probably feels desperate [points to the child figure]. However, there is another part of you standing in front of this vulnerable part, so that I can't get in contact with it [points to the standing figure]. This other part interacts with me like a wall or a shutter. Do you understand what I am talking about? [The therapist waits for the patient's feedback.] Right now I would just like to understand a little bit better why this protective figure is needed here." The function, the biographic development, and the character of the detached protector mode as symbolized by the standing figure can then be explored. For many patients, it is less threatening to discuss their emotional experiences in such a distanced way instead of through a chair dialogue. However, this should be offered mainly to start emotion-focused work with schema modes. In the long term, the therapist should always motivate the patient to start dialogues with real chairs as well. The "real chair" format activates much more intense emotions, which seems to be a major prerequisite for actual emotional change.

Including a coping mode in chair dialogues with parent and child modes   Apart from the chair-dialogue formats described above, coping modes can be included in other chair dialogues as well, such as one in which the patient fights the punitive parent mode or gives comfort to the vulnerable child mode from the chair of the healthy adult. When these dialogues elicit strong emotions, patients sometimes switch into the detached protector mode. They may then express avoidance motives, like "This is all too much for me, actually, and I have no idea why we have to do this," or, "I would really like to leave the room now." When the emotional process is not impaired severely by such statements, the therapist might just validate them briefly: "That's quite a stressful exercise, I know! You're doing a great job!"

However, when this mode increases and interrupts the flow of emotions, it should be taken as an activation of the detached protector coping mode. Generally, coping modes must be validated and appreciated by the thera-pist. In the context of a chair dialogue, this can easily be done by adding an additional chair for the activated coping mode. This chair represents the perspective of the coping mode, and the patient is asked to take a seat in it and express this perspective. Usually, avoidant coping modes mainly intend to avoid intense negative emotions as they are too difficult. In the context of a chair dialogue aiming at parent and/or child modes, the therapist should validate the coping mode by giving it a voice but try to continue with the more emotional work afterwards. In some cases, however, it may not be possible to simply continue the dialogue with child or parent modes after a brief validation of the coping mode. In such cases it may be necessary to set the focus on the coping mode once more: to discuss pros and cons again, or to conduct a two-chair dialogue between the coping mode and the healthy adult mode.

Case example: direct bypassing of a coping mode

After a couple of sessions, Phillip and his therapist have developed a closer relationship and Phillip feels well represented by the schema mode model. He generally feels that his problems are very well conceptualized with this approach. However, in one of the later sessions he once again displays quite a strong overcompensatory state. He starts the session by criticizing the clinic's administration, and explains at length how he would solve the problem. The therapist decides to go for a direct bypass of the coping mode: "Phillip, I see that your overcompensation mode is really strong today. You're in this narcissistic state we discussed in the last session. Do you agree?" Phillip briefly nods but tries to continue. The therapist interrupts him again: "Do you know why this mode has been triggered today? Did something stressful happen to you? I guess there must be some emotional issue behind this mode?" This intervention helps the patient to step out of the mode. He explains that another patient criticized him in the occupational therapy session for his overcontrolling behavior. Phillip felt hurt, like he had his back against the wall.

The therapist suggests working directly with the vulnerable child mode which has obviously been triggered by this situation: "This was very hard for Little Phillip, right? I imagine that you felt bullied and ashamed, like when you were young?" Phillips agrees. "I would suggest doing an imagery exercise with these feelings. Is that OK?" In the following imagery rescripting exercise (see Section 6.3), the emotions of "Little Phillip" are changed so that he no longer feels ashamed and isolated, but like a member of the group.

Confrontation versus "direct bypassing" of a coping mode   When a coping mode pops up in therapy, the therapist usually has two basic options for how to work with it. First, the therapist can confront the patient with the coping mode and explore it using one of the strategies described in this section. With these interventions, the functions of the coping mode are discussed and the patient is motivated to reduce this mode in a stepwise manner. Particularly in the early phase of the therapy, it is useful to deal with coping modes this way, since the therapeutic relationship is not yet very close. In psychodynamic terms, it is necessary to deal with the defense mechanisms first.

However, when a good therapeutic relationship has been established and the patient has already opened up with the emotions of the vulnerable child mode in the therapeutic situation, we have the second option of directly bypassing the coping mode. Direct bypassing means focusing immediately on the vulnerable child mode or the punitive parent mode that is activated behind the coping mode. In psychodynamic terms, the therapist can break through defense mechanisms when they are already familiar with the patient's inner emotional experiences. With direct bypassing, the therapist addresses the coping mode only briefly, and immediately proceeds to more emotional issues: "When you started talking about last night, you switched into the detached protector mode. Why? What happened last night which triggered this mode just now?" We always assume that the activation of a coping mode is triggered by emotional stress and that it's most important and effective in the long term to reduce these stressful emotions via emotion-focused techniques such as imagery rescripting exercises. Therefore, we always focus as directly as possible on the negative emotions related to dysfunctional parent or child modes when the patient is able to bypass the coping mode and relate to these emotional triggers (see Chapters 6 and 7).

5.4   Behavioral Techniques

On the behavioral level, the main goal is to help the patient activate and increase healthy modes and healthy behavior patterns and to decrease dysfunctional modes. This includes feeling and expressing important needs more adequately. Depending on the patient's actual symptoms, symptom-related intervention techniques can play an important role. When, for example, OCD symptoms or self-injury have the function of detaching the patient from negative emotions (detached protector mode), the therapist can offer behavioral techniques (such as exposure in vivo with response prevention to reduce OCD rituals or skills training to replace self-injury) to help the patient deal with these symptoms. This is especially important if the dysfunctional coping is triggered in a (semi-)automatic fashion, or if patients feel a lack of control over these behaviors, for instance if a patients report that dysfunctional coping is triggered automatically and has the character of an addiction or a compulsion. However, if no healthy way of dealing with the negative emotions is developed, the isolated use of behavioral techniques is likely to fail. Thus, the application of behavioral techniques to address coping modes should go hand in hand with the development of healthy ways to deal with the emotions triggering the the dysfunctional coping mode.

5.4.1   Increase healthy modes and decrease dysfunctional modes

Socially withdrawn patients with a strong detached protector mode should become more active socially on the behavioral level. They should increase activities which make them feel connected and close to others, and should learn to express their feelings more clearly. Of course, we do not expect the patient to make social contact and display intense feelings all the time. Sometimes patients believe that "showing more of their feelings" mainly refers to the expression of vulnerable feelings. It can be helpful to explain to such patients that joint activities with others foster the experience of contact and closeness and related positive feelings, rather than negative feelings. These can be everyday activities such as sports or exercise, cooking or baking, working together, helping somebody, and so on. In fact, any activity which might be suggested for positive activation in CBT for depression is suitable. Related patient materials such as lists of positive activities can be used too.

When a patient has a strong avoidant protector mode, decreasing avoidance has the highest priority. Typical behavioral techniques are CBT techniques such as homework assignments and exposure exercises. The therapist should validate and verbally reinforce the patient when they manages to overcome avoidance. Note that very avoidant people avoid not just social activities but all kinds of intensive stimulus, including spicy food, emotional books or movies, and so on (Taylor et al., 2004). Behavioral homework assignments can refer to such issues as well.

5.4.2   Teach the patient to express their own needs more adequately

When in coping modes, patients are usually not able to express their needs adequately. In detached or avoidant coping modes, it is usually hard for people to realize their needs at all, let alone to express them. For these patients, it is important that they learn to express more of their needs. Related homework assignments might be to suggest their favorite leisure-time activities to family members or friends, or to ask for support at work or at home.

Patients with strong overcompensating modes, on the other hand, typically express their needs in an exaggerated, distorted, aggressive, or overly dominant way. Paradoxically, this often leads to less fulfillment of these needs, since other people are put off by this mode and become unwilling to care for the patient or support them. These problems are discussed using cognitive techniques such as pro-and-con lists, while social skills training can help to teach these patients a friendlier and more adequate expression of their needs. Video feedback might be very helpful, too.

5.4.3   Exercise the expression of needs in the therapy session

The therapeutic relationship is a good setting for the patient to exercise a more adequate expression of their needs. The therapist should explicitly encourage the patient to use this setting for such expression: "It would be great if you were to learn to express your needs in a way that lets other people understand what you want of them. At the same time, it is important that you are friendly with others, because they will then be much more motivated to help and support you. Both these issues have been quite complicated for you so far. Often you do not manage to express your needs at all; but when you do, you are usually in your overcompensating mode. This mode might put other people off, and make them draw away from you. That makes you feel vulnerable, and you draw back yourself and won't express anything about your needs anymore, right? I would be very happy if you were to use our therapy sessions as an opportunity to learn more about the adequate expression of your needs. I will always try to take care of your needs; but we should both look for opportunities for you to openly express your needs, too." When patients manage to express their needs in a more adequate way within the therapeutic relationship, the therapist should always reinforce them verbally: "Do you realize that you just expressed what you need from me in a very nice way? That's fantastic!"

When patients manage to express their own needs within the therapeutic relationship, their subjective experiences should be reflected upon. Note that the expression of needs can be a satisfying experience in many situations, but it may also be connected with at least some degree of frustration, because the therapist (or another person in the patient's life) does not completely meet the need, since this would be beyond their limits. It may be important to discuss realistic limits with the patient: We hardly ever get all our needs perfectly met. However, it is not necessary for all needs to be perfectly fulfilled in order to be psychologically healthy. Rather, it is important that most of our needs are fulfilled to a substantial degree, but some degree of frustration tolerance is necessary too.

5.4.4   Behavioral techniques related to specific symptoms

Severe symptoms related to coping modes should usually be treated on the behavioral level using the usual symptom-related or symptom-specific CBT techniques. For example, binge-eating attacks can be part of a detached protector or a detached self-soothing mode. In some cases, severe symptoms decrease with emotion-focused interventions aimed at the vulnerable child mode, but in many cases we also need behavioral interventions. Note that behavioral symptom-related techniques can be related to the mode model, just like emotion-focused and cognitive techniques.

Case example: behavioral interventions to reduce a detached protector mode in OCD

Lucy, a 29-year-old OCD patient, suffers from control compulsions related to contagion anxieties. The symptoms started after the death of her mother, when Lucy was 13 years old. When confronted with images or memories of her mother, Lucy uses compulsive rituals to calm heself down (OCD as part of the detached protector mode). In exposure with response-prevention exercises, Lucy starts feeling intense grief and sadness. Her therapist suggests combining exposure and imagery rescripting by working with the childhood memories related to grief and sadness that pop up when compulsive rituals are prevented in the exposure exercise.

OCD symptoms, for example, can be part of a coping mode—such as the perfectionistic overcontroller or detached protector—with the functions of overcompensating and avoiding intensive emotions. In some cases, OCD symptoms might improve via imagery rescripting exercises aimed at the vulnerable child mode alone. However, in many cases it will be necessary to use behavioral techniques (such as exposure with response-prevention) first, before the feelings of the vulnerable child mode can be accessed at all. The feelings of the vulnerable child mode should then be treated with adequate techniques in addition to exposure. The following two case examples demonstrate these two approaches.

Similarly, substance abuse related to a coping mode can be treated with specific behavioral techniques, especially when repeated empathic confrontation with the substance abuse doesn't work and the abuse seems to have become rather autonomous. When patients show self-injury behaviors or dissociative symptoms as part of the detached protector mode, dialectical behavior therapy (DBT) skills can be temporarily used to replace these problematic behaviors as part of the work with the detached protector mode. However, as opposed to the highly structured and manualized DBT skills training (Linehan, 1993), we would rather look for skills more tailored to each patient individually, and use most of these only temporary until the healthy adult mode is strong enough to deal with emotions and stress in a healthy way. Note that in the view of the schema-therapy model, some of these skills are, although less dysfunctional than for

---

Case example: imagery rescripting as the main intervention for OCD

Maria, 35 years old, has obsessions regarding ordering, which typically increase when she feels insecure in a social situation. Emotionally, she often feels lonely, disconnected, and like she doesn't belong in groups, which is related to the experience of being bullied and excluded when she was a schoolgirl. She does a series of imagery rescripting exercises related to exclusion and bullying in therapy. Afterwards, her obsessions have markedly decreased without the use of additional interventions targeting the obsessions more directly.

instance self-injury, still detaching. Although the detached protector can be useful in some circumstances, we also want to develop other ways of dealing with emotions and stress.

5.5   FAQ

(1) The confrontation part of schema therapy seems to be rather direct.
Isn't this approach sometimes a bit rude?

It is indeed often necessary to be clear and direct in schema therapy, particularly when confronting an overcompensation mode. This may feel strange to therapists who have a self-image of being only nice, friendly, and caring with their patients. However, you should remember that a problematic coping mode is usually a big issue for the patient: it damages—and eventually ruins—their relationships. It is the job of the therapist to help their patients understand their most damaging interaction patterns. If the most damaging pattern is an overcompensation mode, therapists should not shy away from confronting it.

Sometimes therapists feel rather bad when they use these confrontational techniques. The therapist's own modes, particularly guilt-inducing punitive parent modes, can block them from confronting their patients with critical issues. The therapist's punitive parent mode might have messages such as, "You always have to care for the well-being of others," or, "Your patient must always feel good during your sessions." A typical biographical background for such a mode in a therapist is a parent with psychological problems, such as a depressive mother, for whom the therapist felt responsible as a child. If this is the case, the therapist should try to understand this pattern in themselves better in order to be more relaxed about confronting their patients. Also note that confrontation in schema therapy is not belittling, aggressive, or overly critical. It should be either playful (e.g. with narcissists) or empathic.

(2) What can we do when a coping mode is strongly reinforced?

Coping modes can be very rewarding for patients, particularly the overcompensating, stimulating, or attention-seeking ones. These are related to stimulation, attention, or feelings of control and power, often in combination with lax discipline and procrastination over annoying duties as part of undisciplined or impulsive child modes. Detached and avoidant modes can also be very rewarding, because of their immediate anxiety-reducing effects, and can therefore be addictive. Note that patients may experience these modes as very rewarding even when they are able to see their disadvantages, or even when they question them ethically. Strong reinforcement by a mode decreases the willingness to change it.

As in "classical" CBT, it is important to consider the positive and negative reinforcement of symptoms and modes and discuss this with the patient. This is part of the cognitive pro-and-con discussion detailed in Section 5.2. This intervention is meant to motivate the patient to reduce their coping mode, but if the mode is strongly reinforced and the pros are powerful, the patient may end up deciding not to. We would certainly recommend that the therapist discuss the motivational situation with the patient again in such cases; however, if patients are clear about their decision, the therapist should accept it. Sometimes the decision against reducing a coping mode is a decision against therapy at all. In that case, the therapist should offer the patient the option to return if they change their mind, but should not try to coerce them into staying in therapy.

Of course, therapists have to consider their limits, too. When a patient reports illegal or extremely self-damaging activities but does not want to change them, the therapist may eventually have to decide not to offer any treatment for as long as the patient is unwilling to change these patterns: "You just told me that you see no reason to give up prostitution and drug use. I see no way to change your emotional problems without making changes in these areas of your life. I don't see a point to therapy under these circumstances. I will be happy for you to return to therapy if you decide to make a change in the future." However, if a patient is willing and able to work on the underlying (vulnerable) child modes, the therapist should temporarily tolerate (which is not the same as accepting) the coping modes. With adequate work on the child modes, the need for the patient to use the coping modes will reduce, and the motivation to address them will increase.

(3) What can you do when a patient stays silent instead of engaging in the therapeutic process?

Problems in the therapeutic process are conceptualized in schema therapy using the mode model whenever possible. When the patient remains silent during sessions, this silence would usually be conceptualized as an avoidant or detached protector mode. It must be limited to reduce its damaging influence in therapy. One way to set limits on such a mode is to engage the patient actively in therapy, by asking them frequently for feedback. The therapist can also validate the mode and explore its background: "You often stay very silent in our sessions. Why? Do you have to protect yourself against something?" If these strategies are not effective in reducing the silence, more active limit-setting may be necessary: "How should we continue? If you do not participate in therapy, I will not be able to help you."

6

Treating Vulnerable Child Modes

Intense negative emotions are related in the schema mode model to vulnerable or abandoned/abused child modes. Patients usually avoid or overcompensate for these emotions by means of coping modes. A central idea in dealing with vulnerable child modes is that patients should approach and process these emotions—this enables them to change their emotions in a positive way within emotion-focused interventions (imagery rescripting exercises and chair dialogues). The patients' psychological problems are thus treated at the root.

In short, the main goals with vulnerable child modes are to validate them, to process (traumatic) memories, emotions, and cognitions associated with them, and to help patients experience them within a caring and stable therapeutic relationship. Furthermore, patients are supported in caring better for these parts of themselves. They are encouraged to take their needs more seriously in everyday life. Often patients' needs are not well met within their unhealthy relationships. Thus, caring for vulnerable child parts can require the establishment of healthier interpersonal relationships. Within and outside interpersonal relationships, better meeting the patients' own needs usually reduces dysfunctional coping, such as surrendering, avoiding, detaching, self-soothing, or abusing and denigrating others.

Schema Therapy in Practice: An Introductory Guide to the Schema Mode Approach,
First Edition. Arnoud Arntz and Gitta Jacob.
© 2013 John Wiley & Sons, Ltd. Published 2013 by John Wiley & Sons, Ltd.

6.1   Reparenting and Extra Reparenting in the Therapeutic Relationship

When the feelings of a vulnerable child mode pop up in the therapy session, the therapist should validate and welcome them very warmly. Limited reparenting includes praising the patient and offering emotional support. Eventually the therapist might offer "extra reparenting," for example by giving transitional objects to the patient, offering a teddy bear in the therapy session to soothe the patient, and so on. In the original schema therapy approach by Young et al. (2003), "extra reparenting" also included offering the patient a phone number on which they could reach the therapist outside usual office hours. Many therapists did not feel comfortable with this standard, since they did not want to mix up their work and private lives. Nadort et al. (2009) therefore investigated the effect of crisis support outside office hours in patients with BPD, for whom this intervention was thought to be particularly important. No influence on the treatment effect was found. As a consequence, this standard has been taken out of the protocol for the treatment of BPD. An email address to which patients can send their messages when in their vulnerable child mode might be a good alternative, however, as it offers the patient a low-threshold connection to the therapist, without the therapist being bothered outside office hours. Therapists have often reported that patients have begun to report vulnerable issues in emails before they felt able to share these directly in the session.

However, some patients may appreciate having a phone number so they can listen to the therapist's voice on the voicemail message. Other methods utilizing the voice of the therapist can be helpful too. The theapist might record a message for the child mode on the patient's cell phone, so the patient can easily listen to it whenever they need to. Imagery rescripting exercises can also be recorded for the patient. In schema therapy for patients with BPD, all sessions are recorded anyway, and patients are asked to listen to them as part of their therapy homework (Arntz & van Genderen, 2009).

6.1.1   Cognitive techniques

On the cognitive level, patients often have to learn about the normal needs and normal rights of children, and to relate these to themselves as children. Traumatized patients often assume (implicitly or explicitly) that they are themselves guilty for the abuse they experienced, or feel that they were responsible for solving complicated family conflicts. Such unrealistic cognitions can be reduced using cognitive techniques. Cognitive treatment techniques can also be used to reduce desperation and hopelessness connected to vulnerable child modes.

6.1.2   Emotional techniques

The main emotion-focused technique in the treatment of vulnerable child modes is imagery rescripting. In imagery rescripting exercises, the patient enters a traumatic memory in imagery related to their current negative feelings. This image is then changed in such a way that the needs of the child (or the patient at another age) are fulfilled. Negative feelings, such as threat, anxiety, shame, guilt, and disgust are reduced, and safety and safe attachment are increased.

6.1.3   Behavioral techniques

On the behavioral level, it is important that patients terminate any current abusive relationships, since these can have the same damaging effect on the patient as abusive relationships in their childhood. These patterns must be reduced in the patient's life. If a relationship is not abusive but does not meet many of the patient's most important needs, it is important that the patient gives higher priority to their own needs, and communicates them better to others. We assume that the therapeutic relationship can offer the patient the best opportunity to exercise and experiment with an adequate expression of their own needs. Sometimes it might be the first relationship in which the patient has tried to understand and communicate their needs. After having positive and corrective experiences with the expression of their own needs in the therapy situation, the patient should try to express their needs more clearly in other relationships as well. Group therapy can be particularly meaningful in this context. The group setting offers many different relationships within therapy which the patient can use to learn to feel safe and to express their own needs. Just as the therapist is meant to become a parent figure by reparenting the patient, other group members can adopt sibling roles.

6.1.4   The therapeutic relationship

When the patient is in a vulnerable child mode, the main task of the therapist within the therapeutic relationship is to validate and care for the patient's emotions and needs. This relates to all kinds of therapy situations and therapeutic techniques. Whenever a vulnerable child mode pops up, the therapist should react in a very warm and caring way. Often it is helpful to explicitly address the negative emotions related to the vulnerable child mode as "important emotions which should be appreciated, taken seriously, and processed" (see the next case example). The therapist should react to all of the patient's vulnerable feelings in this way, whether they appear during discussions with the therapist (inside or outside therapy) or in the middle of an emotion-focused intervention technique (imagery exercise or chair dialogue).

Case example: validating the vulnerable child mode in the therapy session

Lucie, a student with avoidant behavior patterns and BPD, calls her therapist during office hours. Her desperate emotional state becomes clear as soon as Lucie says her name. The therapist immediately addresses her feelings and validates her: "Hi, Lucie. I can hear that you feel really bad right now. It's great that you've called me! What's up?" The patient explains that she just got an email from the university saying that she may not be allowed to take her exams as scheduled. She won't know the final decision until tomorrow, since the university office has already closed for the day. She continues: "I know that you can't really help me and that you're very busy, but I didn't know what else to do."

The therapist focuses on reparenting by soothing Lucie and validating her feelings, but keeps the conversation brief—or else it would not be *limited* reparenting (reparenting within the limits of a normal therapeutic relationship). Patients can usually tolerate these limits so long as their emotions are sufficiently validated. Even though the limits of the therapeutic relationship may be painful for patients, they are usually well aware of them.

Therapist: Lucie, I am sorry, but I can't actually help you right now, other than by talking with you for a few minutes. I have to see another patient soon, and after that I have to run to pick up my children from day care. We will have much more time in our next session, the day after tomorrow. If we need more time than I have now, I can call you tomorrow. However, I am happy that you called me. Maybe I can help you to calm down a little

	bit. I think it's very important that you do not feel completely alone in this situation.
Lucie:	Yes. I think that's actually the reason why I called you.
T:	Perfect. I think so, too, and I really appreciate it. I understand that the message that you might not be allowed to take your exams is very upsetting to you. Am I correct?
L:	Yes. I really don't know what to do. What should I do now?
T:	I feel that it is not important right now to do something, but rather to share with me what emotions were triggered when you heard about this. Can you try to share them with me?
L:	I am so stressed. Panicky . . . I feel like I have no control over the situation. They will just throw me out of the university There's nothing I can do . . .
T:	OK. Now I understand better why the message is so alarming for you. As I understand it, the message is that they cannot guarantee that you will be able to take the exams. And although the decision is still open, it has given you such an overwhelming feeling of uncertainty and lack of power that you feel panic and the need for support. I guess Little Lucie, your vulnerable child mode, has been triggered by this, and you feel as powerless again against overwhelming negative things as you did when you were a little child. Is that possibly happening here?
L:	Uhhh . . . [Thinks for a moment.] Yes, I think you are right . . .
T:	OK, this will help us to understand what is happening with you emotionally when you feel so upset. And also to understand what you need. What is it that you need?
L:	I guess I need clarity. This is just a vague and sort of threatening message . . . It gives me the feeling that my fate is entirely at the mercy of others . . . I need some influence . . . And I need support.
T:	Absolutely, and both are completely healthy needs. It is wonderful that you can share them with me. And I can offer you help with them. I have to take a look at my

watch . . . I'm so sorry I can't help you more at the moment, but I understand that the panicky feeling of Little Lucie is very strong and you have this feeling of "I need help now!" However, I can offer you the following options: (1) you can send me an email and I'll respond to that first thing tomorrow morning; (2) I can make some time, say 15 minutes, tomorrow around noon, to call you and we can discuss this further; or (3) we can do both. Do any of these sound good to you?

L: I'll send you an email . . . I think it will help me to share my feelings with you some more . . . Can I tell you by email whether I need a call tomorrow?

T: Sure!

L: OK.

T: How do you feel right now?

L: Less upset. But I am a bit afraid that the panic will start again later on . . .

T: No problem. Just email me then . . . and let me know if you need me to call you tomorrow. Thanks for calling, and please send me your email. Take care, Lucie.

The therapist should deal warmly with and validate the emotions related to vulnerable child modes, both in discussions with the patient inside and outside of therapy sessions and in emotion-focused exercises. With regard to emotion-focused interventions, the therapist should care warmly for the patient's child mode and fight against the punitive parent modes in chair dialogues and imagery exercises. Limited reparenting in an imagery rescripting exercise is demonstrated in the next case example, and more detailed instructions for imagery exercises can be found in Section 6.3. In chair-work exercises, the therapist should always talk very warmheartedly and caringly with the vulnerable child part of the patient, and validate the related feelings and needs (see the case example on limited reparenting in chair dialogues).

Limited reparenting in the therapeutic relationship is central to schema therapy. The experience of a safe and supportive therapeutic relationship is important to healing the maladaptive schemas at the basis of personality disorders. The safe attachment offered by the therapist is

Case example: caring for a vulnerable child mode in an imagery exercise

Lucie imagines a scene of her mother making fun of her as a 7-year-old girl because she doesn't understand her homework and has made a "stupid mistake." Her mother doesn't help her, and instead laughs at her and withdraws sneeringly. In the mental image, Little Lucie sits at her desk; she feels lonely, sad, unloved, and is longing for understanding, love, and support from her mother. The therapist enters the image, saying: "Now I'm entering the room. Can you picture me there?" The patient nods. "First I approach you, Little Lucie, and sit down at your side. What would you like me to do? Is it OK if I stay where I am, or should I hug you, or would you like to sit on my lap?" The patient says that Little Lucie would like to sit on the therapist's lap. "OK, please sit down on my lap. I give you a hug: 'Hello, Little Lucie, I'm sorry that you are so sad. You're a lovely little girl. It's completely normal to misunderstand something at school and to make some mistakes in your homework. That's actually part of learning new things! You just need somebody to explain it to you again. That's absolutely normal and happens to everyone from time to time.'"

Case example: limited reparenting in chair dialogues

Alan often surrenders to his wife's needs, even if his own needs are very different and he feels badly treated by his wife. The therapist suggests a chair dialogue to help Alan focus more on his needs in the relationship. The biographical background of his compliant surrender mode is a very similar relationship between Alan and his mother. His mother lost her husband early and as a little boy Alan felt responsible for supporting her emotionally. Accordingly, he did not learn to focus on this own needs and to ask others for emotional support himself; this problematic pattern is now repeated in his marriage.

In the first phase, the chair dialogue deals with Alan's demanding mother mode, which forces him to always focus on his wife's needs and desires. Alan becomes very sad when experiencing the high impact of this demanding mode. His sadness is regarded as an indicator of his vulnerable child mode. The therapist's goal in the chair dialogue is to decrease the impact of the demanding mode and to soothe the sad child mode. Both methods should help Alan to give higher priority to his needs, to communicate them more directly, and to set clearer limits. To approach these goals, the therapists explains from the healthy adult chair that every human being has the right to care for their own needs and that it is not healthy to focus solely on the needs of others. The therapist first says this in a strict voice to the demanding mother mode's chair, and then in a warm and caring voice to Little Alan's chair: "Little Alan, you are a lovely boy and I am happy that you are here. Listen: your rights and your needs are OK! It is important that you show what you need. We will do everything here to help Healthy Adult Alan to care much better for you; then you will not feel as sad anymore."

The patient starts crying and says how good it feels to hear this. The therapist validates these feelings, and repeats the "message to Little Alan." They then try to find out whether Alan is able to feel (at least some) anger when in the chair of the angry child mode. When the vulnerable child mode feels accepted and gets attention, it is often easier for the patient to feel anger, which would actually be quite helpful for Alan in his current situation.

supposed to counteract any unsafe attachment experiences the patient had in their childhood. It is important to reflect upon reparenting in the therapeutic relationship—and its pitfalls—with the patient. Sometimes patients will show dependent relationship patterns and wish that the reparenting by the therapist will never end. However, reparenting involves helping the patient to become an adult and to be autonomous in feeling and expressing their own needs. Consistent dependent patterns block this process and must be addressed. The limits of the therapeutic relationship can be an important issue in therapy and should be openly discussed.

6.1.5 The limits of limited reparenting: helpful reparenting versus supporting a dysfunctional dependent pattern

Limited reparenting—validating, soothing, and supporting the patient—is a central agent of change in schema therapy. It is supposed to help the patient build up trust in the therapist and learn to feel safe in the therapeutic relationship. However, learning to trust and feel safe with the therapist is only the first step. In the next, the patient has to try out healthier patterns in other relationships as well. The more the patient manages to strengthen healthy relationships outside therapy, the less important the therapist becomes.

The therapist is regarded as a model for addressing and meeting the patient's own needs. The patient is supposed to internalize this healthy adult model. This will help them to care better for themselves and to set clearer limits in everyday life. Again, the more the patient manages to build up such healthy patterns, the less important the therapeutic relationship becomes.

Sometimes patients are quite surprised by how strongly they are supported by the therapist regarding their needs and their rights, within chair dialogues or imagery rescripting exercises for example. Schema therapists take quite a different position here to cognitive therapists. We suggest openly explaining the nature of the therapeutic relationship in schema therapy in order to help the patient understand why the therapist is so supportive and nurturing. By discussing the therapeutic relationship, we help the patient to reflect upon the nature of their own relationships and the balance of rights and needs between each partner within them. This provides a basis from which the patient can take responsibility for healthier patterns in their relationships.

Case example: explaining limited reparenting in the therapeutic relationship

Alan reflects upon the chair dialogue with his vulnerable child mode (see Section 6.1.4): "It feels great to be comforted by you. It is similar to the imagery exercise in our last session, when you entered the scene and cared so nicely for Little Alan. I felt absolutely safe and secure, which I actually never did as a child. However, it's also a bit frightening. Isn't there a risk that I become completely dependent upon you?" The therapist responds: "You're pointing to a very important aspect of schema therapy. We assume that you were not able to learn how to feel safe when you were a child, since you never experienced safeness, as you just said. Thus you also did not learn to address your own needs and to ask for support from someone else. Instead, you learned only to surrender to the other person in your relationships, as you're doing in your marriage today. We assume that you first have to experience that relationships can be safe and supportive. Only when you are able to feel safe can you start to behave more self-confidently in relationships such as marriage. I want to offer you a therapeutic relationship which helps you to experience and internalize safety and care. It may be that you will sometimes feel a bit emotionally dependent. However, as soon as you feel safe here, you will be able to transfer this feeling step by step to other people as well. Usually this development occurs automatically over time. Then it will be more and more possible for you to stand up for your needs and to set limits on others. In the long term, you will not need me anymore, because you will be able to care for yourself much better than you can now, and you will no longer feel dependent upon me."

Patients with BPD need a particularly close therapeutic relationship, at least for some time. Within this close relationship, limited reparenting is possible. The patient can then develop the experience of safety and safe attachment which was not available in their childhood. For that reason, the risk of dependency or too-close attachment to the therapist is generally not regarded as a problem in schema therapy. However, it is of course absolutely necessary to stay within the limits of a professional relationship. It would, for example, not be regarded as suitable to have phone calls with a patient each night, to constantly give them extra appointments, or to have excessive physical contact with a patient.

Dependent behavior patterns in the patient   The course of the therapeutic relationship over time has to be reflected upon. Sometimes dependent patterns in the patient turn out to be a problem only after a while. Patients with dependent patterns in their relationships may gratefully accept emotional support from the therapist from the very beginning of therapy. Accordingly, interventions with limited reparenting work very well with these patients early in therapy. However, in the longer term such patients may not take steps toward developing autonomy in expressing their own needs outside the therapy. This is typical of patients with a strong dependency schema and/or with symptoms of a dependent personality disorder. Therapists often sense this through countertransference; they may feel somehow tired or resigned after a while, and the therapy process can get stuck.

It's vital to openly address such situations in therapy. Therapists often feel very uncomfortable confronting their patients with dependent patterns. However, without this confrontation the therapy might not be helpful, or it could even be damaging for the patient in the long term—dependent relationship patterns can actually be stabilized when the therapist does not address them in time. When the therapist confronts the patient with dependent patterns, it is first important to validate these patterns as understandable—perhaps dependency has been the only way for the patient to secure support from others since their childhood. Without validation, the patient may experience this confrontation as a reproach, which can quickly trigger the punitive parent mode: "I want to share an observation with you that I made in our last session. When we do emotional interventions like imagery rescripting or fighting your punitive parent mode in a chair dialogue, they usually work really well. That's great! These exercises are meant to help you find an emotional basis from which to take better care of yourself and your needs in your everyday life, which is something I think you have trouble with at present. [Wait for patient's reaction.] Sometimes we see that patients haven't learned to take care of themselves in their childhood because they were not allowed to communicate their needs, and that they have developed very dependent patterns as a coping strategy. Dependency means that you always need somebody else to care for you and take over responsibilities for your needs, because you feel that you will never manage on your own. I wonder whether such a pattern might play a role in our relationship?"

It is important to reflect on whether reparenting leads to an increase of self-care and the healthy adult mode in the patient over time. When this is not the case, dependent patterns may play a role. The therapist should confront the patient empathically with this issue.

Combination of borderline and dependent personality traits   The combination of borderline personality pathology and dependent personality traits is rather common and poses a special dilemma for the therapist. In this situation, therapists may find themselves having a conflict between reparenting the vulnerable child mode and limiting dependent patterns. Reparenting the vulnerable child mode is a very important part of schema therapy in BPD over a long period of the therapy (Arntz & van Genderen, 2009). However, dependent patterns are often not clearly identifiable at the beginning of therapy. They are usually associated with high compliance on the part of the patient regarding therapeutic advice, and thus such patients do not seem to be "complicated" at the beginning of therapy. (A high number of prior therapies without clear effect can be an indicator of dependent patterns in the patient.) Thus therapists often offer a high level of reparenting to these patients. They may then find it very hard to confront dependent patterns after they become clearer over the course of therapy, as this means switching from a mainly caring and supportive style to a more autonomy stimulating and limit-setting one.

It is clearly not helpful to strive for the goal of stopping dependent patterns in the very beginning of therapy. Borderline patients with dependent patterns should be confronted with their dependent parts when these parts actually inhibit therapy progress. When the therapist decides to confront patients with their dependency, they should on the one hand set limits on the dependent parts of the patient, while maintaining a very warm and caring attitude towards the vulnerable child parts on the other. The best way to do this is to distinguish between emotional dependency and functional dependency. We usually explain to the patient that it is OK to feel emotionally dependent upon the therapist for some time during therapy. Emotional dependence means feeling that it would be hard to live without the support of the therapist at that moment. At the same time, it is important that the patient becomes functionally more independent and autonomous. Functional dependency means actually needing the therapist's practical support for nearly every step of the patient's life. Developing functional independency—in other words, autonomy—might include establishing other relationships in addition to the therapeutic relationship, becoming socially more active, looking for supportive people who are willing to help the patient in everyday life, and so on.

Chair dialogues are an important means by which to help patients understand their dependent parts. In a chair dialogue, the dependent part of the patient (either a dependent child or compliant surrender mode, according to the mode's main affect) gets its own chair. It can thus be expressed, understood, and validated. The patient can learn to identify and understand its patterns. Furthermore, the patient should not feel merely criticized, since the dependent part is introduced as "one part of the patient," which they may not have been aware of before. The therapist should be particularly validating and caring in this intervention. They should make sure to schedule enough time for the issue, because the patient might have problems understanding it or might feel criticized at first anyway. This is particularly important with patients with BPD who are quick to feel punished and criticized. It is important that the therapist clearly explains that they do not want to punish the patient: "You are important to me, and Little X is particularly important", but that they do not avoid the confrontation: "I regard it as very important that we discuss these dependent patterns, since they may have quite an impact on your life. This impact may sometimes be confusing for you, since sometimes dependency has very positive short-term effects but very negative long-term effects." For patients with BPD and dependent patterns, the differentiation of emotional from functional dependency is always recommended.

6.1.6   Limits of the therapeutic relationship

The concept of limited reparenting suggests a very close therapeutic relationship. However, the therapist is responsible for setting adequate limits upon it. These limits should eventually be openly discussed with the patient. The issue of limits is probably—at least at first sight—less important in therapeutic approaches with a more neutral therapeutic relationship, such as the classical psychoanalytical relationship or the Socratic attitude adopted in cognitive therapy. However, clinical experience with personality-disordered patients tells us that adequate limits in the therapeutic relationship are vital even in other therapeutic approaches.

It is extremely important that a schema therapist knows what "traps" they are prone to. If a therapist tends for example to be overly protective with patients, they should reflect upon whether they instrumentalize the schema therapy approach in order to justify overprotective behavior or to take over too much responsibility for patients. A basic rule in schema therapy is that the therapist may offer any kind of support within emotional interventions such as imagery rescripting exercises with vulnerable child modes—all the needs of the vulnerable child mode should be fulfilled *within the imagery*, if necessary through the person of the therapist, including by offering physical contact to the child, taking the patient as a child to the house of the therapist, adopting the vulnerable child into the therapist's family, killing the abusive perpetrator, and so on—however, this "perfect care" is restricted to imagery exercises, which are supposed to help the patient acquire the feeling of safety and to bring about the emotional processing of childhood traumas. It is not necessary—and it would definitely be beyond reasonable limits—to do such things in reality! This is, by the way, usually completely clear for patients without discussion.

However, if a patient asks the therapist to do things beyond the limit of the therapeutic relationship, the therapist should first validate these needs—"It's understandable, and actually it's probably even true, that you think it would be much nicer for you if we were to become real friends"—and acknowledge the (frustrating and depriving) reality of the patient's life—"You are indeed lacking positive social experiences and you are in need of good friends who care about you"—but then clearly address the realistic limits of the therapeutic relationship: "However, I can only offer you support in our therapy, not in a private friendship. That's reality, even if it may sometimes be hard for you."

Case example: discussing the limits of the therapeutic relationship

Patient: I really like you. You are the first person that really seems to understand me. I really feel accepted by you.

Therapist: Thank you. That is nice of you to say. I also like you, and think we collaborate very well in therapy.

P: I would like to have you as a real friend. I feel that we could get along very well. I mean, not just in therapy, but also outside. Why don't you come to my house and I can show you my paintings? You are always so interested in my painting.

T: Many thanks. That is very flattering. But I'm afraid I don't have the kind of feelings towards you that are necessary for friendship. I really like you, but I would like to restrict our meetings to therapy. Perhaps if we had met outside treatment, but that's not how it happened. So thank you for your invitation, but I cannot accept it . . . How is that for you? [The therapist continues to explore what this rejection means for the patient, and corrects any misinterpretations, but also allows and validates primary emotional reactions. Therapists should take care not to fall prey to countertransference by blaming the patient for developing feelings towards them that they cannot meet.]

Physical contact in the therapy situation   With regard to physical contact, we suggest being cautious. Depending on the culture, it might be completely normal, or even indicated, to shake hands at the start and end of each session, or to give an occasional hug. Here schema therapy doesn't want therapists to be distant. However, the contact should not be erotic, and any doubts should be discussed in (peer) supervision. It may happen that a patient feels very supported by the therapist's holding their hand. As long as this clearly aims at supporting the vulnerable child mode, and as long as both the patient and the therapist feel perfectly comfortable and relaxed with it, this may be a helpful and effective intervention. However, we would not recommend going further by giving the patient long and intense hugs, holding their hand during imagery exercises, and so on. Patients learn to feel safely attached in imagery exercises. Intense physical contact is not necessary and could be more complicated than helpful for the patient. If the patient asks for physical contact that the therapist feels is uncomfortable, the therapist should respect their own boundaries and explain this to the patient: "I understand that you need this, but I would feel uncomfortable with it. The reason that I won't do this is not that your question is wrong, but that this is my personal boundary." The therapist should check what emotions (and modes) this evokes in the patient. Note that the therapist explains the decision to the patient based on personal arguments, not on professional rules like "That is forbidden." Clarifying one's behavior through personal reasons helps to build the kind of therapeutic relationship that is central to schema therapy.

6.2   Cognitive Techniques

Emotion-focused techniques and the therapeutic relationship are the most important in treating vulnerable child modes. However, cognitive techniques can at times be important too. These techniques help patients understand the functions and the needs of the vulnerable child mode and learn more about its development in their life. Furthermore, the actual implementation of changes in everyday life can be supported by cognitive techniques.

6.2.1   Cognitive restructuring

Cognitive restructuring can be used to reduce hopelessness connected with vulnerable child modes. Typical cognitions of the vulnerable child mode in need of restructuring are: "Nobody likes me, nobody will ever love me," "I am completely worthless," and "I am a failure." In a vulnerable child mode, a patient may have distorted cognitions like: "Mary didn't look at me when she said 'hello'; obviously she doesn't like me anymore." Such cognitions can be the topic of chair dialogues. However, it is also possible to use typical cognitive techniques for the treatment of depression, such as Socratic dialogues, questioning biased interpretations, and so on.

6.2.2   Psychoeducation

With regard to the vulnerable child mode, psychoeducation mainly aims at teaching patients that their needs and emotions are normal and understandable. Humans need to feel attached and safe with others; if these needs are not adequately met, the feelings of the vulnerable child mode pop up. Little children are not responsible for taking care of their own needs; it is the task of their parents to understand and meet them. When parents abuse their child or ask too much of them, it's not the child's fault. Sometimes patients tell us that they were "difficult" children; even though this might partly explain difficult childhood experiences, the child cannot be held responsible for such problems. Instead, the parents are responsible for getting support and help for their child. Table 6.1 summarizes the main content of psychoeducation targeting vulnerable child modes.

Psychoeducation can be used in combination with different interventions. It is usually part of explaining the mode model to the patient. The therapist explains how dysfunctional schemas developed and why the patient has maintained them. Sometimes patients ask for psychoeducation because they want to find out in therapy why they have always felt in some way bad, lonely, or guilty.

Table 6.1 Psychoeducation for vulnerable child modes

Children are basically wonderful and valuable—even when they are a strain, make mistakes, or don't behave perfectly.

Children are basically good. No human being is born a bad person.

When a child is abused, hurt, or ignored by their parents or other people, the child is not to blame. Although the reasons other people behave this way might be understandable (they may be unable to cope with their own problems), the child is never to blame.

When parents are overstrained with their children, it's their job to get support. A child cannot take responsibility for solving difficult family situations.

All children have feelings and needs. They need support, help, love, and care. Children have a right to get these needs met to an acceptable degree. When these needs are not met at least to some degree, a child may not be able to develop into a healthy, adult person.

Needs and feelings are basically good.

Often it is understandable (with hindsight) why parents were not able to care well for their children; they may have been overstressed, have had psychological problems, and/or have been mistreated or abused themselves when they were very young. However, children cannot take this external perspective when they are being treated badly: they simply suffer and get damaged.

6.2.3   Emotion-focused techniques

Psychoeducation is often important in the context of emotion-focused methods. Often vulnerable child modes (= the patient as a child in imagery) express guilt or the feeling of being overly responsible for a complicated situation within imagery rescripting exercises. They may for example say, "But I am a bad child, that's why I didn't deserve better treatment." In such cases the therapist should provide psychoeducation within the imagery exercise, either as a general comment or as a comment from the healthy adult figure in the image: "Little Susie, I understand that you feel you are bad because that is what you have been told all your life. But children are never bad from birth. Like every other child, you are basically good. You are very valuable just the way you are."

6.2.4   Chair dialogues

Psychoeducation can also be part of chair-work exercises. When the therapist expresses care and empathy for the vulnerable child mode from the chair of the healthy adult, they can include psychoeducative elements: "You're a good child! No child is born as a bad child. Sadly, some children are told by others that they are bad. I want to help you understand that you are basically good and valuable, just like every other child." In the context of an emotion-focused exercise, such statements are expressed in a warm and caring tone of voice.

6.2.5   Schema flashcards and other written materials

As in "classical" CBT, written materials can be very helpful in implementing change in everyday life. Cognitive interventions focusing on self-esteem are particularly useful, such as diaries regarding positive events. Worksheets can help patients to understand their everyday emotional and schema-mode processes. The so-called "schema flashcard" is used to summarize the patient's everyday experiences in terms of schema modes and their cognitive and emotional implications. Alternative interpretations can also be elaborated (see Table 6.1 for a worksheet). You can either use a worksheet for a schema flashcard (Table 6.2), or write it up on a piece of paper or a postcard.

Table 6.2   Schema flashcard

Schema Flashcard

Identify the current feeling

Right now I feel (emotion) . . . .
since (trigger points) . . . .

Identify the mode

This is probably the following mode: . . . .
I developed this mode as a child because (biographical background)
. . . .
My typical coping reaction (avoid, overcompensate, surrender) is . . . .
(typical coping behaviors) . . . .

Reality testing

Although I think that (negative cognition) . . . .
reality says that (healthy cognition) . . . .
Proofs: . . . .

Alternative behaviors

Although I feel like doing (dysfunctional behavior in this mode) . . . .
. . . .
I could try to (healthy alternative) . . . .
. . . .

Case example: schema flashcard

Lucie and her therapist develop the following text for a schema flashcard: "When my friend Maria does not call me when we have not seen each other for a couple of days, I feel completely alone and lonely, as if nobody will ever be interested in me again. These feelings belong to Little Lucie, my vulnerable child mode. It is completely understandable that I feel this way since I was very lonely as a child. However, it is not true anymore: I have several friends, including good friends whom I can trust and who honestly like me. I can, for example, rely on Martha to listen to me when I have a problem. Joe just told me how much he likes spending time with me. The other girls from the choir like me at least a little bit, or else they wouldn't invite me to their birthday parties. In order to feel less sad and lonely in the current situation, I could either take action by calling Maria myself, listen to the CD from our last choir concert to remind myself of my friends there, or just go out for a jog or a little walk to help me calm down."

Schema flashcards should contain the following points:

- Current negative thoughts and feelings evoked by an everyday event and the (vulnerable child) mode they are related to.
- Typical coping behavior related to this mode.
- Reality-testing and healthier, more adequate interpretations of the current event.
- Suggestions for more functional coping (including emotion-regulation skills, if necessary).

6.3 Emotion-Focused Techniques

The central emotion-focused techniques in treating vulnerable child modes are imagery exercises and chair dialogues. In this section, imagery techniques are explained in detail. More detailed information regarding chair dialogues can be found in Chapter 8.

Imagery techniques can be used as both a diagnostic and a therapeutic tool. Diagnostic imagery exercises are always used at the beginning of schema therapy. In these exercises, current negative feelings are used as a starting point for exploring biographical memory images related to them. Patients are asked to recall memories with their parents and with all other people (family members, peers, etc.) who were problematic for them in their childhood. Diagnostic imagery exercises resemble the starting phase of imagery rescripting exercises (see Section 6.3.2), but without the rescripting part.

Keep in mind that a person's parents are not always the main cause of their psychological problems. Punitive or self-devaluating introjects can be related to other people, such as bullying peers. Many patients report aggravating circumstances in their childhood outside the scope of human influence, such as severe diseases, loss of family members, or problems with physical appearance (overweight, severe acne).

6.3.1   Goals of imagery exercises

The main goal of imagery exercises is to establish new emotional patterns. Patients with chronic psychological disorders typically experienced traumatic or abusive situations in their childhood. As a result, they have difficulties experiencing positive emotions related to safe attachment such as safety, security, and protection. Instead they feel threatened, ashamed, helpless, abandoned, and so on, even in non-threatening situations. In imagery rescripting exercises, threatening memory images are processed and changed. Negative emotions are replaced with positive emotions such as safety, security, joy, and pleasure.

With regard to specific negative emotion, imagery rescripting exercises are particularly suitable for changing feelings of anxiety, threat, disgust, shame, and guilt. These emotions can (and should) be substantially reduced using imagery rescripting exercises. Regarding feelings of sadness, however, clinical experience shows that it may sometimes be more important to validate and accept sadness, and go along with the patient in working through a mourning process, than to try to reduce it through imagery rescripting. Patients often avoid stressful or traumatic childhood memories because they believe that reliving them will make them feel sad about their "lost childhood." It seems to be important to face and validate this sadness.

Validating and accepting sadness (as opposed to reducing it) does not conflict with the general goals of imagery rescripting exercises, since sadness can exist alongside positive feelings such as safety, security, and safe attachment. A sad child can be soothed in imagery (or in a chair dialogue) by the therapist in the role of a warm and caring helping figure. Shame, anxiety, and threat, on the other hand, are not compatible with safety and consolation. If these emotions are in the foreground, their source must be eliminated in an imagery rescripting exercise before the therapist can soothe the vulnerable child mode.

> Feelings of anxiety, threat, shame, guilt, and disgust can be quickly changed using imagery rescripting exercises. With regard to sadness, it may be more important to focus on the process of mourning. However, consolation and support should be offered for sad vulnerable child modes.

6.3.2 *Imagery rescripting exercises*

In imagery rescripting exercises, an emotionally stressful situation is accessed via mental imagery. Usually past (childhood) experiences are the focus of imagery rescripting exercises, but they can also be applied to current or even future situations. When the patient feels the painful feelings related to the situation in question, the image is changed in such a way that negative emotions (guilt, shame, threat) are replaced by positive ones (attachment, safety, empowerment, joy). Imagery rescripting is a very flexible and creative technique. The exact content of an imagery exercise can never be completely predicted. However, the emotional process can be clearly defined and guides the actual content of the exercise. Hackman et al. (2011) offer a thorough introduction to this treatment technique. Table 6.3 provides an overview of the imagery rescripting process.

Each step of this process will now be explained in more detail. Typical problems and possible variations will be discussed.

(1) Provide relaxation instruction During imagery exercises, patients should if possible close their eyes. If a patient is too scared or feels uncomfortable closing their eyes, they may instead fix their gaze on a point on the floor or the ceiling. Sometimes patients feel more comfortable

Table 6.3 Imagery rescripting process overview

---

(1) Provide relaxation instruction, optionally with a safe-place image.

(2) Access the current stressful situation and related negative emotions in imagery.

(3) Affect bridge: keep the feeling, but wipe out the image of the current situation; access instead an emotionally stressful memory image associated with the emotion (most often a childhood image).

(4) Briefly explore the childhood situation ("Who's there?" "What's happening?"); focus on the feelings and needs of the child.

(5) Introduce a helpful figure who cares for the child's needs and changes the situation in such a way that the child feels safe and that its needs are met.

(6) Once the immediate threat has been taken away, deepen the feelings of safety and attachment.

(7) Optional: transfer the emotional solution in the childhood picture to the original image/situation.

Case example: imagery rescripting

Focus on the current emotional problem

Jane (see Section 2.1.3) feels stressed and is threatened at work by a new colleague. The new colleague tends to put herself in the foreground and thus dominates the social situation in the sheltered workshop. Jane feels inferior, victimized, threatened, and lonely. She both fears and hates the new colleague. The therapist suggests an imagery rescripting exercise. Jane closes her eyes, relaxes briefly, and imagines a stressful situation with the colleague. Everybody is having coffee during the morning break. The colleague seems at first to approach Jane, but then ignores her. Jane feels tensed, frightened, and angry. The therapist asks for her emotions and related physical sensations in order to focus her attention upon them.

Affect bridge

The therapist asks Jane to wipe out the current picture and let a childhood memory come up instead which is associated with the current affect.

Elaborate a childhood memory

Jane gets an image of herself as a 12-year-old girl on the way home from school on a hot summer day. She is wearing her favorite colorful, long skirt. Her classmates make fun of her: "Jane shouldn't wear such a colorful skirt! Look at her fat arse!" Little Jane feels frightened and ashamed. She needs "somebody who can tell the others how horrible they are. Everybody has their shortcomings. And I don't want to be so lonely."

Introduce a helpful figure and meet the child's needs

The therapist enters the scene and gives Little Jane a hug. Then they stop the classmates: "It is sad how you treat Jane. You are so many, and she's on her own. You're unfair and cowardly!" The patient likes this intervention and wants her teacher to join in and listen, too. When she was a child, she was always too ashamed to tell him about the bullying. The teacher enters the scene and the therapist explains Jane's desperate situation. The teacher reassures Jane that he will help her in the future. However, the patient is still a bit mistrustful. Therefore, the therapist promises Little Jane they will accompany her on her way to and from school next time in order to see how things develop.

Increase feelings of safety and attachment

The therapist asks Little Jane what she would like to do now. Little Jane wants to go to a shop and look for a nice summer skirt. Afterwards she'd like to go to the park and eat ice cream together. These activities are carried out in the imagery exercise and are deepened by sensory details (imagine the taste of the ice cream, the color of the flowers, the warm sun, etc.), until the patient feels good and safe.

if the therapist closes their eyes, too. In the long term, almost all patients eventually feel safe enough to close their eyes for imagery exercises.

A general relaxation instruction is usually given to start an imagery exercise: "Please take a comfortable position and concentrate on your breath for a minute." Some therapists use a safe-place image—an image of the patient in a place in which they feel safe and secure—as a starting point (sometimes also as an end point) for imagery exercises. The safety related to the safe-place image is supposed to help the patient deal with the potentially threatening emotions induced by the imagery exercise.

For severely traumatized (BPD) patients, finding a safe-place image can be very difficult since the patient may not feel safe on their own anywhere. In such cases it might be too stressful for the patient (and too time-consuming for the therapy session) to both find a safe place and conduct an imagery rescripting exercise. Searching too long for a safe place can also be frustrating and stressful for the patient, reminding them of their inability to feel safe.

In our view, increasing positive and safe feelings is the main goal of imagery rescripting exercises; therefore, the additional use of a safe place isn't absolutely necessary, and is up to the preferences of the therapist and the patient. Furthermore, the patient should experience the therapeutic relationship itself as a safe place. If they don't feel safe there (yet), they will not be willing or able to do emotionally intense imagery exercises in any case.

(2) Access an image associated with difficult emotions   To actualize stressful emotions, the patient pictures themselves in a currently stressful situation. If possible, the patient should take the field perspective—that is, see the situation through their own eyes (not as an external observer). Sometimes patients start talking in detail about a current situation with their eyes closed, but don't really put themselves into it. In such cases the therapist should briefly explain that the focus is on emotions and ask related questions: "I think I understand the kind of situation now. How do you feel right now, being in the situation?" If the patient still won't focus on their emotions or gives only general answers—"I find it horrible"—the therapist can directly address possible relevant feelings: "What feeling is present? Do you feel sad, anxious, or ashamed? Do you maybe feel lonely?" Particularly in the first few imagery exercises, when the patient is not yet familiar with this technique, direct questions may be necessary. Exploring physical sensations can also be helpful in focusing on emotions: "Do you sense this emotion in your body?"

These strategies help the patient to increase their emotional experience. However, some patients—particularly those with BPD—won't stand emotions above a certain level of intensity. When this level is exceeded, they can react by ending interpersonal contact, opening their eyes, or dissociating from the emotional experience: "I don't know why, but the feeling just disappeared." In such cases, the emotion should be increased just as much as the patient can stand, and the next steps of the imagery rescripting exercise should be taken rather quickly.

In this step, the patient should enter emotions which create difficulties in their life. However, since imagery rescripting is not an exposure technique, it is not necessary to stay in these feelings for very long—the next step of the exercise can be introduced as soon as the patient has "got the feeling": "Do you now feel the emotions we have been talking about?"

(3) Affect bridge The patient returns to their childhood memories with a rather general instruction: "Please wipe out the current scene now, but keep the feeling. See whether an image pops up from childhood." Often childhood scenes pop up which have already been discussed in the early sessions, but different images may appear as well. You should be open to any image the patient accesses.

However, sometimes patients report no images at all: "I can't think of any memory." The therapist should relax in such cases; it may take some time until suitable images develop: "It doesn't matter if nothing's come up so far. Take your time and see what happens." If the patient starts to get nervous, the therapist might ask about general childhood pictures, such as photographs: "Do you have photos of you as a child? Can you see one of these pictures in your mind's eye?" In our experience, all patients have at least some kind of visual representation of themselves as a child. When the patient remembers a photograph, they are asked to "fill this picture with life," to enter the scene and take the perspective of the child. If the patient developed intense emotions during the first phase of the exercise, in the vast majority of cases it will be possible for them to enter related childhood memories and feelings within an adequate timeframe.

(4) Explore the childhood situation, focusing on the child's feelings and needs When the patient has got access of a childhood memory, they should briefly describe the scene. The therapist needs to know who is involved and what the main problems are. However, it is not necessary to understand each detail. If a patient starts to explain the situation in great detail, the therapist should focus back on the child's feelings in the situation: "How do you feel?", "How are you?" It's particularly important to ask about the child's needs: "What do you need right now?"

Imagery rescripting is not an exposure technique. The patient has to experience the traumatic situation only to the point where they are in contact with the negative feelings related to it. It is not necessary to relive the complete trauma. A patient who has been repeatedly sexually abused by her brother does not need to reexperience the abuse in great detail in the imagery rescripting exercise. It is sufficient to go as far as the point at which the patient starts to feel threatened—"I hear him coming upstairs and I know what he will do to me. I feel completely helpless, I'm at his mercy."— and then start the rescripting. This nonexposure approach reduces emotional stress for the patient. It helps the patient not to dissociate, but to stay in the exercise. An empirical investigation of this approach as compared to exposure therapy in patients with posttraumatic stress disorder (**PTSD**) showed similar effects on anxiety. However, the imagery rescripting procedure had a stronger effect on other problematic emotions such as anger, guilt, and shame, and patients were more willing to undergo the exercises than exposure exercises (Arntz et al., 2007).

(5) Rescript the image through the use of a helping person The actual rescripting of the traumatic situation in the exercise may be creative and even a complete fantasy. The limits of reality are not valid in an imagery exercise. The only rule is that the helping person fighting the perpetrator has to win. Accordingly, the child mode of the patient must feel safe and well at the end of the exercise—at least, much safer and better than in the beginning.

The helping person
In an imagery rescripting exercise, we always need a helping person. Regarding the choice of an adequate helping figure, different opinions are found in the literature. We don't agree with some articles that state that only the patient as an adult is appropriate as a helping person (e.g. Smucker et al., 1995). Others suggest not using helping persons who actually exist in reality (Reddemann, 2001). However, no empirical studies have been conducted so far regarding the effects of different helping persons. In schema therapy, all kinds of helping persons are welcome, and the approach is rather pragmatic: the helping person used in the rescripting phase must be able to protect and help the child in such a way that the central needs of the child are met.

The choice of the helping person depends on the patient's healthy adult mode. Basically, we differentiate between three different classes of helping person. When the patient's healthy adult mode is still weak, the patient is often not able to name any helping person at all—from a psychodynamic perspective, they are not able to develop good inner objects which can serve as helping persons. In such cases, the therapist should put themselves in the imagery scene as a helping person to model a healthy adult and to help the patient build up good inner objects.

For patients with a stronger healthy adult mode (or patients who have already undergone imagery rescripting exercises with the therapist as a helping figure), other helping figures can be used. These are usually not (yet) the patient as a healthy adult themselves, but somebody else who is neither the patient nor the therapist. These "third-party" helpers can be either real people or fantasy figures (for example, movie characters or fairytale characters), depending on the preferences of the patient. Real figures might be relatives or friends, such as a caring granny, a good aunt, or a close friend. It doesn't matter whether the helping person is still alive or not. We use both people from the patient's childhood and people the patient knows today— they must only be suitable for communicating safeness and security to the patient's vulnerable child mode. Therefore, it's probably not recommendable to use people with whom the patient has an ambivalent relationship, such as an ex-friend the patient is still in love with. When the therapist does not agree with the use of the helping person suggested by the patient, they should explain why and discuss it with the patient.

Patients with a sufficiently strong healthy adult mode can act as a healthy adult in the imagery rescripting exercise themselves, and take care of their own vulnerable child mode. If you do not know which kind of helping person to choose, try it out. If the healthy adult mode of the patient enters the scene and deals adequately with the situations, everything's fine. However, if the patient as an adult intervenes but is scared of the perpetrator, or dislikes the child, the healthy adult mode is not strong enough and the therapist or a third-party helper is needed. If the patient cannot imagine any third-party helper strong enough to deal with the perpetrator, the therapist should enter the scene.

Some patients with very weak healthy adult modes and severe childhood trauma will not accept a person other than themselves entering the imagery rescripting scene when they start imagery work. This might indicate "obsessive autonomy"; possibly the patient as a child experienced help from third parties as worsening an already bad situation and understand-ably drew the conclusion that they would rather do everything by them-selves. For example, Nicole (see Section 1.3.3) insisted on helping Little Nicole in imagery rescripting exercises herself as a healthy adult and did not want the therapist to enter the image. In such cases it is important that the therapist insists on entering the imagery situation as a helpful person anyway. It's vital that the patient learns to accept help and care from somebody else. This may frighten the patient at the beginning and should therefore be thoroughly explained. In the case of Nicole, social workers had visited her family when she was a child repeatedly, and this was not a positive experience for Nicole, since her mother often decompensated after these meetings. Thus Nicole learned to mistrust possible helpers.

When the weak healthy adult mode of a patient requires the therapist as a helping figure in imagery rescripting exercises at the beginning of therapy, they should be replaced by third-party helpers and finally by the patient's healthy adult mode over the course of therapy. That is, after a couple of imagery rescripting exercises with the therapist as a helping figure, the patient should be encouraged to use a third-party helper, and later on to act themselves as the healthy adult in the imagery rescripting exercise.

This sequence (therapist as helper, third party as helper, patient's own healthy adult mode as helper) can be varied flexibly. When the patient feels insecure entering the scene as a healthy adult, the therapist may suggest doing the rescripting together—that is, both the patient as a healthy adult and the therapist enter the scene. Then the therapist can take care of the vulnerable child mode while the patient's healthy adult supports them with advice and feedback; or the patient's healthy adult can intervene while the therapist offers support.

> We differentiate between three types of helping figures in imagery rescripting exercises, which are chosen according to the strength of the patient's healthy adult mode. In severely disordered patients, the therapist takes the position of the helping person; patients with a strong healthy adult mode enter the scene as a healthy adult themselves. A "third-party" helper, be it real or a fantasy figure, is an intermediate step. Another intermediate step is joint rescripting by the therapist and the patient's healthy adult mode.

(6) Develop attachment, comfort, and safety Comfort and safety are mainly induced by images of the patient's child mode being comforted by the helping person, or of the two of them playing and having fun together. Typical images are related to nature, play, and safe family situations. In severely disturbed patients, it may be necessary for the

therapist to take the patient to the therapist's own (fantasized) family in order to offer a safe and caring environment.

Positive emotions can be deepened by focusing on related physical sensations—"Can you feel this relaxed feeling in your body?"—and instructing the patient to enjoy and retain their feeling. They may also be anchored using hypnotherapy techniques (finding a symbol, song, movement, etc. connected with the positive feeling).

6.3.3   The process of rescripting

The goal of imagery rescripting exercises is to reduce guilt, shame, and threat, and to induce feelings of safety and healthy attachment. The process of the exercise is oriented towards these goals. It is important to understand which emotions are induced in the vulnerable child mode by the punitive or demanding parent mode. Patients with borderline or antisocial personality disorders, for example, typically imagine aggressive, abusive, and very threatening parent modes, which primarily induce threat and anxiety. These parent modes have to be fought by dramatic means in order to eliminate intense anxiety. On the other hand, patients with avoidant or dependent personality disorders often don't imagine very aggressive and dangerous parent modes—instead, their parent modes usually induce feelings of guilt when the vulnerable child mode expresses the patient's needs. A typical scene might be a depressively crying mother who will feel even worse if the child leaves the house to play with friends instead of taking care of her.

These different parent modes have to be fought differently, too. When dealing with an aggressive perpetrator, it may be necessary to include several policemen in the rescripting to put the perpetrator in prison, or even to kill them. However, when the parent mode is a guilt-inducing depressive mother, it might be better to explain that the mother has a depression. Although she may not know better, the child cannot take responsibility for her and help her, as she needs professional care. The therapist should explicitly reassure the child that they will take care of the mother, relieving the child of the responsibility, and tell the child that they will take the mother to a clinic or to psychotherapy.

After disempowering the parent mode, feelings of safety and healthy attachment are built up in the imagery exercise. Particularly with severely disordered patients, when the therapist has to step in to model the healthy adult mode, it is often necessary to take the patient's vulnerable child mode to the therapist's (fantasized) house in order to offer an alternative and safe family environment. When the main goal of the rescripting scene is to absolve the child mode of responsibility for the depressive mother, however, the patient's child mode might rather feel like playing with other children, in order to feel accepted and get important needs met. Such child modes often feel isolated, and lack fun and play. It may not be necessary to offer them an alternative family, however, since placing the responsibility for the mother on somebody else might be the most important issue.

Case examples

Susan (see Section 1.1), a patient with avoidant and dependent personality traits, often feels completely overwhelmed by everyday social tasks. In the imagery rescripting exercise, she remembers herself as a 10-year-old girl in the kitchen. Her mother is in deep depression, and sits at the table crying. Little Susan feels responsible for comforting her. She also feels guilty because she would rather be playing with friends outside. In the rescripting phase, the therapist enters the situation. The therapist hugs the child, validates Little Susan's feelings, and explain to the mother that it is important for Little Susan to have friends and to play with children of her own age. The mother, however, feels nervous and more depressive about Little Susan leaving the room. The therapist states that the mother is herself responsible for taking care of her depression and promises both the mother and Little Susan that (s)he will arrange an appointment for the mother in the outpatient therapy service. Afterwards, the thera- pist accompanies Little Susan to the playground. The therapist sits on a bench and watches Little Susan playing with other children.

Carmen, an emotionally unstable 36-year-old patient with social phobia, wants to rescript a rape at age 16. The rape happened in a car on the way home from a party. The perpetrator was the ex- friend of her sister, who had offered her a lift home. Carmen enters the rape scene as a healthy adult. She pulls the perpetrator away from Abused Carmen and drives back to the party with both Abused Carmen and the perpetrator. At the party, she publicly accuses the perpetrator of the rape and thus achieves his social exclusion. She is supported by other guests, who fully believe her. This makes her feel safe again.

Claus, a 20-year-old patient with BPD, often feels threatened, frightened, and unfairly treated. A current emotional-trigger situation leads him into a biographical image of a vacation in Italy with his family. He got home a little late one day. To punish him for being late, his obviously sadistic uncle imprisoned him in a dark and tiny cellar and threatened to not let him eat with the family. Little Claus was afraid of starving and being abandoned in the cellar. In the rescripting phase, the therapist enters the situation, rescues Little Claus, and confronts his uncle. Since the uncle reacts aggressively, a group of six policemen is introduced to the image. They arrest the uncle and put him in the local prison for the rest of Claus's vacation. Afterwards, the therapist takes Little Claus to the beach, where they eat ice cream together and have fun with other children.

Nick, a 42-year-old alcohol-dependent patient is currently in the detox clinic. He craves alcohol when he feels overly responsible for others. His sense of responsibility is associated with sadness, guilt, and feelings of being overstressed. In an imagery rescripting exercise focusing on these emotions, the patient immediately imagines himself as a six-year-old boy at his father's deathbed. He knew before that his father was very sick, but he was not prepared to see him dying. He is alone with his father, because his mother died four years ago. He feels like he should cope with the situation "like a man," and should help his father and not show any distress. Apart from sadness and desperation, he experiences pressing and overwhelming feelings of responsibility. In the rescripting phase, the uncle and aunt with whom he lived after the death of his parents enter the scene. They cared very well for him as a child. In the imagery rescripting, the aunt takes over responsibility for the situation and takes care of Nick's father. The uncle leaves the room together with Little Nick. He reassures Nick that a six-year-old child can never be responsible for such a difficult situation. This sad exercise finishes with an image of Little Nick and his uncle sitting on a bench in front of the father's house after the father has finally died. The uncle validates Little Nick's grief and comforts him.

Aggression in imagery rescripting   In an imagery rescripting exercise, any suitable means of fighting the punitive parent modes can be used, as long as it helps the vulnerable child mode to feel less threatened. This includes aggressive fantasies such as fighting a perpetrator physically, or even killing them. We generally assume that any kind of fantasy (including an aggressive fantasy) which helps people to cope with stress may be part of an imagery rescripting exercise. Since psychologically healthy people sometimes experience aggressive or revenge fantasies, we don't see a reason not to use such elements in imagery rescripting exercises. Furthermore, clinical experiences are encouraging. However, particularly with forensic patients, many therapists feel uncomfortable with imagery rescripting in which aggressive behavior is acted out in fantasy. They are afraid that this might encourage their patients to display more actual aggression in real life, and even disinhibit aggression. We have not experienced any negative consequences of aggressive imagery rescripting ourselves so far. In a study of imagery rescripting in the treatment of PTSD, where taking revenge and aggressively defending oneself was allowed in the rescripting phase, the imagery rescripting led to a stronger reduction of anger problems and a greater increase in control over acting out anger than the gold-standard treatment imaginal exposure (Arntz et al., 2007). However, the question of whether aggressive imagery rescripting is helpful or dangerous has not directly been investigated empirically as yet, especially in populations with aggressive problems. Thus we don't know for sure whether undesirable side effects might appear after aggressive imagery rescripting exercises.

A particular dilemma arises when the patient asks the therapist to perform an aggressive act (e.g. killing a perpetrator) with which the therapist feels uncomfortable. Again, it is important that therapists

---

Case example: revenge fantasies in imagery rescripting

Sally, a 35-years-old woman with subthreshold BPD symptoms, was sexually abused by her cousin when she was a child. In an imagery rescripting exercise dealing with these memories, she feels intense hate and takes revenge in fantasy by castrating the cousin in a very painful and cruel way. Afterwards her interpersonal and emotional problems improve tremendously.

respect their own boundaries and share these with the patient, without condemning the patient or forbidding the patient from having the act completed in fantasy. In such cases, other people than the therapist will have to carry out the act.

If the therapist has doubts about possible acting out of aggression following imagery rescripting, it is important that they explain the aim of imagery rescripting (which is primarily to bring about changes on an experiential, and not a behavioral level) and explicitly ask (or even insist) that the patient not take any actions in the real world as yet, and that they discuss any action plans in therapy before they are carried out.

We have often found that patients are dissatisfied with extreme aggressive fantasies. In such cases, we have suggested the patient rewind and try out another action. One patient first killed her sadistic mother in fantasy, but then decided this was not satisfying. After rewinding, she put her mother in jail and taped her mouth shut so that she couldn't comment and had to listen to what the patient had to tell her. The patient was much more satisfied with this scenario. This suggests that therapists don't need to be too anxious about extreme scenarios, as patients often express a wish to do something else after trying them out.

Jointly choosing the process of rescripting   The actual rescripting process should be developed spontaneously by the therapist and the patient together. However, the therapist should suggest elements for the rescripting process if the patient has no idea what to do, or is very afraid of the punitive parent mode. The patient's emotions should constantly be monitored by repeatedly asking for the current feelings and needs of the vulnerable child mode and the reactions of the punitive parent mode in the rescripting phase. When a particular action does not have the desired effect, the therapist can "rewind the tape" and start a new version of the rescripting phase. When the patient feels guilty for fighting the parent mode after the exercise, the therapist has to explain that we do not fight real people within such exercises; instead we fight the inner parts of the patient that make them suffer today.

Note that a patient may suggest solutions for the rescripting phase which correspond with their typical coping mode. Thus avoidant patients may suggest hiding in their room until a parental conflict has run its course or fleeing from an aggressive father, or a patient with daydreaming as a self-soothing coping mode may suggest entering a typical daydream. When a solution suggested by the patient seems to be related to a coping mode rather than to the healthy adult mode, the therapist should suggest alternative solutions. Again, when a rescripting process takes a wrong turn, it can always be corrected by "rewinding the tape" and starting a new fantasy.

Variations in the process of rescripting   The process of an imagery rescripting exercise can vary according to the content of the patient's mental images. When the exercise starts with a current negative affect, the affect bridge technique connects the current emotion with a stressful memory image. In some cases an affect bridge will not be necessary, because the biographical materials and images to be rescripted are already clear. This is true for many patients with PTSD and related intrusive memories, and patients with other diagnoses may report pervasive and recurring mental images too. In such cases, the imagery rescripting exercise can start immediately with the recurring mental image.

Case examples: "rewinding the tape"

Susan rescripts the memory of a horrible and life-threatening sexual assault. She wants to kill the perpetrator with a huge knife. However, after the therapist and two policemen have done so, she is disgusted by the bloody image. The tape is rewound, and the perpetrator is weighted with stones and thrown into a deep river. Now Susan feels relieved and safe.

Jane uses intense daydreaming as a self-soothing mode. In the very first imagery rescripting exercise, she suggests leaving the traumatic image and entering her usual daydreams. The therapist does not agree with this course of action and suggests doing something with the therapist and Little Jane instead. Jane feels offended: "You don't accept my daydreams." The therapist briefly interrupts the exercise to explain that her daydreams are a coping mode, and that in imagery exercises, new, helpful emotional processes are supposed to be established. Jane agrees and is able to continue the exercise as suggested by the therapist.

On the other hand, particularly in patients with less severe disorders, it is often possible to add another phase to the rescripting exercise. After the rescripting phase, the patient reenters the emotional situation which was the starting point of the exercise. The patient then either experiences this situation with the positive affect developed in the rescripting phase or changes the situation in a similar way to how they changed the biographical image. Note that this should not be done with more severely disordered patients. For these patients, rescripting a memory image is stressful enough, and they would be overstressed (and possibly emotionally over-whelmed once again) by adding another phase. Furthermore, clinical experience shows that rescripting of biographical images often leads to behavioral and emotional changes in current situations even when these current situations have not been the focus of an imagery exercise.

6.3.4   Variations on imagery techniques

Imagery techniques can be varied in many ways (see Hackmann et al., 2011). Imagery rescripting of traumatic childhood memories is the most frequently used format, but later traumas, current emotionally difficult situations, and even future situations can be the focus of imagery rescripting exercises too.

If the real-life situation of the patient is still traumatizing, establishing their current safety takes priority. In such cases, imagery rescripting can be used to help the patient build up the strength to stand up for their rights and to change or eventually end damaging relationships.

Case example: imagery rescripting with a current situation

Jane is very ambivalent regarding a scheduled day trip with her colleagues. On the one hand, she is looking forward to it, but on the other, she is afraid of feeling insecure or of being rejected by the group. The therapist suggests preparing Jane for the trip with an imagery exercise. Jane imagines herself on the (future) day trip in a scene which could induce feelings of rejection: two colleagues having a talk without her. Although she knows on the cognitive level that this is a normal situation and does not indicate that her colleagues dislike her, she still feels rejected and unlovable. In the rescripting phase, a close friend of hers joins the scene and gives her a brief hug. The friend is very relaxed with the colleagues because she does not interpret their talk as a sign of rejection. With this image, Jane feels safer and more relaxed.

6.3.5 Comforting vulnerable child modes with other emotion-focused techniques

The comforting interventions used in imagery rescripting can also be realized with other treatment techniques. The central goals and basic principles of the therapeutic relationship—comfort, strengthen, and heal the vulnerable child mode—always stay the same. Similarly, it's always important to ask the patient for feedback regarding these interventions and answer their questions. Exercises should be adapted to the patient's needs and preferences. Note that by giving feedback and discussing emotional experiences related to the treatment, the patient takes over a rather high degree of responsibility for the therapy. This is desirable, as it balances the high responsibility the therapist accepts within the reparenting relationship approach.

Caring for the vulnerable child mode in chair dialogues Chair dialogues (see Section 8.3.1) in schema therapy follow the same rules as imagery rescripting exercises. As in imagery exercises, the vulnerable child mode can be validated, soothed, and comforted in chair dialogues, and just as the patient and therapist fight the punitive parent mode in imagery exercises, so they fight a punitive parent mode in a chair dialogue. The therapist may for example first talk to the chair of the punitive parent, then answer back to this mode's damaging messages, and finally throw the chair out. Afterwards, the therapist may address the (chair of the) vulnerable child mode in the following way: "Little X, I am happy to see you here and to get in contact with you. You are a lovely child, and your needs are absolutely important."

Audio files and transitional objects Any technique that comforts the patient can be used within this framework. The use of transitional objects is particularly helpful, such as (soft) toys or postcards with personal messages from the therapist. These objects help patients to stay in contact with the vulnerable child mode (and with the therapist, even when they are not present). Furthermore, they are supposed to help the patient internalize the therapist as a healthy adult mode.

The same applies to audio files. The therapist can for example record the "message to Little X," and give it to the patient. Most patients have cell phones with a microphone function, which can be used for audiotaping. The patient can then listen to the audio file at home when they feel bad or when they find it hard to carry out therapeutic homework related to caring for the vulnerable child mode.

There are parallels between these schema-therapy techniques and some of the behavioral skills in DBT for BPD (Linehan, 1993). Many of the "skills boxes" of borderline patients in DBT contain pictures of good friends, postcards with encouraging messages, and other comforting items. Such objects should be individually implemented in the patients' lives.

6.4 Behavioral techniques

On the behavioral level, patients learn to more adequately accept, express, and fulfill their own needs. This involves accepting that human needs are normal and important; you can be psychologically healthy only if at least some of your needs are met. This is in line with the basic assumptions of humanistic therapies. Note that expressing needs does *not* mean expressing every emotion and every need instantly and directly. Needs must be expressed to a degree appropriate for the social situation. Social skills training may therefore be recommendable for some patients.

The therapeutic relationship in schema therapy is seen as a safe place to exercise the expression of the patient's emotions and needs. The therapist should reinforce the patient in expressing their needs and emotions adequately and healthily. Social skills can be trained within the therapeutic relationship too. When the patient advances in expressing their own needs within the therapeutic relationship, social skills training should then focus on expressing their needs and emotions in other relationships. However, if a particular relationship is abusive, the patient might instead be encouraged to end it. Sometimes patients do not manage to end abusive relationships in the initial phase of treatment. In such cases, ending the relationship should stay on the therapy agenda, since the patient will not be able to develop feelings of safety and healthy attachment while it is still going on.

However, emotion-focused methods must first be used to help the patient understand their right to set limits.

Behavioral techniques in the treatment of the vulnerable child mode resemble the CBT treatment of depression. In addition to social skills training, positive and reinforcing activities are established. The patient should do things that make them feel safe, satisfied, or happy. This includes both small steps, such as indulging themselves with a hot bubble bath, and larger steps, such as renewing an old hobby. To connect these behavioral techniques with the mode approach, we ask the patient for activities that would be fun for their happy child mode. What does the happy child like to do and with whom, and what did it like to do earlier in the patient's life?

6.5   FAQ

(1) Is it always necessary to close one's eyes during imagery rescripting exercises?

Imagery exercises are emotionally more intense with closed eyes. However, if a patient isn't able to close their eyes at first, you shouldn't be too strict about it. Usually patients get familiar with these exercises and can close their eyes after a while. If a patient doesn't close their eyes for a long time, you should ask why and eventually adapt the procedure. Some patients find it much more relaxing when the therapist closes their eyes as well, or when the therapist and patient sit back to back for the exercise. Most patients are able to close their eyes after a while.

(2) Isn't it dangerous when aggressive acts are performed in imagery rescripting exercises, for example when a perpetrator is killed?

The emotional process is the main criterion for evaluating an imagery exercise. When a patient feels safe only when the perpetrator is killed, we would suggest having him killed in the rescripting phase. However, when the patient does not want to deal violently with a perpetrator, you should look for another solution. When a patient is able to feel safe without aggressive acts in imagery, that's also fine.

Therapists often find it hard to support a patient in taking revenge or exerting violence in the imagery rescripting phase. They may feel morally negative about it, or they may be afraid that imaginary revenge will decrease the patient's barrier against actual aggression in real life. However, one can also argue that striving for revenge is very normal: many people experience revenge fantasies when they are angry or feel unfairly treated. Usually such fantasies do not lead to open aggression. They may even reduce the pressure to overcompensate aggressively in real life.

Arntz et al. (2007) found a stronger effect of imagery rescripting as compared to mere exposure therapy on reduction of anger and increase of anger control in PTSD patients. Since aggressive imagery rescripting was present in this study, these data speak in favor of using aggression in imagery exercises. Furthermore, we have never heard of any case in which fantasized aggression in an imagery rescripting exercise has triggered real aggression. However, we cannot fully answer this question as yet, since studies are still underway (Seebauer, personal communication).

(3) Is the use of aggressive fantasies in imagery rescripting exercises recommended for patients who have already been violent in real life (such as forensic patients)?

There is an ongoing discussion regarding this question. Some therapists are strictly against using aggressive fantasies with forensic patients, while others favor it and report good clinical experiences with aggressive fantasies even in severe forensic cases. This is finally an empirical question that has not been studied yet.

(4) Do patients understand the difference between imagery exercises and reality, in particular when the therapist takes the patient to their family in the rescripting phase? Might this trigger overly high expectations in the patient regarding the therapist and the therapeutic relationship?

According to our experience, patients readily understand the difference between imagery exercises and reality. However, with imagery rescripting exercises that include closeness between the patient's vulnerable child mode and the therapist, the patient may get in contact with their need for interpersonal closeness in general. This is actually a goal of imagery rescripting exercises: the value of love and attachment is a frequent topic in the rescripting phase.

Intense imagery rescripting exercises with high closeness between the patient's vulnerable child mode and the therapist are mainly important for BPD patients, since less severely disordered patients are able to experience closeness between their vulnerable child mode and their own healthy adult mode. In borderline patients, intense longing for closeness is typical in any case. This is not merely the result of imagery intervention, but rather a feature of this patient group. According to the schema therapy model, the experience of attachment in imagery rescripting exercises helps the patient to experience the feelings they actually need. Furthermore, it introduces the issue of longing for attachment explicitly in the therapy situation. Indeed, patients sometimes say that they long for the therapist even when they are not present. Borderline patients experience intense attachment needs whether the therapist works with imagery rescripting exercises or not. When the patient can openly address this, it becomes an issue of discussion in the therapy. This offers an opportunity to discuss the relationship on a healthy level: severely disordered patients usually have deficits here, and it is possible to learn. Sometimes a patient may experience their longing for the therapist as problematic: "I listened to our last imagery rescripting audiotape last Sunday, when I felt really bad; to be honest, I got really angry at you, because you were having fun with your family in reality, while I only got this lousy tape." In such cases the therapist should on the one hand validate the patient's attachment needs—"I can absolutely understand you when I think about your feelings of loneliness; it would certainly be wonderful for you to live in a healthy family, such as mine."—and on the other, stress the real limits of the therapeutic relationship: "However, unfortunately I cannot offer you such a family. But I hope I can help you to grow so that the chances are higher that you will be able to start one yourself."

(5) Some therapists feel intuitively uncomfortable about offering borderline patients an intense relationship in imagery rescripting exercises. Shouldn't they follow their intuition and offer only as much as they feel comfortable with?

It is certainly important to critically reflect upon the content of imagery rescripting exercises. Imagery rescripting exercises aim to care for the vulnerable child mode; thus attachment and closeness must be tailored to the patient's vulnerable child mode. You should offer everything you'd offer your own small children, including hugging and protecting the child, and even offering an alternative family if the child's own family is unsafe. However, your offers should not focus on the relationship with the healthy adult part of the patient, and of course any kind of sexualized intimacy is unacceptable.

Since the goal of the rescripting phase is to increase safety and healthy attachment in the patient's vulnerable child mode, the needs of the child mode guide the process. If the child mode feels safe only with the therapist, the patient should experience this in the rescripting phase. Thus, we do not allow the personal preferences of the therapist to guide the image, but rather the needs of the child. Imagery rescripting is a potentially very powerful technique which should be used as effectively as possible. Some elements, including taking the child mode to the therapist's family, may be vital for a positive outcome and the therapist should be prepared to make use of them. Note that the therapist's home and family can be fantasy images.

If a therapist hesitates to offer these elements, we would first suggest that they try them out anyway. Like patients, therapists have to get used to these techniques, and they may feel unfamiliar at first. After using imagery rescripting with intensive reparenting for several patients, the therapist will usually start to feel more relaxed about it. The feeling of the therapist's own limits being threatened will disappear as they experience that it's "just an exercise, like any other."

However, if the therapist does not even feel able to try it out, or still feels uncomfortable after a number of trials, they should try to understand the reasons for this discomfort. Sometimes therapists feel under pressure to offer the same (or at least much more than they usually would) to the patient in reality as they offer in imagery rescripting exercises. This is irrational, and might be an expression of a guilt-inducing parent mode of the therapist. The limits of the therapeutic relationship do not depend on the content of imagery rescripting exercises!

Sometimes therapists instead feel uncomfortable because they have been trained with another therapy model that has different guidelines for the therapeutic relationship. Imagery rescripting elements, such as taking a vulnerable child mode to the therapist's family, may conflict with these guidelines. In such cases, the therapist has to decide whether they are willing to change some of their routines and accept the guidelines of schema therapy.

(6) Is it always necessary to use a safe-place image in imagery rescripting exercises?

Many therapists like the exercise of the safe place and use it a lot in imagery rescripting exercises. It can be used at the beginning and/or the end of an exercise. However, in our view it is actually unnecessary.

Paradoxically, the more disturbed patients are, the less they are able to develop a safe-place image, despite urgently needing one. Finding a safe place is nearly impossible for many patients with BPD, at least at the start of therapy. In such cases, we don't use the safe-place image. On the other hand, we do everything we can to strengthen positive and safe feelings at the end of the imagery rescripting exercise. Thus, the imagery rescripting exercise itself (and the therapy in general) becomes a safe place for the patient.

(7) How do you address child modes in the imagery scene?

We always address child modes informally, like we do with real children. If you usually call a patient by their last name, you should use their first name when talking to the child mode. If you use a language that distinguishes between formal and informal forms of address, the informal version is appropriate for the vulnerable child mode.

(8) When can you actually begin the imagery work? How much should you work at the therapeutic relationship beforehand?

The general rule is to start as early as possible with imagery rescripting exercises. When this technique is introduced early in therapy, the patient quickly gets familiar with it. Diagnostic imagery exercises can be used in the second or third session. If possible, therapeutic imagery exercises with rescripting should also be applied early in therapy, once the mode model has been established.

However, since strong coping modes block emotions, many patients with more severe disorders are unwilling to work with imagery rescripting techniques early in therapy. In these cases, it's necessary to work with the coping modes first. This can take a lot of time—up to 1 year in patients with BPD (Arntz & van Genderen, 2009).

In these patients, imagery techniques can be introduced slowly, step by step. The patient may want to keep their eyes open in the first few exercises, or you may decide on a time limit—for example, starting with exercises with a maximum duration of 10 minutes. You might start with a focus on positive imagery—for example, imagining only the final scene of an imagery rescripting exercise, after discussing the first parts of the exercise verbally. When the patient gets more familiar with imagery techniques, the standard imagery rescripting exercise can be implemented in a stepwise manner.

(9) How should you react when a patient completely refuses to do imagery work?

First you should clarify whether the patient has understood the idea behind this technique. Some patients report somewhat strange experiences with imagery interventions from earlier treatments. Furthermore, patients sometimes (implicitly) hold the idea that imagery work contains lots of emotional processing, but not emotional change. If they experience their emotions as very stressful, they will understandably not be keen to process them without limits. Such experiences or ideas should be discussed; if necessary, the process of imagery rescripting as used in schema therapy should be explained more thoroughly.

However, when there is no such understandable reason as to why the patient rejects imagery work, the rejection should be regarded as part of a detached protector mode. That is, you should assume that the patient is actually afraid of intense emotional experiences, and needs to protect themselves. In such cases, the basic schema-therapy principles of treating a detached protector mode are applied (see Chapter 5). That is, you should validate the patient's anxiety. If the patient is afraid of particular memory images, imagery exercises can be introduced step by step, starting with "easier" images. Very mistrustful patients might even expect to actually be traumatized during imagery exercises—they worry the therapist might attack them, or an evil person might enter the room as soon as they close their eyes. In such cases, you should discuss how the patient could be made to feel safer in this situation. You could lock the door, for example, or the patient could leave their eyes open. If the patient feels ashamed at the thought of you watching them undergoing an emotional experience while their eyes are closed, you can close your own eyes as well, or sit back to back with the patient.

Sometimes patients are afraid that the punitive parent mode will "fight back" after an imagery exercise with reparenting. You should take this seriously and discuss possible solutions, such as a brief phonecall or email contact some hours after the imagery exercise, or a recorded message against the punitive parent mode.

Only in very resistive cases, or in very fragile patients (e.g. patients who get lost in a torrent of images), should you accept the idea of doing schema therapy without imagery rescripting exercises. Imagery rescripting is a very powerful technique and must not be easily given up upon. However, in some cases we have found that drama techniques do better than imagery rescripting. For some reason, some patients respond better to drama techniques than to imagery, and drama techniques offer a good alternative (Arntz & Weertman, 1999). Note that it is not only patients who avoid emotion-focused techniques, but also therapists. Take care that you and the patient do not agree on joint avoidance . . .

(10) What about the risk of decompensation by imagery rescripting exercises? Can it happen that the patient is completely flooded with difficult emotions?

Earlier experiences with a less structured use of emotion-focused techniques, for example in Gestalt therapy, showed a risk of decompensation in emotionally unstable patients. Therefore, these techniques were not recommended for severely traumatized patients until recently. However, the emotional process of imagery rescripting exercises is highly structured and is guided by the therapist. The therapist constantly monitors the patient's emotions by asking for the child mode's feelings and needs. Furthermore, fighting the scary perpetrator—if necessary with the help of the therapist— is essential to imagery rescripting exercises. Without this guidance, the risk of destabilization by traumatic memories would indeed be high, since in these patients the punitive parent mode (and related feelings of self-hatred and pervasive threat) is usually very powerful. The guiding therapist makes sure that the scope for the punitive parent mode is very limited. As soon as feelings of threat come up, the therapist actively starts powerful rescripting, if necessary with violence—by using weapons, policemen, and so on. There is only one rule for imagery rescripting exercises: the therapist always has to be the winner when fighting the punitive parent mode! Furthermore, the next priority is to soothe and comfort the vulnerable child mode, which strengthens the patient and weakens the punitive parent mode further. If the therapist follows these guidelines, they will stay in control of the emotional process, and the patient will not be overwhelmed by negative feelings and will not decompensate.

The biggest problem is not decompensation, but avoidance of intense emotions. Patients with high emotional instability usually have a strong detached protector mode. In imagery rescripting exercises, such coping modes come up when the patient explains the emotional situation in great detail (including irrelevant details), opens their eyes repeatedly, dissociates when emotions increase, and so on. Usually the most difficult task for the therapist is not to avoid decompensation, but to focus the patient on their emotions and keeping them in the exercise.

(11) How do imagery exercises work when patients take (sedative) psychotropic medications?

Sedative psychotropic medications such as benzodiazepines and sedative neuroleptics block intense emotions. Imagery rescripting may have a weaker or no effect when the patient is sedated. Giesen-Bloo et al. (2006) found post hoc that schema therapy was much less effective in patients with BPD when they took additional psychotropic medication. From a clinical perspective, this may be caused by a lack of emotional intensity. However, this has not been tested in a randomized controlled trial as yet.

(12) How should you deal with patients with many different traumatic memories?

Severely disordered patients often need many sessions with imagery rescripting exercises, focusing on different situations and different emotions. For example, Jane (see Section 2.1.3) reported a range of different problematic childhood memories: her mother was cold and dismissive, probably overstressed by the difficult family situation; her father was verbally aggressively when he was drunk; her classmates bullied her for being overweight.

In such cases, the patient and the therapist can make a list of situations that need to be treated with imagery rescripting exercises. You should start with a less severe situation, and generally follow the patient's preference regarding the order.

(13) What does it mean when the affect bridge leads to a pleasant childhood memory image?

Sometimes the childhood image that comes up after the affect bridge is not negative, even though the exercise started with a negative emotion. One simple reason may be that the intervention is not suitable because the negative emotional impact of the problematic situation is fully explained by the situation, and is not related to a life pattern.

However, sometimes pleasant images pop up when the current problem clearly is linked to a life pattern. In such cases, imagery rescripting is probably a suitable intervention, but you must find out the meaning of the pleasant picture. In our experience, such pleasant childhood situations often show the child in a coping mode rather than in the vulnerable child mode. This should be discussed with the patient. You can either directly ask the patient whether the pleasant image might be a coping situation, or you can explore the situation further in imagery in order to discover a coping mode. You could ask the patient what they would like to do now, or you could for example suggest leaving the situation and getting in contact with a parent figure who is not present. Often the patient's emotions will then change and the vulnerable child mode will pop up after all.

Case examples: coping situations in childhood memory pictures

Case 1: self-sacrifice

Simone, a 38-year-old physician, is often afraid about her family's safety when she is travelling to conferences. Beginning with these feelings, she pictures herself as a child in the living room of her house. Her mother is present as well. The scene is peaceful; Little Simone does not have intense feelings. Clearly, fear related to the current emotional problem is not present. The therapist suggests changing the scene in order to understand what's happening. She asks the child mode in the memory image what she would like to do now. Little Simone would like to go out and play in the garden because the weather is beautiful. The therapist asks her to do so. However, when Little Simone leaves the house, anxiety pops up. She is scared that her mother, who is emotionally unstable and chronically depressive, might feel bad or even harm herself while Simone is absent. Little Simone feels very responsible for her mother's emotional well-being. Changing the image in the imagery exercise demonstrates that the patient's child mode is stabilized by staying with the mother and taking care of her; when this coping pattern is interrupted, anxiety pops up, resembling her current fears about her family. Furthermore, the childhood coping situation also mirrors Simone's self-sacrificing style, which plays an important role in her current life situation too.

Case 2: withdrawal and self-soothing

Barbara, a 44-year-old patient with chronic eating-disorder (anorexic/bulimic), alcohol-abuse, and BPD features, felt unfairly treated and rejected recently. To cope with these feelings, she drank alcohol, which led to an eating attack. In an imagery exercise beginning with her current feelings, Barbara finds herself as a 10-year-old girl snuggled in her bed. She eats chocolate and feels OK. The therapist explores the meaning of the chocolate. It turns out that the patient has stolen the chocolate from her mother and that she is about to eat the whole bar: "I need it to feel good." She is also afraid that her mother will find out about her theft and punish her harshly. This image demonstrates the importance of eating as a self-soothing coping style early in the patient's life. Furthermore, by adding the mother to the image and shifting the focus of the imagery exercise to the interaction between Little Barbara and her mother, the vulnerable child mode and the punitive parent mode appear onstage.

(14) How should you deal with a patient talking nonstop during the imagery exercise (for example, explaining lots of irrelevant details)?

Particularly in their first imagery exercises, patients will not be used to this treatment technique. They need instructions on what to do, and what not to do: "It's actually not necessary that I know all these details—your feelings are much more important. Please take some time and try to sense your emotions, as if you were in the situation right now. Thank you."

(15) How should you deal with a patient who rejects the idea of the therapist entering the scene in the rescripting phase?

The therapist should not ask for permission to enter the scene, but simply step in. If you ask the patient for permission, there's a high risk of not getting it; however, the same patient will often feel relief when you enter the scene directly and without asking for permission.

Some patients will still reject the idea of the therapist in the image. Again, this can have different reasons and should be discussed with the patient.

In the best case, the healthy adult mode of the patient is strong enough to do the rescripting without the help of the therapist. The presence of the therapist may thus be a bit awkward, since the patient does actually not need them. This applies when the childhood image is only a minor threat, when the patient's healthy adult is quite strong, or when the patient is not very severely disturbed. Simone has a high level of functioning, for example, and suffers only from minor symptoms. In her case, the therapist will not be necessary in the rescripting phase, since Simone's healthy adult mode is capable of resolving the situation.

In the worst case, however, the patient has no trust at all in other people and prefers to stay on their own. Superficially, these cases come across rather paradoxically, because the worse the childhood situation is, and the more support is needed, the more the patient rejects the therapist's participation. In these cases you should discuss the need for trust with the patient and jointly find a way to include the therapist in rescripting scenes. This will help the patient to learn to put trust in others.

Case example: a mistrustful patient rejects the therapist in rescripting

Nicole, a forensic patient with borderline and antisocial personality disorder (see Section 1.3.3), absolutely does not want the therapist to enter the rescripting scene to help Little Nicole with her devaluing and aggressive mother. To understand the high intensity of Nicole's rejection, the therapist and the patient try out a brief (diagnostic) imagery exercise with the therapist entering the child-hood image. Little Nicole gets very scared when the therapist appears, as it reminds her of the visits of social workers from the youth office. Nicole grew up in a very antisocial family, well known by the local youth office. Thus social workers came from time to time to make sure that things were in order. Their intention was to help the family, and they often criticized the mother. However, these visits were of no help, since the whole family pretended that things were OK, even though they actually weren't. Furthermore, the mother often decompensated with rage at having been criticized after such visits. For the patient as a child, these visits were more dangerous than helpful. This association explains Nicole's rejection of third parties in imagery rescripting scenes.

Once this has been understood by Nicole and her therapist, they discuss how to solve the problem. The major point for Nicole is that the therapist should treat her mother with respect and offer her help instead of just criticizing her.

Sometimes child modes mainly reject the therapist's appearance in imagery because the punitive parent mode is very strong. These patients are either afraid that the punitive parent mode in the image (for example, the abusive drunk father) will harm the therapist or else feel guilty for allowing the therapist insight into their usually well-protected family situation: "You must not let anybody know what's happening here." In these cases, we assume that it is the punitive parent mode that rejects the help of the therapist, rather than the vulnerable child mode. Therefore we explain to the vulnerable child mode that the punitive parent mode is against the therapist and ask the patient to let the punitive parent mode say things against the therapist. Then we disagree with the punitive parent mode about the vulnerable child's needs and fight its devaluation of the vulnerable child's neediness.

Case example: a punitive parent mode rejects the therapist in rescripting

The therapist enters the situation in the imagery rescripting phase.

Patient: "That would feel good, but it's not allowed!"
Therapist: [Linking the rejection with the punitive parent mode:] It is the opinion of your violent father that I should not be allowed to protect you, right? Can you let your father say this in the image?
P: My father says: "Who the hell are you? What do you want here? You don't have anything to do with our family, leave our house!"
T: [Talking to the father:] I see this completely differently. It is very important that I get involved in this situation. You're threatening and abusing your daughter horribly and I will not accept this anymore.

(16) How should you deal with a patient who gets into the vulnerable child in the imagery situation, but then becomes suicidal or does not stop complaining?

First, it is important to validate the suffering of the vulnerable child mode. In most cases, validating the child and fighting the punitive parent opens the way to soothing the child and developing positive emotions. However, sometimes this option is blocked, and the vulnerable child mode does not open up, but instead becomes suicidal, does not stop complaining, or seems to be stuck in a very pessimistic state. This is rather typical in patients with compliant surrender and/or avoidant coping modes, who avoid acknowledging their needs even in the imagery rescripting situation. To solve this problem, and continue the exercise, you must briefly deal with this coping mode. In most cases it is sufficient to quickly explain to the patient that developing positive solutions is an essential part of the exercise. This short explanation can usually be given during the exercise. When the "stuck state" of the child mode is more severe, the therapist may have to interrupt the intervention briefly and explain to the patient that they must collaborate in looking for positive solutions. This might mean bypassing their own (dependent/avoidant) barriers. Usually this procedure is sufficient to help the patient continue the intervention more constructively. Note that only patients who are able to let down their coping modes will begin imagery exercises anyway; these patients are usually also able to continue the exercise when they get stuck in their coping mode halfway.

(17) What should you do when a patient first agrees with an extreme action in the rescripting phase (for example killing a perpetrator), but then decides they dislike it?

In general, imagery rescripting is a very creative technique. Any solution can be tried out; if the patient happens to dislike it, you should simply look for another solution ("rewind the tape"). Sometimes patients address their discomfort with a particular part of the rescripting only after the exercise. In that case, a new exercise with another ending should be scheduled for another session. It is easier when a patient addresses their discomfort during the exercise—then you "rewind the tape," go back to the point where the discomfort started, and try out another solution (see the case examples labeled "rewinding the tape" in Section 6.3.3).

(18) Sometimes the patient is not a child in the memory image, but an adolescent. Does reparenting fit with an adolescent mode, too?

Imagery rescripting can basically be used with any emotional problem. However, it is vital to respond to the specific emotional problem represented in the image. Sometimes interpersonal or emotional problems are related more to problems with autonomy and less to a lack of attachment and safety. Related memory images are not threatening parent modes, but rather parents blocking the healthy autonomy of the patient as an adolescent (for example, an overprotective mother). Accordingly, the central unmet need is not attachment, but autonomy and independence. The therapist (or another model of the healthy adult) should focus on the right of the adolescent to be autonomous in such cases; they might discuss this issue with the overprotective mother, or invite the patient's adolescent mode to go their own way and create images of feeling free and independent.

(19) A technical question: how do you produce audio files?

Many MP3 players have a microphone function and can be used to record audio files as well as listen to them. They are quite cheap; some patients buy one to use just for therapy recordings. Most cell phones have a microphone function, too. We usually ask patients to look for the microphone function on their cell—they usually have one, although they may not be aware of it. Since most people carry their cell phones most of the time, the patient will usually have the audio files to hand.

7

Treating Angry and Impulsive Child Modes

Enraged, angry, undisciplined, and impulsive child modes are subdivided into two categories, with some overlap. Angry or enraged child modes are present when anger or rage is in the foreground, with strong, sometimes uncontrollable "hot" affect. People in impulsive and undisciplined child modes also focus on their own needs in an exaggerated way; but instead of anger, the wish for gratification—to experience positive emotions—is associated with these modes, and people in these modes are rather undisciplined, spoiled, or impulsive. The typical emotions and affects of these categories are listed in Table 7.1.

The therapeutic approach differs depending on whether this child mode is more angry/enraged or undisciplined/impulsive. It is always important to validate the affect related to this mode, and the (unfulfilled) needs behind it. However, the patient has to find more adequate ways to express these feelings and needs. Particularly with undisciplined/impulsive child modes, it is also important to confront the patient with the undisciplined or spoiled character of the mode and to stress that in the long term, taking responsibility and being disciplined at least to a degree is very important.

Schema Therapy in Practice: An Introductory Guide to the Schema Mode Approach, First Edition. Arnoud Arntz and Gitta Jacob.
© 2013 John Wiley & Sons, Ltd. Published 2013 by John Wiley & Sons, Ltd.

Table 7.1 Typical emotions and affects of angry, impulsive, and undisciplined child modes

Affect	Emotions	Example
Anger	Feels unfairly treated. Expresses frustration and anger	The patient is disappointed that the therapist is 5 minutes late and is verbally angry
Rage	Can lose control over aggressive behavior. In extreme situations, others can be hurt or even killed. In short, behavioral expressions of anger dominate, including severe aggression	When somebody provokes the patient, they sometimes get blind with rage, hitting the person they're annoyed with, or destroying their belongings in the heat of the moment. Later they regret it
Impulsivity	Follows own needs without regard to longer-term consequences for themselves or others. Patients feel in a sort of happy, "why bother?" mood. Sometimes driven by rebelliousness	The patient sees shoes in a shop window and buys them right away, "because I just *must* have them." They don't care that their bank account is already in the red
Lack of discipline	Is lazy, can't organize themselves to do boring tasks, doesn't care about obligations and responsibilities	The patient does not care about unpaid invoices, filing their tax returns, and so on. Often their mother steps in to avoid negative consequences. The patient knows that their behavior is not OK, but just "doesn't want to be bothered with all this stuff"
Obstinacy	Others often feel that they are angry; however, on the behavioral level, obstinate and negativistic patients don't openly express anger, but rather refuse everything and reject everybody. Obstinacy can be part of angry or undisciplined child modes	The girlfriend of a patient says in a joint session that she wonders how to find a good solution for when her sister visits. She is aware that the patient does not like her sister, but she would like to find an acceptable compromise. However, whenever she touches on the issue, the patient becomes obstinate, closes up, draws back demonstratively, and refuses any constructive discussion

Pamperedness	Seems to be rather spoiled in their undisciplined child mode	The patient does not follow the rules of the inpatient psychotherapy ward. However, they expect others to care for their needs, to adapt to their schedules, and so on. They behave like a spoiled child who does not understand that you have to conform to social standards and rules in daily life

> Enraged/angry child modes are connected with intense "hot" negative affect, while impulsive/undisciplined child modes are rather undisciplined and spoiled, and more related to achieving positive affect. Emotional work is the most important for angry/enraged child modes, while impulsive/undisciplined child modes also require empathic confrontation and limit-setting.

7.1 The Therapeutic Relationship

7.1.1 The therapeutic relationship with angry/enraged child modes

In dealing with an angry or enraged child mode, the balance between validation and confrontation is of particular importance. This defines "empathic confrontation," an important therapeutic strategy in schema therapy. The main principles of the therapeutic relationship for angry or enraged child modes are:

(1) Validate feelings of rage and anger.
(2) Let the patient ventilate anger.
(3) Consider other feelings, such as vulnerability, desperation, and helplessness; they often come up after anger has been ventilated.
(4) When patients display less anger than is adequate or expected, help them to experience anger and support anger expression.
(5) Keep in mind that punitive parent modes may be activated when the patient is in angry/enraged child modes; limit the punitive parent mode if necessary.

(6) After validation, confront the patient with the dysfunctional parts of their angry or enraged child modes.

(7) Encourage adequate expression of anger, while limiting punitive parent modes.

Validate and ventilate rage and anger   When an angry or enraged child mode pops up, the therapist should validate the related feelings and asks the patient why they are angry. When anger is activated in the therapy session, it may have been triggered by the therapist or the treatment institution. The patient should get the opportunity to ventilate all the reasons for their anger. When a patient mentions one or two causes of their anger, the therapist should thoroughly explore whether more reasons are present. It may be that earlier experiences led to the irritation and anger, but that the patient has suppressed them out of fear. It is important that the patient also ventilates this hoarded anger. By ventilating anger, patients usually calm down, and more vulnerable feelings appear. This technique is particularly important for patients with BPD; a more detailed description of the technique and its meaning in this condition is given in the manual *Schema Therapy for Borderline Personality Disorder* (Arntz & van Genderen, 2009).

Case example: ventilating anger

Therapist: Steve, you seem to be angry. Can you tell me why?

Steve: Well, actually, I didn't want to talk about it. But it's really frustrating that I always have to wait for you!

T: You're angry that you had to wait for me today, and that you have had to wait for me before as well. Are there more issues you are angry about?

S: Well, when I'm late, you address it in a way that makes me feel guilty. However, when I have to wait for you, you don't seem to feel very guilty!

T: I understand that you feel it's unfair: you are blamed for being late, but I am not. Are there more things you are angry about?

S: . . .

Rage and the punitive parent mode   Often the expression of anger or rage was not accepted when the patient was a child. Parents often punished rage and anger, either aggressively (i.e. through physical abuse) or by making fun of the child, depriving them of love, or inducing guilt ("Mum is very sad when you are angry"). Later in life, the experience or expression of anger activates a punitive parent, which devalues or punishes the patient for expressing anger. This punitive mode has to be anticipated and limited by the therapist. To do so, the therapist basically pronounces the right of the patient to be angry and to express anger. Everybody should be able to feel anger when their needs are not met, and everybody has the right to express anger. We do not suggest expressing intense anger at all times and everywhere—it is only important to help the patient understand that rage and anger are normal and important feelings: they help us to feel when our needs are not met.

Limit destructive expressions of anger or rage   When the anger expression of the patient is destructive (i.e. the patient bawls at the therapist and humiliates them), the therapist should communicate their personal

---

Case example: anticipate and limit a punitive parent mode

Therapist: Steve, it is important that you can express your anger here. As you told me, your father punished you harshly for being angry when you were a child. I wonder whether your punitive parent mode gets activated now when you tell me why you're angry at me.

Steve: [Nods.]

T: Your anger is a very important feeling. It may happen though that you do not find the perfect way to express it. This can be disadvantageous for you and I would like to help you find more adequate ways of expressing anger. You are free to feel and express anger here! Your punitive parent mode is not right when it says that you should be blamed for being angry!

S: . . .

reaction and limit the destructive anger expression: "Steve, you have criticized me quite harshly. I can understand your criticism and I appreciate it when you stand up for your rights when your needs are not met in therapy. However, your way of criticizing me is very unpleasant. I feel humiliated and my personal reaction is to draw back and distance myself from you, rather than to stay close to you."

Setting limits to destructive rage is important when the patient is unable to wind down by ventilating anger, or when they are very aggressive or threaten the therapist. If the patient does not calm down when the therapist sets limits, step-by-step consequences may be necessary. This is in accordance with the treatment of enraged children. When the patient gets enraged, they might be asked to leave the session for a couple of minutes to calm down in the waiting room, for example. The session can then be continued. However, according to our experience, such measures are usually not needed, as the combination of validation and empathic confrontation is sufficient. Anger or rage can usually be reduced well by these strategies, and the related feelings of vulnerability and helplessness can be addressed.

Encourage a more adequate expression of anger   Although we validate and ventilate the patient's anger and limit punitive parent modes related to anger, we often do not evaluate the patient's anger expression completely positively. When a patient expresses anger inadequately, they should learn to express it in a more appropriate way. Behavioral techniques which focus on social skills training are helpful in this respect.

Often, the feelings of the vulnerable child mode are hidden behind the angry child mode—for example, abandonment, rejection, or worthlessness. Thus an important goal of schema therapy is to get "behind" angry or enraged child modes, and to meet the needs of the vulnerable child mode. When vulnerable child modes pop up behind enraged or angry child modes, they are treated as described in Chapter 6.

The therapeutic relationship with enraged child modes   Enraged child modes hardly ever turn up in the actual therapy session. However, patients sometimes report behaviors which are obviously related to enraged child modes, such as spontaneous physical violence against other people in the heat of an argument. Whenever a therapist becomes aware of such problems, they should focus on limiting them.

Case example: developing a more adequate expression of anger

Therapist: Steve, it's understandable that you get angry when you have to wait for me. I am sorry that I made you wait again today, even though you already told me that you really dislike it when I am late! I was late because I have a busy schedule today, but that does not mean that you shouldn't be angry with me, since it is my responsibility to maintain a realistic schedule. Anyway, wouldn't it be great if you could find a good way to express your anger? It's not good if you just try to ignore it, and get into your compliant surrender mode. However, when you react very angrily, with the angry child mode, it may be a bit over the top. What might be a good compromise? What would the healthy adult mode say?

Case example: limiting an enraged child mode

Paul, a 38-year-old alcoholic (currently abstinent), had an extremely violent father who was also an alcoholic. The father is still alive, but lives in another city. Sometimes he calls Paul when he is drunk, and either humiliates Paul or asks him for money. In these situations, Paul sometimes becomes very angry. He says that he would probably attack his father if he met him in person, as he has done in the past. Sometimes he feels a strong urge to drive to his father's house in these situations. The therapist and Paul agree that the therapist should temporarily keep the key to his father's house. Paul feels that this will reduce the risk of him driving there in rage. Furthermore, Paul and his therapist agree that this enraged mode should be the next focus of therapy. The therapist will return the keys when Paul is reliably able to control his rage.

7.1.2   *The therapeutic relationship with impulsive/undisciplined*
child modes

As described above, angry and enraged child modes often stem from the
childhood experience of being punished for the expression of one's own
needs and feelings. By contrast, impulsive and undisciplined child modes
seem to have somewhat different roots in childhood. Patients with strong
impulsive or undisciplined child modes often report that they were rather
spoiled as children, and that they were not taught to take responsibility.
Sometimes they may have been overburdened, too (e.g. being left alone
with a severely ill parent). In any case, they did not learn to take
responsibility for themselves and others appropriately. Note that some
patients have both angry and impulsive/undisciplined child modes. They
may report both kinds of childhood experience (e.g. the father was
aggressive and punitive when he was drunk; but when he was sober, he
was sorry for his drunken behavior and spoiled the child inappropriately).
In such cases, the impulsive/undisciplined child modes can often be
understood as being driven by rebelliousness against maltreatment and
lack of care. It is important to check this with the patient and, if the patient
agrees, to repeatedly empathically confront the patient with the fact that it
is completely understandable and justified that they should rebel against
maltreatment, but that their chosen action is, in the present circumstances,
not very adaptive and does not lead to meeting the patient's true needs.

   The following list summarizes the basic therapeutic relationship strategies with impulsive or undisciplined child modes. Limited reparenting of
impulsive or undisciplined child modes comprises limit-setting and teaching of discipline, in addition to validation and care—much like the role of
parents, who also have to combine care and support for their children with
the setting of appropriate challenges and limits. In this section, we will
discuss the distinctive features of the therapeutic relationship depending
on whether the child mode is undisciplined, impulsive, or obstinate (the
latter is somewhere in between angry and undisciplined child modes).
However, note that we often see a mixture of these characteristics, rather
than purely undisciplined or impulsive features.

(1) Explore the needs connected to the mode.
(2) Validate these needs.
(3) Confront the patient with the dysfunctional fulfillment of needs in
     this mode: the impulsive child mode goes for "too much"; the

undisciplined child mode avoids responsibility and endeavors too much. Alternatively, ask the patient to reflect on the degree to which their actions lead to fulfillment of their true needs.

(4) Model and teach the patient healthier ways of fulfilling their own needs.
(5) Model and teach the patient healthy discipline.
(6) Set limits if necessary (on potentially harmful impulsive acts).

Impulsivity Impulsive child modes mainly go in for hedonistic needs (having sex, drinking alcohol, buying or stealing nice things, having fun, and so on). It is easy to understand and validate these needs, since a certain degree of hedonism is healthy and pleasurable. Everybody should have at least some opportunity to fulfill their hedonistic needs. However, the impulsiveness of an impulsive child mode is potentially damaging to the patient themselves and to others (unsafe sex, spending too much money). Thus the problems connected with this mode should be highlighted and the therapist should help the patient to find more realistic (and more limited) ways of fulfilling hedonistic needs. Often the impulsive action only leads to a poor substitute for the real need: having sex with a stranger cannot really replace intimacy and love; getting drunk with a group cannot replace real friendship; shopping and spending money does not lead to happiness and a fulfilled life, and so on.

Lack of discipline The main goal of undisciplined child modes is to avoid stress, responsibility, and annoying or boring tasks. The main task for the therapist is to explain to the patient that annoying tasks and obligations are part of every successful healthy adult life. Most people don't like to do their taxes, but it is necessary. Thus the focus with this mode is on setting limits and helping the patient to develop discipline.

Pamperedness Sometimes patients come across as very spoiled when they are in their impulsive child mode. They can be demanding in a rather childish way. They consider it normal to fulfill their needs without regard to the consequences for themselves or others; however, they may not be particularly impulsive in the sense of acting spontaneously and inconsiderately first and then regretting it later. These more spoiled child modes are also related to a lack of discipline and an overemphasis on hedonistic needs, and the same principles can be applied as with clearly impulsive or undisciplined child modes.

Case example: validating and confronting an undisciplined child mode

Therapist:　How did you get on with your homework?

Patient:　I know I promised you I'd exercise twice this week, but I just didn't feel like doing it.

T:　Why not?

P:　I don't know, I just didn't manage to pick myself up and go out.

T:　I wonder whether your undisciplined child mode got activated. We already discussed the fact that your parents did not teach you enough discipline when you were a child. Unfortunately, that's quite a problem for you today. Do you think your undisciplined child mode played a role in your not doing your homework?

P:　Well, possibly, yes.

T:　What are the pros and cons of this mode, in your view?

P:　Well, I don't do things that bother me. However, I don't really achieve my longer-term aims.

T:　You're perfectly right! Do you agree that it seems to be important to reduce the influence of this mode in your life?

7.1.3　Excursus: obstinacy

Sometimes a patient will seem to be angry, but the therapist cannot motivate them to ventilate anger. The patient reacts irritatably instead, and the therapy process gets stuck. In such cases, obstinacy may be the main problem. Obstinate people seem to be angry, but are not willing to express their anger. When the therapist encourages them to express their feelings, they withdraw and reject the therapist. Thus strategies for the treatment of angry child modes do not work well. If a patient is obstinate, they will not collaborate in the therapy. Strategies for the undisciplined child mode are not useful due to the patient's general refusal.

According to clinical experience, obstinacy is often strong in people whose autonomy was not accepted when they were adolescents (e.g. their parents did not accept their privacy when they had a visitor) or in those who were often put under (emotional) pressure (e.g. their mother usually started crying when they criticized her, leaving them feeling guilty and stopping the argument). As obstinate patients tend to reject any therapeutic intervention, we suggest focusing on the obstinacy itself. In doing so, the therapist should address the following points with the patient:

(1) People learn to react with obstinacy when their autonomy is not accepted in adolescence, or when they are put under emotional pressure as children or adolescents. Under such circumstances, obstinacy is often the most functional reaction; it's understandable that people with such experiences should develop obstinate interaction patterns.
(2) With regard to social interaction, obstinacy is mainly associated with the rejection of others. When somebody is obstinate, they tend to refuse whatever others try to do or to say. When another person tries to get closer, rejection increases.
(3) This marks an important difference between obstinacy and other emotions. When somebody is sad or anxious, another person can help them (e.g. by soothing, giving safety), thus creating a positive experience which may help the sad person to cope with complicated feelings. With obstinacy, it is different. You have to decide against your obstinacy before somebody else can give you support.
(4) It would therefore be useful for the patient to give up their obstinacy (at least for the moment), and to share their underlying frustrations and anger with the therapist.

Alternative possibilities include:

(1) If the therapist senses that the demanding or the punitive parent plays a role, they should address this parental mode (without asking the patient's permission) and express anger. In this way, the therapist models anger expression and shows that it is safe to be angry at these parental modes.
(2) It might be helpful for the therapist to suggest to the patient that they may be frustrated or angry because they were treated in a specific way and they couldn't express these feelings openly. It helps when the therapist has specific details of the maltreatment.

In the schema mode model, obstinacy often fits with an "obstinate child" mode, resembling an angry child mode. Like an angry child mode, the obstinate child is frustrated that its needs and its autonomy are not accepted. If obstinacy is very persistent, though, and always comes up when the patient faces new challenges, it may fit instead with an avoidant protector mode. In any case, the integration of obstinacy in the mode model should be discussed with the patient.

Conflicts between undisciplined/impulsive child modes and demanding parent modes   Demanding self-related cognitions ("I don't do this well"; "I should push myself more"; "I should do better") are usually regarded in schema therapy as demanding parent modes. The treatment aims at reducing these modes. However, when impulsive or undisciplined child modes play a role, the picture can be different. Self-demanding cognitions may reflect a realistic and healthy view of the actions of the impulsive/undisciplined child mode and their social consequences. Accordingly, the affect related to statements such as "My lack of discipline is not good," "I should make more effort," or, "In the long run this will not have a good outcome," is not necessarily self-punitive. Instead, patients may say these things in an adult way: they are aware that they match the evaluations of others (parents, friends, colleagues, bosses, or the therapist). In these cases, it is important to conceptualize this aspect of the patient as part of the healthy adult mode. It should not be the goal to fight this voice, but instead to strengthen it, at the same time as limiting the impulsive or undisciplined child mode.

7.1.4   The therapeutic relationship when patients do not express anger

The angry child mode is associated with an exaggerated expression of anger. However, more often we see patients who instead have problems expressing anger. Anger is not exaggerated, but they are unable to address it at all. In these cases, the therapist often experiences anger through countertransference, while this feeling is completely inhibited in the patient. The therapist may even feel that the patient is angry as well, but the patient will deny it when directly asked. This occurs particularly when situations in which anger would be a healthy reaction are discussed (e.g. a female patient talks about verbal abuse by her husband, saying, "I'm not angry—that's just the way he is").

Extreme anger suppression is—just like the inappropriate display of anger with angry child modes—often connected with the childhood experience of being punished for the expression of anger. Anger expression

Case example: anger seems to be an issue, but the patient denies it

Patient: [In slightly irritated tone of voice:] The homework you gave me was pointless. How am I supposed to have a talk with my neighbor when I can't even leave my apartment?

Therapist: It sounds as if you are angry at me because your homework assignment was inappropriate.

P: Angry? Not at all. I'm only sad, because I don't feel understood.

T: I sensed some anger when you said it was "pointless." Usually people use this word when they are irritated or angry.

P: No, I only feel sad.

Case example: biographical background of anger suppression

Evelyn, a 52-year-old OCD patient with avoidant and dependent personality disorder (see Section 2.1.3), is unable to address anger. However, her OCD symptoms serve the function of setting limits when others are invasive. When she dislikes her boyfriend's behavior, she does not become angry, but her OCD symptoms increase. Via symptoms she either controls him (e.g. tells him where to sit in her apartment) or cuts off contact with him (e.g. "cannot" tolerate him in her bed). The therapist senses Evelyn's suppressed anger, as her interaction patterns become very passive-aggressive in such situations. However, when asked, she does not report anger, only helplessness and sadness.

In a diagnostic imagery exercise focusing on this pattern, Evelyn starts with a current situation. She feels badly treated by a nurse on the inpatient ward, but does not feel anger, and ignores the nurse instead. In the related biographical image, Little Evelyn is five years old. Evelyn's mother is very depressed; her father is drunk and enraged, and shouts aggressively at Evelyn and her mother. Little Evelyn would like to talk with her mother about problems at school—some classmates are bullying her, and Evelyn is both angry and afraid of them. But it is not possible to talk with her mother because she feels so bad and is threatened by her husband. If Little Evelyn were to bother her with her own problems, her mother might start crying or even leave the house and perhaps never come back (Evelyn's mother often threatened to leave the family). Furthermore, Little Evelyn is frightened of her violent father. Evelyn knows that he has a gun and is very scared that he might use it. This biographical image explains why Evelyn is afraid of expressing anger and why she does everything to suppress and avoid it.

may even have been vitally threatening for these patients. Their parents showed rage or punished family members severely for the expression of feelings or needs. Such parents are frequently severely psychologically disturbed themselves, often with alcohol-related problems.

In such cases, ventilating anger does not play a role since the patient is simply unable to do it. Instead, the main goals are to encourage the patient to experience anger, to explain that anger is a normal feeling, and to help the patient in developing a more accepting attitude towards anger. Whenever the patient displays a touch of anger in the therapy situation, they are reinforced. However, it is important to distinguish genuine anger from an angry protector mode. When an angry protector mode is present, it should be limited, rather than reinforced.

Case example: reinforcing anger expression in therapy

Therapist: Evelyn, you just said that you don't want to be both-ered with these questionnaires again. Wow, I hear anger in your voice, that's great! It's important that you learn to express anger, but we discovered that is hard for you, as expressing anger was really dangerous in your childhood. Thus it's great that you took a step forward here. Please tell me more about what you are angry about!

Unfortunately, patients like Evelyn frequently choose difficult partners. They often manage to find partners who resemble their parents. Evelyn, for example, was married for more than 15 years to a violent and aggressive alcoholic, with whom she has a son. She had intended to separate from him long before she actually did so, but for many years she was afraid that he'd kill both her and their son if she attempted it. After leaving this man, she found another complicated partner: her current boyfriend is an alcoholic as well, and is verbally abusive. With such a partner, the patient may indeed be well advised not to express anger openly, as it might lead to a harmful reaction. As these patients are often quite lonely, they may not be willing to leave their partners. Thus therapeutic changes usually take place in very small steps and may require a lot of time.

7.2   Cognitive Techniques

Cognitive techniques are used to explain and discuss the biographical backgrounds of all modes. Table 7.2 summarizes some typical biographical factors of angry or impulsive child modes, based on our clinical experience. As always, this list is not exhaustive, and other factors may be relevant too.

7.2.1   *Cognitive techniques with angry or enraged child modes*

On the cognitive level, the adequacy of anger or rage has to be addressed. The patient needs to learn a healthier appraisal of the following issues: how should you express anger, what kind of anger expression is socially accepted, and will it yield the desired results? If a patient mainly suppresses anger, intensive cognitive work is necessary to discuss the meaning and the importance of anger and to help the patient develop an accepting attitude towards anger.

Function and development of rage   Anger is an important feeling, as it shows us when needs are not met. Thus it helps us to focus on our needs when they are frustrated. Children learn to feel and express their anger adequately when (1) they have healthy models of anger expression and (2) they have a safe environment in which to express feelings and needs. Usually patients with an angry or enraged child mode and/or with suppressed anger had neither. Their parents or peers either expressed anger or rage in a threatening way or suppressed their anger themselves. Some patients experienced a combination of these extremes, such as

Table 7.2   Typical biographical background factors of angry or impulsive child modes

Modes	Biographical factors
Angry/enraged child modes	Experience of being unfairly treated (by family members or peers); physical or sexual abuse; being punished for the expression of needs or feelings
Enraged child modes	Extreme violence, violent crimes; often raised in severely disturbed and/or criminal families, with physical abuse, often including physical abuse of the patient
Impulsive child modes	Lack of guidance, limits, and structure; parents either deprived the child of its needs or were overly permissive. Some patients report a mix of depriving and overly permissive reactions. Often social models were impulsive, too
Undisciplined child modes	Undisciplined or spoiled social models; spoiled by parents and/or did not learn to take responsibility in age-appropriate ways. Again, patients may have experienced a mix of deprivation and pamperedness
Obstinacy	Lack of age-appropriate autonomy as an adolescent, and/or (emotionally) overwhelming inappropriate social demands

Evelyn, whose father displayed threatening rage, and whose mother suppressed her anger and surrendered to her father, and instead used complaints to articulate her own feelings and needs.

Healthy parents express anger in a way that communicates their needs, but without threatening or devaluing others; their relationships are not damaged by normal conflicts. Furthermore, they also validate the feelings and needs of their children and do not punish anger expression. Note that parents can punish their children's anger expression either directly or in a more subtle way, by making fun of their angry children or by depriving them of love.

> Anger shows us when own needs are not met and helps to express them. To develop an adequate expression of anger, a child must not perceive anger as threatening and must not be punished for the expression of anger or rage.

7.2.2   *Cognitive techniques with impulsive or undisciplined child modes*

When impulsive or undisciplined patterns are in the foreground, the main cognitive task of the therapist is to confront the patient with these patterns and discuss realistic limits. Usually the development of these modes can be understood from the patient's biography. Parental figures inadequately spoiled the child and did not set healthy limits, or else they restricted the autonomy of the child inappropriately, provoking obstinacy.

Many therapists find it hard to openly address sensitive issues like pamperedness or obstinacy with patients. However, these are very important topics which need to be discussed in therapy. Patients should be encouraged to reflect upon their spoiled or impulsive behavior patterns, which are often strongly reinforced in the short term: people in such modes can often push through their needs effectively and manage to avoid boring or annoying tasks, which are done by others. Since it is often regarded as socially awkward to address pamperedness, these patients do not necessarily know how others perceive their impulsive or undisciplined behaviors (although partners, teachers, or family members such as siblings may be more open). Others often decide to draw away from the patient, rather than explain that they dislike their lack of discipline. Thus, such patterns damage many relationships in the long term. Furthermore, they are usually associated with a lack of long-term target achievement in various life domains.

In any case, because of the positive short-term effects of impulsive or undisciplined behaviors, high motivation is needed on the part of the patient to successfully change these patterns. Therefore, the therapist has to be very clear about their problematic nature in order to support motivation as far as possible.

Case example: discussing the pros and cons of an undisciplined child mode

Toby often behaves in a very spoiled manner. His mother clearly pampered him too much as a child. Toby reports that he was always "Mom's Crown Prince." The following dialogue is related to his last homework assignment—the therapist asked Toby to pay his invoices and start doing his taxes.

Therapist:	Did you finally start to do your taxes this week?
Toby:	Oh, that's so boring and annoying, and I'm horribly busy. Fortunately, my girlfriend started it, since it's becoming really urgent.
Th:	It would actually be quite stupid of you to do it yourself, right?
To:	[Grinning.] If you want to put it that way, yes.
Th:	[With a serious voice:] That's an important consideration when somebody has an undisciplined child mode like you do. Others take your responsibility if it's becoming urgent. That's actually quite a comfortable arrangement for you.
To:	[A bit embarrassed.] That's right.
Th:	You don't need to be embarrassed, as this is actually quite normal. We call it short-term reinforcement.
To:	Yes, I remember that you said that before. Problems that are highly reinforced don't melt away on their own.
Th:	Exactly. That's the big advantage of your spoiled child mode: so far you have always found someone who will help you out. When you were an adolescent, it was your mother; now it's your girlfriend. Do you see any disadvantage to this system?
To:	Yes, of course! I sometimes feel silly when my girlfriend takes over all my duties and I don't do anything for her in return. And I feel a bit like a dependent child. I don't have any reason to feel proud of myself.
Th:	That sounds right. I completely agree. I wonder whether these considerations will help you to increase your level of discipline.

The therapist might suggest having a chair dialogue with the spoiled child mode and the healthy adult mode. This might help to intensify the healthy adult mode (and thus motivation for change) on an emotional level. Such a dialogue should be combined with a behavioral homework assignment requiring the patient to show more discipline. This chair dialogue is described in the next section.

7.3   Emotional Techniques

Regarding emotion-focused interventions for angry and impulsive child modes, chair dialogues are a very useful treatment technique. The most common chair dialogue formats with these modes are dialogues between the angry or impulsive child, the healthy adult mode, and the punitive or demanding parent mode.

When the patient punishes themselves for experiencing or expressing anger, the main goals of such a dialogue are to help the angry child to become visible, to validate it, and to support the patient in experiencing and expressing angry feelings. Accordingly, the punitive parent mode should be limited, as the expression of anger does not deserve punishment. This intervention is described in detail in Chapter 8.

When impulsive or obstinate child modes are in the foreground and the punitive parent mode does not play a central role, the main goal is to reduce the impulsive/undisciplined child mode. The healthy adult mode should also be strengthened and the patient should be encouraged to take responsibility and to engage themselves in more annoying or boring tasks. The following case example describes a chair dialogue with Toby's undisciplined child mode (see Section 7.2).

Case example: chair dialogue with an undisciplined child mode

Therapist: I would suggest a chair dialogue regarding this issue. Do you agree? [Stands and puts two chairs facing each other, one for the undisciplined child mode and one for the healthy adult mode. The patient takes a seat on the undisciplined child chair.] Well then, please let your undisciplined part explain why things are so good the way they are!

Toby: [On the undisciplined child chair:] Life's fantastic the way it is! Doing my taxes is boring—it's no fun at all—and Marina is doing a great job. I'll invite her for dinner to say thanks—that's fun for both of us—and everybody will be happy!

Th: Brilliant! Now change chairs please.

To:	[After changing to the healthy adult chair:] You're taking it quite easy, though!
Th:	Can you please talk in the first person?
To:	I am taking the easy way out. I know Marina hates to do my stuff. She's simply more disciplined than I am. She is justly angry at me and in the long run I'll ruin our relationship. I know quite well how frustrated she is about me being so spoiled.
Th:	That sounds good. What action plan would this side suggest?
To:	Unfortunately, it's my job to do my crap. I must become more disciplined in the future.
Th:	Great! What's does the spoiled side have to say to that?
To:	It doesn't say anything else. It knows that's true.
Th:	Does it really give up so quickly? May I take a seat on the undisciplined chair? [Takes a seat on the chair of the undisciplined child mode and talks from that perspective, exaggerating its point:] Take it easy, man! Marina won't leave you, she's reliable—she's even talked about marriage! Remember how boring your taxes are. Everything's OK as long as I don't have to do them myself! Maybe she's a bit frustrated, but she'll soon get over it.
To:	[Stays on the chair of the healthy adult:] No, that's not OK! Even though she's so helpful and will probably help again, that's not the way I want to be. I don't want to use others because I'm too lazy to do things myself.

The therapist can try to strengthen the patient's healthy adult mode by taking a seat on the dysfunctional mode's chair. From this chair they can challenge the patient's healthy side. Don't forget to agree on a behavioral homework assignment following such an exercise! If a patient repeatedly fail to do their homework, you could consider offering the next appointment only after they have done it. Thus you will model a healthy relationship in which both sides are responsible for their tasks and set limits on the patient's undisciplined child mode: "It sounds great that you are finally willing to do your taxes yourself. I suggest that you call me to schedule our next appointment after you have done your taxes."

7.3.1 Exercising anger expression

Patients with anger suppression and anger avoidance should be encouraged to express anger in chair dialogues. This is discussed in more detail in Chapter 8. The goal in such dialogues is for the patient to experience anger and to accept it as normal.

Other exercises can also be used to increase the experience and expression of anger (such as boxing or other martial arts exercises). In schema therapy for groups with BPD patients, exercises combining aggression and fun are used (tug-of-war, pillow fights). Exercises from body therapy can be useful as well. For example, in one such exercise the patient places a rope on the floor, marking their personal space. They can see how it feels when the therapist accepts (by staying outside of the are marked by the rope) and does not accept (by crossing the rope) this limit. The emotional and behavioral reactions of the patient can then be discussed. Farrell & Shaw (2012) list more suitable exercises you can try.

It is also important that the patient learns to detect irritation and anger earlier, and to express them at a suitable time, instead of suppressing them until things have built up so much that they explode.

7.4   Behavioral Techniques

On the behavioral level, exercises for an adequate expression of anger are applied in the treatment of angry/enraged child modes. Social skills training with video feedback is helpful here. For patients with strong angry or enraged child modes, the focus is on learning to express anger more appropriately. In patients with suppressed anger, however, social skills training mainly aims at expressing anger at all.

When impulsive or undisciplined child modes are in the foreground, behavioral work is mostly related to increasing discipline and reducing impulsive behaviors. Homework assignments are particularly important. When a patient tends to be obstinate, behavioral work must be prepared with intensive cognitive work; obstinate patients will not follow any homework assignment anyway, until they have decided to stop their obstinate patterns. Finally, with a lack of discipline that is not driven by rebelliousness, it might be important to use operant conditioning to change the reinforcement of the (lack of) activities. For instance, the patient can apply self-reinforcement by rewarding discipline (e.g. first clean the kitchen, then have a coffee and watch television), and sometimes by "punishing" lack of discipline (no pleasant activities if the is duty post-poned, giving money to a charity they disagree with, and so on).

7.5 FAQ

(1) How do you distinguish between different anger-related modes (e.g. angry child, angry protector, bully and attack)?

The social and psychological functions of the different modes guide such destinctions. This is explained in detail in Chapter 2.

(2) Some patients find the experience of anger so threatening that they refuse to approach this emotion. How do you deal with such a problem?

This is typical in patients with severe and chronic disorders, such as long-lasting cluster-C disorders and BPD. In the clinical impression, suppression of anger is often at the core of many of these patients' problems (e.g. a patient who has severe flashbacks of sexual abuse, but refuses to let the therapist fight the perpetrator in imagery rescripting because "you're not allowed to fight my granddad"; in everyday life the patient is very easily threatened, but "never gets angry, just scared"). This may be combined with dependent patterns (the dependency of a helpless child mode or avoidant protector or compliant surrender mode; e.g. a patient who always needs a friend to accompany them on visits to their doctor, as they are afraid to to stand up for their own needs). In such cases, the therapist should be very clear regarding the central meaning of anger and rage. If the patient keeps refusing to deal with anger, they will probably not be able to make substantial progress in therapy.

   Note that "dealing with anger" can be divided into many small steps with these patients. Usually you start with cognitive work regarding the meaning of anger, including Socratic dialogues, pro-and-con lists, and so on; emotion-focused work comes later, as is usually much more threatening for the patient (albeit more helpful in the long term).

Emotional work is also introduced stepwise. For example, chair dialogues may be preceded by similar dialogues using Playmobil figures. The therapist should be prepared to model healthy anger expression for a long time with these cases. Altogether, focusing anger may play a major part in the therapy of these patients.

(3) Do patients usually have either an impulsive or an angry child mode, or can both exist in the same patient?

Patients with a strong angry child mode, particularly those with BPD, often experience both intense anger and a lack of discipline/impulsiveness. This corresponds with the diagnostic criteria of BPD, which include both impulsivity and anger-related problems. Accordingly, both problems developed early in these patients' lives: on one hand, anger expression was dangerous; on the other, healthy models teaching an adequate expression of needs and appropriate discipline and limits were lacking. In the treatment of these patients, strategies for both angry and undisciplined child modes have to be combined. Often they are driven by a similar motive; that is, rebelliousness against former, present, or expected maltreatment. Framing this in such terms helps the patient to better understand these modes, and helps the therapist to remain empathic. On one hand, dysfunctional parent modes punishing the expression of emotions have to be reduced. On the other, healthy demands regarding discipline should be reinforced and encouraged. Don't expect quick therapy success in these patients, as they usually suffer from severe disorders requiring longer treatments.

8

Treating Dysfunctional Parent Modes

The central goal with dysfunctional parent modes is to reduce and limit their influence, if necessary by fighting them. The optimal goal would be to get them out of the patient's system, and replace them with healthy and functional moral standards and values. The more punitive they are, the more they must be fought. With interventions related to dysfunctional parent modes, the patient learns to reduce self-devaluations and build up self-esteem and healthy and balanced self-evaluations. Self-hatred is reduced, and both the positive and negative sides of the self can be accepted. A fundamentally positive self-evaluation is an important precondition for accepting one's own mistakes and shortcomings. Only when people can basically accept their shortcomings can they begin to improve them.

8.1   The Therapeutic Relationship

In the therapeutic relationship, the therapist limits dysfunctional parent modes when they pop up. They offer a model for a positive and balanced self-evaluation. Furthermore, limited reparenting is itself an antagonist to punitive parent modes.

Patients with a punitive parent mode tend to interpret neutral comments (or the absence of comments) from the punitive parent perspective: "When I get a new haircut and nobody praises it, I feel that everybody hates my haircut." Any comments the therapist makes may also be interpreted from this perspective. The therapist should pay attention to this risk and repeatedly refer to it in the session, thus setting limits on the punitive mode. Any misinterpretation related to the punitive parent mode in the

Schema Therapy in Practice: An Introductory Guide to the Schema Mode Approach, First Edition. Arnoud Arntz and Gitta Jacob.
© 2013 John Wiley & Sons, Ltd. Published 2013 by John Wiley & Sons, Ltd.

Case example: setting limits on the punitive parent mode in therapy

Jane (see Section 2.1.3) didn't manage to do her last therapy homework: preparing a job application: "It's so stupid that I coulnd't do it! I'm such a failure!" The therapist sets limits on the dysfunctional parent mode by questioning this overly negative self-evaluation—although avoiding the job application is obviously a problem. "It's a pity that you didn't manage to do it and we have to find a way for you to get along better. However, it's not true that you are a complete failure—that's your punitive parent mode talking. You manage many things quite well. If the punitive parent mode always takes over when you make a mistake, you will mainly be discouraged. In the end you won't be willing to try anything challenging anymore, right?"

session is suitable for cognitive techniques aimed at correcting the cognitive distortions associated with this mode.

In schema therapy, limited reparenting and empathic confrontation go hand in hand. On one hand, patients are provided with care. On the other, patients are empathically confronted with critical patterns such as dysfunctional coping modes or a lack of discipline. Discussing these sensitive and critical issues often triggers punitive parent modes: "You don't like me—nobody likes me, because I'm so avoidant and boring!" Thus therapists should always try to limit the punitive parent mode when critical issues are addressed. The therapist can use the reasoning that they are only confronting the patient with these critical issues out of good intentions as they are genuinely interested in helping the patient.

Therapists often avoid difficult confrontations because they are afraid to trigger the punitive parent mode. With empathic confrontation and limited reparenting, critical issues can be addressed by balancing confrontation and care.

Case example: balancing empathic confrontation with limited reparenting

Lucie (see Section 6.1.4) tends not to take responsibility for her everyday life, including her studies. She is formally continuing her studies, but gets into an avoidant coping mode whenever she is confronted with a problem. Thus she has hardly participated in any classes in the last few years. She is already 5 years over the regular period of study, and will probably be unable to ever finish her course. However, she is unwilling to discuss her perspective realistically (probably because she has no idea what else to do); instead she sees different physicians and therapists, complains about depressive symptoms and burn-out, and asks for new antidepressant medication and inpatient treatment. This pattern is conceptualized as a compliant surrender/avoidant coping mode. Confrontation with such a problematic coping mode will probably trigger Lucie's punitive parent mode.

Therapist: [Explains that Lucie may show dependent behaviors in order to avoid a realistic view of her studies.]

Lucie: [Punitive parent mode gets triggered.] Now I feel completely wrong again! You are right that I am a failure and that it's only dependent and childish of me to run to my doctor over my depressive symptoms. I'm too stupid to finish my exams!

T: [Does not change the topic, but tries to bring in reality and to point out the punitive parent mode.] Lucie, you are right that I am kind of criticizing you—I just asked you whether you might avoid confrontation with the reality of your study, for example by behaving in a dependent way instead of taking responsibility, and that is a critical question indeed. However, I did not say that you are a failure or that you're stupid! I care a lot about you and I genuinely want to help you. That's the main reason I'm addressing this sensitive issue of dependency. However, I sense that perhaps your punitive parent got activated. Am I right?

L: Yes, because you were critical. Every time somebody is critical towards me I start to feel a complete failure and a fool . . .

T: Yes, I think you might be right. So it is important that we start to address your punitive parent side, in order that you can learn to deal better with critical remarks, and have less need to avoid them and to avoid confrontation with reality. So, although I know your study is a very sensitive issue, I will continue to suggest putting it on the agenda, because I think it's of the highest importance for you. I want to help you, and I don't devalue you!

L: I can see that, but it doesn't feel that way . . .

T: I understand, as your punitive parent gets activated by it. Your healthy side understands that we should address your study and your dependent ways of dealing with problems, but you seem so afraid of the punitive parent side that you would rather avoid it. Although I understand it is unpleasant in the short term, I think we should work on no longer avoiding addressing these issues, as we cannot solve them by avoiding them. And I think we should now give priority to dealing with the punitive side, so that you become less afraid of it. When we accomplish that, you will become less afraid of addressing difficult issues such as your study. Do you understand what I mean?

8.2   Cognitive Techniques

Cognitive interventions aim at changing the punitive parent mode's black-and-white thinking style about the self and others—"I am completely bad, others are perfect"—and at increasing self-esteem. All "classical" cognitive techniques from CBT are appropriate. The following list gives an overview of suitable cognitive interventions for dysfunctional parent modes. Again, this list is certainly not exhaustive.

(1)   Educate the patient about the development of high or low self-esteem.
(2)   Analyze the biographical background of the dysfunctional parent mode.

(3) Restructure extremely negative self-evaluations: reduce black-and-white thinking style and look for alternative interpretations.

(4) Encourage the patient to keep a positive diary: schedule at least one positive item daily.

(5) Ask the patient to list their positive characteristics.

(6) Ask the patient to observe what others like in them.

(7) Use schema flashcards (Table 6.2) for everyday situations related to the punitive parent mode.

Patients usually experience the messages of dysfunctional parent modes as egosyntonic. They need to learn (as part of psychoeducation) that self-esteem and self-evaluations develop to a large extent through social feedback. No child is born with the self-evaluation of being a failure, or of not deserving any good. Healthy and well-balanced self-evaluations develop when parents teach their children that they are basically worthy and lovable. Everybody has some shortcomings, but that does not undermine the basic worth of every human being. However, when children experience rejection, deprivation, or abuse, they are at risk of developing a punitive parent mode and very low self-esteem.

8.2.1 Biographical development of dysfunctional parent modes

Social evaluations are not only communicated by parents. Peers, teachers, trainers, friends, and others contribute to the self-concept people develop in childhood and adolescence. Dysfunctional parent modes develop when social feedback or the way a child is treated, no matter by whom, is negative or devaluing. On the cognitive treatment level, we discuss with the patient the conditions that set the stage for the development of a punitive parent mode in their childhood. Severely disturbed patients in particular often suffered from negative feedback or treatment from several people. Jane, for example, experienced her mother as cold and as demanding too much of her. She told Jane to diet, but did not offer any support apart from pinning diet schedules on the fridge door. The "mother part" of Jane's punitive parent mode is related to statements such as "Nobody loves you," "Nobody is interested in you," "Your needs are not important to anybody." Her father, on the other hand, was impulsive and verbally abusive when he was drunk. He made fun of her with sexualized jokes for being shy with boys. The messages of the "father part" of Jane's punitive parent mode include

"Only sexy women are attractive," "It's embarrassing to be a virgin." Furthermore, Jane was bullied by her classmates for being an overweight outsider. The messages of the "classmate part" of Jane's punitive parent mode are "You are fat and ugly," "People laugh at you behind your back," "You are completely ridiculous."

8.2.2   Dealing with guilt feelings

When the punitive parent mode is questioned, patients often feel guilty. They are scared to talk badly about their parents, and worry that the therapist will get a too-negative picture of them. In many cases, it may have been prohibited to talk badly about their parents when the patient was a child. This adds to guilt feelings evoked by the discussion of parent modes.

When guilt feelings are an issue, the therapist should first explain that fighting the punitive parent mode does not mean that the patient's parents are completely bad. In some cases, parents may indeed have been obviously bad (e.g. sadistic); in other cases, the parents did their best, but were not properly equipped for parenthood or were unable to protect their child against abuse. They may themselves have suffered from psychological problems which decreased their ability to raise their children in a healthy way and offer safe attachment. When we talk about fighting the punitive parent mode, we mainly fight and repel the negative introjects which developed because of certain behaviors by parent figures. When the punitive parent mode is repelled, the patient's self-esteem can increase and they can start to take their own needs more seriously. This leads to increased well-being. The idea of fighting the punitive parent mode does not mean devaluing the parents. However, obvious maltreatment cannot be justified by good intentions, psychiatric disorders, the parents' own childhood, and so on—and nor can its discussion be avoided.

Patients can often—from their healthy adult perspective—understand later in therapy why certain people acted the way they did during their childhood. Jane, for example, understands as an adult that her father, who had himself been severely traumatized as a child in the Second World War, had always been emotionally unstable. Alcohol was both his coping mechanism and a contributing factor to his emotional instability. Her mother was herself unloved as a child and therefore never learned to offer safe attachment to her daughter, or to care well for her husband.

Understanding the motives of parents is certainly helpful. But understanding should never be confused with justification. Also note that in many patients, especially in cluster-C patients, too much and too early understanding tends to increase guilt feelings over the natural anger that is evoked by the maltreatment. Thus, understanding is for later—first the anger should be allowed, and the patient should emancipate themselves from the "brainwashing" that is internalized in the parental modes. Later there might be room for understanding and—though this is a choice for the patient—forgiving. If parents treated their child badly because they themselves were coping dysfunctionally with their own problems, the child still suffered, and their basic needs were still not adequately met. Understanding does not change that.

Psychoeducation regarding these issues can either be communicated within cognitive interventions and/or embedded in emotion-focused exercises such as chair dialogues or imagery exercises. When, for example, a patient in a child mode (in a chair dialogue or an imagery exercise) talks about feeling guilty for criticizing their depressive mother, the therapist can weave in psychoeducation and say to the child mode, "It is nice and important to understand that your mother cannot care for you because she is depressive; however, for you as a child, it is horrible: you are scared, you don't get the care you need, and even more importantly, you get a sort of suggestion that you are guilty of causing her depression, through your mother's rejecting and criticizing you and through not being able to help her."

8.3   Emotion-Focused Techniques

Emotion-focused interventions are supposed to help the patient reduce the impact of the punitive parent mode on their emotions and "felt meaning," and to strengthen the healthy adult mode, including self-esteem and acceptance of the patient's own needs and feelings. The main intervention techniques are imagery rescripting exercises and chair dialogues.

In imagery rescripting exercises, punitive or demanding parent modes are limited in the rescripting phase of the exercise. The healthy adult mode of the patient or the helping person modeling the healthy adult (therapist or third-party helper) limits the dysfunctional parent mode by fighting the perpetrator and/or arguing with a demanding parent figure. The technique of imagery rescripting was described in detail in Chapter 6. In this section, emotion-focused work with chair techniques is explained in more detail.

8.3.1   Chair dialogues

Basics   Chair dialogues have mainly been developed by psychodrama and gestalt therapists (overview in Kellogg, 2004). The basic idea of chair-work exercises is to distinguish different (typically conflicting) parts of the patient. Each part is allocated a chair, and the chairs are arranged in a circle (or opposite each other if there are only two). The patient takes a seat on each of the chairs in turn, adopting its perspective and feeling and expressing its related emotions. When another mode pops up while the patient is sitting on one chair, they change to the chair of the new mode (or the chair is added, if it was not already there). This technique first helps to clarify inner conflicts and ambivalent feelings or behaviors, and second is used to strengthen those modes that need to be increased, and weaken those that need to be reduced, both cognitively, emotionally, and regarding "felt meaning." The main schema-therapy goals of chair dialogues, which are in line with the basic goals of schema therapy in general (see Chapter 4), are as follows:

(1)   Clarify ambivalent feelings and conflicts between modes.
(2)   Validate and comfort the vulnerable child mode.
(3)   Ventilate and validate the feelings of the angry or enraged child modes.
(4)   Validate and set limits on the impulsive or undisciplined child modes.
(5)   Question and set limits on the demanding parent mode.
(6)   Fight the punitive parent mode.
(7)   Reflect upon the pros and cons of, and reduce, the coping modes.

Variations
Two-chair dialogues
Chair dialogues are very flexible. In the simplest format, two chairs are used, representing two different parts of the patient. If a therapist has no previous experience with the technique of chair dialogues, this format is a good beginning. It is suitable for illuminating ambivalent feelings or inner conflicts. This format can be used within any model; in schema therapy, two-chair dialogues usually comprise one "schema chair" and one "healthy chair"; within the mode model, one chair represents the healthy adult and the other represents a dysfunctional mode. If you are not sure what modes to involve at the beginning of the exercise, you can just start with two chairs and see which modes appear when the patients takes a seat on them.

Typical areas of application are ambivalent feelings regarding social relationships, problems at work, and so on (see the following list for typical starting points of two-chair dialogues). Each of the perspectives expressed is represented by one of the two chairs. For example, regarding the first statement in the following list, one chair would represent the plan to leave, the other chair the motivation to stay.

- "I have been thinking about leaving my boyfriend for about a year now, but somehow I just never manage it . . . "
- "I would really like to participate in this seminar. But I am already way too late for registration, as always . . . "
- "I have been looking for an apartment to buy for over 2 years now. I've seen some really nice ones, but I just can't seem to decide . . . "
- "My boss always delegates annoying tasks to me. I would really like to be more assertive, but somehow I never manage . . . "
- "It would be good for me to exercise again. I just have to push myself a bit more . . . Next year I'll run a marathon for sure!"

Chair dialogues with three or more chairs
The schema mode model allows for all possible combinations of modes in chair dialogues. We often start with a "discussion" between a dysfunctional parent mode and the healthy adult mode. When these different perspectives are processed, intense feelings may emerge as well (either vulnerability or anger); these feelings are connected to their respective child modes, and a chair for each activated child mode is added to the chair circle. As a variation of the chair dialogue between healthy adult and punitive parent mode, some patients imagine the actual person on the punitive chair who implemented the punitive parent mode in their childhood. It is then a discussion between the patient and this person. The content and effect are usually the same as when the patient has a discussion with the punitive parent mode itself.

Another typical start for a schema-therapy chair dialogue with more than two chairs is a discussion between the healthy adult mode and a coping mode, with the aim of understanding (and later reducing) the coping mode. In this context, another chair for the vulnerable child mode may be used to reflect how the vulnerable child mode feels when the two different modes (healthy adult and coping mode) are activated.

All chairs used in a chair-work exercise represent parts of the patient that are currently activated. However, it's not always necessary or recommendable to actually let the patient take a seat on each of the chairs. The longer a patient sits on a chair, the more strongly its mode is activated. By contrast, if a patient keeps away from a chair, the mode gets less activated and the patient can keep some distance from it. This is particularly recommendable when a patient first start with chair exercises, when they need a lot of safety in the therapy situation, when they are easily overwhelmed by their emotions, or when they suffer from an intense punitive parent mode. In such cases you may allow the patient to keep their seat on the usual therapy chair, and just tell you what the different modes on the different chairs say. As a next step, the patient can take a seat only on the chairs of the vulnerable child and the healthy adult, but not on that of the punitive parent mode, in order to prevent intense activation of and identification with the latter. Thus chair work can be begun in small steps and is adapted to the emotional problems and capacities of the patient.

The therapist takes a very active role in schema-therapy chair dialogues. They participate in the game, play different modes themselves, have discussions with the different modes, and so on—mostly as a model for the healthy adult mode. The therapist may, for example, limit the punitive parent mode or even put its chair out of the therapy room, which is a powerful act symbolizing that the punitive parent mode should be eliminated from the patient's system. Similarly, the therapist may—while sitting on the patient's healthy adult chair—validate and comfort the vulnerable child on its chair.

Some typical schema-therapy chair-dialogue exercises include the following:

(1) Two-chair dialogues to treat any kind of inner conflict or ambivalence; one chair for each perspective.

(2) A two-chair dialogue between a dysfunctional parent mode and the healthy adult mode. The healthy adult limits the demanding parent mode and/or fights the punitive parent mode. Depending on the emotional process of the patient, it may be helpful to add chairs for the vulnerable and/or angry child mode.

(3) A three-chair format with the demanding parent mode, angry child mode, and healthy adult mode. This exercise is particularly helpful for patients with a strong demanding parent mode and conflicts between surrendering to the demanding parent versus expressing anger.

(4) A two-chair dialogue with the healthy adult and vulnerable child mode. The healthy adult comforts the vulnerable child. In this format, the therapist often models the role of the healthy adult mode in the first exercises. As a variation, use only one empty chair for the

vulnerable child mode; the therapist talks to this chair from their normal seat, soothing and comforting the vulnerable child mode.

(5) A two-chair dialogue with a coping mode and the healthy adult mode. This is particularly useful when the coping mode is very dominant in the therapy situation and/or when it blocks important changes in the patient's life.

Introducing chair work in therapy For many patients (and many therapists), working with different chairs sounds kind of weird at first. Accordingly, they may not be very enthusiastic about trying it. Only after their first attempt can patients (and therapists) understand the great potential and impact of this treatment technique. Thus the therapist has to introduce chair-work exercises in a very active and engaged way. They should model all steps of the chair-dialogue exercise, flexibly and dynamically standing up to start the exercise, fetching chairs, modeling modes, changing chairs, investigating the emotional character of different modes, and so on. When the therapist models chair work unselfconsciously, the patient will feel less self-conscious as well. On the other hand, when the therapist stays in their usual chair and instructs the patient to run around in circles, the patient will justifiably feel odd. Like imagery rescripting exercises, chair work should start with short exercises and the patient should always be asked for feedback.

Case example: introducing a chair dialogue in the therapy session

Lucie's therapist would like to do a chair-dialogue exercise to fight the punitive parent mode which was triggered by Lucie's dependent coping. The punitive parent mode accuses Lucie of being a failure. The impact of this mode has to be decreased; it will not be possible to continue addressing her dependency issue in therapy if this mode is always in the way.

The therapist introduces the concept of a chair dialogue by saying, "Lucie, when I addressed your dependent pattern, your punitive parent was triggered and told you that you are a stupid failure. I guess that hearing that, Little Lucie felt quite desperate and lonely, right? At the same time, you know what I am talking about: you are able to reflect on this issue and know it's important—that's your healthy adult mode. I would like to do a chair-work exercise with you to strengthen the healthy adult mode and weaken the impact of the punitive parent mode. Here's what we do in a chair-work exercise: we allocate each of the three modes—Little Lucie, the punitive parent, and the healthy adult mode—to a chair." The therapist stands and arranges three chairs in a circle. "Now I would like you to take a seat on each of the different chairs in turn and to express the perspective and the feelings of the mode on each of them. On which chair do you want to start?"

The course of chair dialogues   In the majority of cases, chair dialogues aim at reducing demanding or punitive parent modes. Just like imagery rescripting exercises (see Section 6.3.2), chair-work exercises have to be adapted to the nature of the dysfunctional parent mode. A chair dialogue with a demanding parent mode focused on achievement often has the character of a discussion, rather than a fight. In this discussion, the healthy adult and the demanding parent negotiate the importance of achievement in the patient's life and their right to pursue nonachievement goals and needs. In chair dialogues with a guilt-inducing parent mode, the central issues are the attribution of responsibility, the patient's right to set limits on others, and the appropriateness of guilt feelings. The healthy adult mode takes the position that the patient is not always responsible for the well-being of everybody around them. Basically, adults are themselves responsible for their own well-being. By contrast, in chair dialogues with an overtly punitive parent mode, it may be necessary to address this mode much more firmly, to cut it short, to deprecate it, to fight it, and eventually to put its chair out of the room. Note that these are general guidelines— individual cases may need adaptations. For example, some very rigid and nonresponsive demanding parent modes may need to be fought, while some punitive parent modes (used to high levels of verbal arguments) may be "taken by surprise" if addressed in a calm, friendly, but decisive way.

The process of a chair dialogue depends on the patient's emotional reactions over the course of the exercise. The more strongly a punitive parent mode dominates, the more the therapist has to protect the patient against this mode and to fight it actively. Thus, the patient sits on this chair for only a very short time, in order to keep some distance from this mode. In severe cases, the patient may not take a seat on the punitive parent chair at all, and instead stay on the chair of the healthy adult or the vulnerable child and report from this distance what the punitive parent says.

The degree of support from the therapist also depends on the nature of the mode. Patients with an intense punitive parent mode usually need a lot of support to fight it. The therapist can provide this by themselves taking a seat on the healthy adult mode chair and limiting the punitive parent, while the patient stays on the vulnerable child chair. To give emotional support, the therapist can display anger towards the punitive parent mode, and put its chair out of the room when it cannot be won over. After putting the punitive chair out, the patient on the vulnerable child chair may receive further emotional support.

When the patient's healthy adult mode is already strong, unrelenting standards are a frequent topic of chair dialogues. In these chair dialogues, the patient argues with the demanding parent mode. The healthy adult asserts the right of the patient to have their needs met and their emotions validated, and to set limits on overly high demands. Again, the affect displayed by the dysfunctional parent mode has to be taken into account. In patients with a strong healthy adult mode, the demanding parent mode is less unforgiving than a severe punitive parent mode. It would be disproportionate to put it out of the room; talking to it with a firm voice is sufficient.

With regard to the distribution of roles in the chair dialogue, with patients with a stronger healthy adult mode, the therapist may do the opposite to what they would do for a patient with a weak healthy adult mode: instead of taking a seat on the healthy adult chair, the therapist sits on the chair of the demanding parent mode and provoke the patient (on the healthy adult chair) with its demands. This triggers the patient to resist it even more strongly from the healthy adult perspective.

Always try to establish the "main message" of the dysfunctional parent mode (see Section 2.1.2). Depending on the character of the mode, devaluations or demands may be related to the patient as a whole or to some specific feature of them (e.g. being a woman, being too emotional, being stupid, etc.). Demanding parent modes may demand high achievement or punitive parent modes may induce guilt and require the patient to put the needs of others above their own.

Note that patients with an enmeshment schema may differ with respect to their demanding parent mode. Their parents didn't help them become (or even kept them from becoming) independent. Thus their demanding parent mode sometimes tells these patients that others would be unhappy if they were to go their own way. The character of the dysfunctional parent mode often becomes clear via the chair dialogue, but it should also be reflected upon with the patient. The following three case examples demonstrate how to adapt chair dialogues to the character of the dysfunctional parent mode in question.

Case example: chair dialogue with a demanding parent mode focused on achievement

Eva cannot allow herself pleasure and rest periods. Her unrelenting standards repeatedly lead to burnout problems. Her parents were themselves high-achievers who worked very hard and did not take care of themselves. Thus they modeled this mode to Eva. She was always the best at school and university; this was nothing to be proud about for her, just normal. Currently she is working on her thesis and can't seem to stay within sensible limits (e.g. she insists on reading all the original papers cited in her thesis completely, even though she knows that hardly any of her fellow students read more than the abstracts). The therapist suggests a chair dialogue between the demanding parent mode and the healthy adult mode.

Therapist: Which chair would you like to start with, to discuss your extreme standards regarding your thesis?

Eva: Well, the demanding chair, I guess. That's always activated. [She takes a seat on the chair of the demanding parent mode.] It's totally obvious that your thesis should be perfect! It's important to read all the literature—including what your professor gives you, as well as whatever you can find yourself. If you don't do that, everybody will be able to see that your preparation was lousy.

T: Fine! What's the other chair saying?

E: [Changes to the chair of the healthy adult.] Come off it! None of my fellow students reads all the literature. Even my mentor said that it's normal to get a brief overview of many papers by reading the abstracts alone. In my professional career after university, it won't matter whether I read 1000 pages more or less now. I'll forget the details anyway. It's more important now to get on with the thesis; I'm losing time and I will get lost in details if I try to meet your [directed at the demanding parent chair] demands! Eventually I'll be completely overwhelmed, I'll have a nervous break-down and have to postpone everything. That'll look much worse on my resume than a less than 100% perfect thesis.

T: Great! What's the demanding parent chair say to that?

E: [Changes chairs again and starts talking from the demanding parent chair.] If you want to start a scientific career, you have to demonstrate to your professor that you understand every detail and that you love to read research literature! [Changes chairs independent of therapist instructions and continues from the healthy adult chair.] But I don't want a scientific career! I already have an agreement with the boss at my internship that I'll get the next job in their clinic. Obviously they don't even care about my thesis—they said I was the best intern they ever had!

T: Perfect! What's the parent chair saying now?

E: [Continues from the chair of the healthy adult.] It's not saying much anymore. It seems to be convinced.

Surrogate materials for chairs when more distance is needed We usually recommend using actual chairs for chair-work exercises, since this brings about the strongest emotional effect. Practical problems like small rooms and so on should not be a reason not to work with actual chairs. If a therapist has a very small office, they can still use small stackable stools.

It should be noted that patients with BPD in particular may initially react with panic when the therapist suggests doing mode work with different chairs. They are scared that they will not be able to stand the emotions related to the exercise and/or will be overwhelmed by the

Case example: chair dialogue with a guilt-inducing punitive parent mode

Vivian is a social worker in a psychiatric outpatient unit. In her job, she sacrifices herself for her clients far beyond any reasonable limits. She even takes over responsibilities for clients which they could (and should) manage for themselves. From a professional/healthy adult perspective, she knows that she should set more limits and push her clients to be independent. However, whenever she sets a stricter limit, she gets a bad conscience, and feels guilty and overly responsible. These feelings are connected with her guilt-inducing punitive parent mode. The following chair dialogue relates to a current situation: Vivian can't set limits on a very dependent patient and ask her to take care of some everyday life issues herself. Other members of her team have got angry at Vivian about this, as they regard her over-responsibility as maintaining the patient's dependency. Vivian starts the chair dialogue on the chair of the guilt-inducing parent mode.

Vivian: You have to care for that poor woman. She is so hard up. Her life is all a mess. You are the only person who cares about her. Nobody else can stand her anymore. When she is incapable of leaving the house to go to the store, it's inhuman to ask her to do it!

Therapist: [Smiling] What does the healthy adult think?

V: [Changes to the healthy adult chair.] Well, that's not completely right. This client is quite good at making other people do her bidding. If I set limits, she'll probably find somebody else to take on the responsibilities. And I don't help her by doing the things she should be doing for herself. To be honest, it would be much better to push her more and encourage her to take responsibility herself. Autonomy in everyday life is a central goal for this client.

T: Great! What does the punitive parent mode answer?

V: [Moves to the chair of the punitive parent mode.] It's just horrible when the poor client feels bad. It's

	inhuman and hard-hearted to accept that somebody you're responsible for feels bad!
T:	Does this actually remind you of your mother? You told me that your mother often asked of you to take care of her well-being. As a child, you felt guilty when your mother was sad.
V:	Yes, I think that's in the same category.
T:	Try to say it from the chair of the healthy adult!
V:	[Changes to the chair of the healthy adult, and addresses the punitive parent chair.] You taught me to feel guilty when others feel bad. Basically, it's nice to be caring. But in some cases I let others blackmail me emotionally. It's important that everybody tries to take responsibility for their own lives themselves as far as possible. This client doesn't want to do it, but it's still my job to help her try. I definitely have to stop reinforcing her dependency!
T:	Perhaps you would like to add: "I have the right to set limits! I am a better social worker when I ask more of this patient!"
V:	Yes, that's absolutely true! It's not my job to take everything over. It doesn't help the client, it's way too much for me, and I don't even get paid for it! And yes, I have the right to say "no" to her! And I refuse to feel bad about that.
T:	Then how should you feel? Tell her!
V:	I will feel proud when I am able to say no!

punitive parent mode. In such cases, it's possible to start with other materials that allow more distance from the emotions than the chairs. Toys are suitable, such as Playmobil figures, glove puppets, tokens, and so on. These items are arranged on the table and the patient explains emotions and cognitions related to each of them. Another way of keeping some distance is to arrange actual chairs in a circle, but for the patient to stay in their normal seat. Instead of sitting on the chairs, they report from this distance what the different modes experience and say. After a patient has

Case example: chair dialogue with a strong punitive parent mode

Michelle, a 20-year-old patient with BPD and a severe eating disorder, was as a child often punished with food deprivation and physical and sexual abuse by her sadistic step-parents. Today she is sometimes unable to eat anything for several days. She feels that she does not deserve to eat; granting herself food leads to guilt, shame, and self-hatred. The therapist suggests a chair dialogue against the punitive parent modes in order to help Michelle feel that she has the right to care well for herself.

Therapist: [Puts three chairs in a circle.] These chairs belong to the punitive parent mode withholding good food from you, to desperate Little Michelle, and to your healthy adult mode. Please stay on your normal therapy chair first and tell me what the three are saying.

Michelle: [Points to at the punitive parent chair.] That's the loudest one. It says I'm just crap and it's silly to think about having a right to eat. I deserve to starve.

T: [Points to Little Michelle's chair.] And how is Little Michelle?

M: She feels awful.

T: [Points to the healthy adult chair.] And what does your healthy adult mode say?

M: I have no idea! I don't feel this part at all.

T: Yes, I can imagine. May I sit on this chair and make some suggestions?

M: [Nods.]

T: [On the chair of the healthy adult mode, talking to the punitive parent chair:] What do you say: Michelle has no right to eat?! Of course she has the right to care for herself, just like everybody! Of course she has the right to eat food she likes! I don't want to hear this bullshit anymore! [To the patient:] How do you feel?

M: Somehow it's good. But I am horribly afraid of the chair over there. [Points at the punitive parent chair.]

T: Yes, I can imagine. I would like to put it out of the room. Do you agree?

M: Yes, that would be a relief!

T: [Still sitting on the chair of the healthy adult, talking to the parent mode chair.] You are so damaging for Michelle, we'll put you out now! [Stands up, takes the chair of the punitive parent resolutely out of the room and closes the door. To the patient:] How do you feel now?

M: Oh, that's much better!

T: Yes, I agree! Would you be willing to take a seat on Little Michelle's chair now? I would like to talk with her, if it's okay with you.

M: [Takes a seat on the chair of the vulnerable child mode.]

T: [On the healthy adult chair, talking to the patient on the vulnerable child chair:] Little Michelle, you are a lovely and valuable girl. Just like everybody else, you have a right to take your needs seriously and to get your needs met. You deserve to eat tasty food, just like every child and everybody else! How do you feel?

M: [On Little Michelle's chair.] It's good to hear that. But it's also a bit strange. I can hardly believe it.

T: Yes, it feels strange because it's new. But I'm glad you can also find it somewhat good! We should do many exercises like this to help you feel that your needs are important.

M: Yes, that would be great. I hardly dare to hope on the one hand; but on the other, it feels like things could change a bit and I might eventually be able to eat without deserving punishment, in the far future . . .

T: That's great to hear. That's a first little step. I have a suggestion: I'll repeat what I just said to Little Michelle and you record it with your cell phone. When you would like to eat, try to listen to the recording first. Maybe it will help you to feel that you deserve to eat; you'd have to try it out, though.

M: Yes, I would like to try that.

> The therapist speaks a message to the vulnerable child mode into the patient's cell phone, in a very warm and caring voice.

become familiar with chair-work exercises using these variations, the therapist may introduce actual chairs in a stepwise fashion.

Protecting the patient from the punitive parent mode   Patients who are very scared of the punitive parent mode are not allowed to sit on the punitive parent chair for long, particularly in the initial chair-work exercises. Often it's best not to let the patient take a seat on this chair at all. Instead, they should report from a distance what the punitive parent mode says. If the therapist does not protect them in this way, patients with intense punitive parent modes tend to get too deeply into this mode when they sit on its chair. Note that these patients are very familiar with the punitive parent mode, and if they were to follow their "natural" emotional process, they would sit on its chair most of the time. It may be necessary to actively stop them and explain why it is important not to get too close to this mode during the exercise.

Accordingly, the amount of speaking time given to the punitive parent mode should be kept brief (although the patient will usually spontaneously elaborate on this mode much more than on the others). When the patient has said two or three sentences from the punitive parent perspective, the therapist should interrupt, summarize, and focus on the other modes, particularly the vulnerable child and the healthy adult modes. When the therapist addresses the punitive parent, the patient never sits on that chair. Furthermore, putting the chair of the punitive parent out of the room helps to protect the patient against from mode.

Modeling the healthy adult mode   Particularly in the first phase of treatment, the therapist often has to model the healthy adult mode. The therapist may sit on the healthy adult chair, with the patient standing aside, or vice versa. Alternatively, the patient may listen to the therapist's healthy adult messages from the chair of the vulnerable child mode or from their usual therapy seat. Never let the patient sit on the chair of the punitive parent mode when the therapist fights and limits it! By contrast, it is recommendable to let the patient sit on the vulnerable child chair when the therapist comforts it and fights the punitive parent. The patient is supposed to internalize the therapist's healthy adult model; to support internalization, the therapist can encourage them to repeat each of the healthy adult's messages in turn (e.g. the therapist soothes the vulnerable child or fights the punitive parent in a chair-work exercise; subsequently the therapist asks the patient to repeat one sentence or comment made by the healthy adult chair which they particularly liked). Listening to recordings of the chair-work exercises as a homework assignment is also useful.

Over the course of treatment, the patient is increasingly pushed into the role of the healthy adult. This is consistent with imagery rescripting exercises for severely disordered patients. In the initial imagery rescripting exercises, the therapist takes the role of the healthy adult mode, but over the course of therapy this role is stepwise assigned to the patient. It's similar in chair dialogues: in the first dialogues, the patient might stay seated on the vulnerable child chair. Subsequently, they get more active in the healthy adult role. As an intermediate step, the patient might stand behind the therapist sitting on the healthy adult chair. In the next step, the patient might themselves sit in this chair while the therapist stands to their side, and so on.

Evoking and modeling anger   Anger is important when it comes to fighting the punitive parent mode. However, patients with suppressed anger must first gain access to this feeling. Anger can be strengthened and modeled well in chair dialogues. The therapist adds a chair for the angry child mode (or for healthy anger) and encourages the patient to take a seat and explore this part of themselves. Such patients are often afraid of expressing anger, as they expect punishment. The model of the therapist can be very helpful here. Playful movement-therapy exercises for the expression of anger and rage (tug-of-war, pillow fights, boxing, etc.) can also help patients experience anger in a safe situation (see also Chapter 7).

It is sometimes easier for patients to fight the punitive parent mode of someone else, rather than their own. The therapist can make use of this by asking questions such as, "What would you think if it was not your punitive parent mode, but the punitive parent of your best friend that said this?" and "How would you feel if this punitive parent mode were to punish your own child?"

Anticipating and preparing for the "revenge" of the punitive parent mode   Often patients are justly afraid that the punitive parent mode will "fight back" when they try to question and fight it in such exercises.

Therapists should anticipate and understand this, and discuss possible solutions with the patient.

It may be good for the patient to stay for a while in the therapist's waiting room after they have completed an exercise to fight the punitive parent, particularly after their first time. The patient can then calm down in a safe situation and perhaps have another brief contact with the therapist in between the therapist's later appointments. Alternatively, or additionally, the patient may be encouraged to write the therapist an email some hours after the exercise. Eventually, a brief telephone appointment can be arranged, which may again be particularly necessary if the patient has completed such an exercise for the first time. The therapist can also give the patient a recording of the fight against the punitive parent mode. The patient can listen to this audiotape whenever they need support against this mode (see the next case example). Trauma-therapy exercises, such as locking the issue in the therapist's cupboard, can be used as well.

Case example: a recording to support the healthy adult mode after a chair-work exercise fighting the punitive parent mode

Therapist: I want you to listen to this tape if the punitive parent mode gets more intense again after our session. I really want to support you—it's fantastic that we've started to fight against your punitive parent mode! Just like everybody else, you have the right to take your needs seriously and to fight against punitive inner parts of yourself. I am happy that you have cooperated with me on this and I will support you however possible. First, I would like to say something to your punitive parent mode. [To the punitive parent mode:] Shut up! Let her alone, don't interfere with her anymore! You only hurt her, you're not right, and you don't have the right to punish her! [To the patient:] Second, in our session we discussed what you can do when you feel bad and threatened by the punitive parent mode. I just want to remind you of our ideas and say that I hope you manage to put one of these suggestions into practice. You could for example snuggle in a soft blanket and

> watch some funny movies; you could call your friend
> Carol or your Aunt Susan; you could listen to the music
> from your vacation in Spain, where you felt so easy and
> relaxed; in the daytime, you could go for a jog, since
> this usually calms you down quite well. Please write me
> an email telling me what you do and how you feel.

Addressing different modes   When we talk about different modes, we usually regard child modes, coping modes, and healthy modes as "parts of the patients." Accordingly, we ask the patient to use the first person when talking on the chairs of these modes in chair-work exercises. However, with dysfunctional parent modes the situation is different. Since punitive parent modes are meant to be fought, the patient should not identify too much with these parts. If we ask people to fight a part of themselves, this automatically implies that something about them is not OK, since it needs to be fought. This may again trigger the punitive parent mode. In addition, we do everything to help the patient distance themselves from the mode of the punitive parent; this includes treating the punitive parent like a third party.

Thus the name of the punitive parent mode is always different from the patient's name. You might call it "the mean peer," "the inquisitor," "the punitive father," or something similar. In a chair dialogue, the patient should talk in the second person when sitting on the chair of the punitive parent mode ("You are a failure," instead of "I am a failure"). This also helps the patient to distance themselves from this mode's messages. When the patient talks back to the demanding or punitive parent mode, the patient should also say "you" to the mode.

Advanced chair-dialogue techniques   Chair dialogues can be used in various therapy models other than schema therapy. Likewise, the schema-therapy model can be integrated with many different chair-work formats. For example, in a chair-work exercise with different parts of a dream, we may find quite a high overlap between the parts of the dream and the modes of the patient. The following list gives some examples of advanced chair-dialogue techniques (see also Kellogg, 2004).

(1)   **"Unfinished business"** When a patient has "unfinished business" with somebody (a friend, family member, ex-partner), ambivalent

feelings usually play a crucial role. In this chair-work exercise, one (empty) chair is assigned to the other person and the patient takes a seat opposite this. They express their ambivalent feelings about this person. The therapist takes care that both sides of the ambivalence are addressed. This exercise should end with some kind of conclusion.

(2) **"Say goodbye"** Similar to "unfinished business"—ambivalent feelings regarding a late person are expressed, and the patient says goodbye.

(3) **Couples therapy** Couples conflicts can often be conceptualized within the schema-mode model. To treat the conflict with a chair-work exercise, the modes of both partners are placed on different chairs. It is often both funny and illuminating when people see their problems from the perspective of their partner's modes.

(4) **Working with dreams** This very traditional chair-work format has been developed by Fritz Perls (see Kellogg, 2004). Different elements of a dream (people, objects, attributes of the situation) are assigned to different chairs. The patient takes the perspective of each dream element regarding both the dream and the dreamer.

8.4   Behavioral techniques

On the behavioral level, reducing perfectionism and increasing positive activities are well suited to fighting the punitive or demanding parent mode. Patients should have more fun and experience themselves through more joyful and positive actions (leisure-time activities, sports, social events, etc.). Social skills for building up new relationships can be helpful. Furthermore, it may be important for the patient to allow themselves breaks from work, to accept their own shortcomings, and to reward their own achievements, instead of always trying to be perfect.

8.5   FAQ

(1) Can chair dialogues be conducted with dolls or similar materials?

It's possible to use materials other than chairs. However, we strongly recommend ultimately using chairs, since they induce stronger emotions than other materials. Playmobil figures and similar materials should be used when the patient is very scared to work with actual chairs.

*(2) Sometimes patients say that the punitive parent mode will never
disappear. How should the therapist react?*

On the one hand, psychoeducation is needed. As with every progress in
psychotherapy, the punitive parent mode will lose ground step by step. On
the other hand, it is important to find out whether the patient is afraid of
expressing anger. Basically, the fight against the parent mode will be won if
the patient only dares to start it. However, to start this fight, the patient
needs to accept and experience anger, which may be blocked by anxiety. If
anger acceptance is a problem, it should be increased in small increments
(see Chapter 7).

*(3) What can you do when the patient in the chair dialogue
empathizes with their mother (or other person responsible for the
punitive parent mode) and refuses to fight her?*

Again, this is a case for psychoeducation: the idea of a chair dialogue is not
to fight the actual mother. Instead, it's meant to fight the damaging
introject which may have been caused by the mother. We acknowledge
that the actual mother may have tried to do her best, but that was
unfortunately not enough.

When the patient was a child, they needed care, not mistreatment.
Whether or not the mother's behavior is (or was for the child) understandable is irrelevant for the needs of the child. As we said, therapists
should be aware of the risk that "understanding" will lead to suppression of
anger and autonomy, to justification of the parent's actions, and to
reinforcement of the introject and the belief that the messages associated
with it are true.

*(4) Sometimes patients feel very alone after the punitive parent has
been thrown out—what can you do then?*

Sometimes patients feel lonely or distressed when the punitive parent mode
is no longer present. Never take the punitive parent mode back in! Instead,
help the patient to accept close contact with their emotions and with other
people in modes other than the punitive parent mode. A chair-work
exercise can be used to reflect upon whether the patient is indeed alone
without the punitive parent mode. This implies thinking about the need for
positive interpersonal experiences. Loneliness is typically related to the

vulnerable child mode; the patient (or the therapist) should comfort the vulnerable child mode from the healthy adult chair. In this context, it is often useful to consider actual people with a positive attitude towards the patient, such as friends, other group-therapy patients, and so on: "Hey, Little Cathy—you may feel alone, but you are not! Many people like you, just think of X. You don't need the punitive parent to be in contact with somebody. You can actually be closer with others without the punitive parent mode, since it always blames you for every conflict or problem!"

(5) What can you do when the patient doesn't manage to enter the healthy adult mode?

Patients with BPD are typically unable to experience the healthy adult mode in the beginning of therapy, even when they are sitting on its chair. Thus the therapist or the patient group models the healthy adult. While the therapist is modeling the healthy adult, the patient sits either on the vulnerable child chair or on their usual therapy chair, or stands behind the therapist. Over the course of therapy, the healthy adult mode will develop step by step.

(6) What can you do when the patient feels weak and helpless while on the healthy adult chair?

These feelings indicate a switch to the vulnerable child mode. Thus, another chair for the vulnerable child mode is added. The patient takes a seat there and the intervention focuses on comforting the vulnerable child mode. It is of course possible to ask the patient to return to the healthy adult chair after the vulnerable child has been comforted.

(7) What can you do when the patient does not develop anger while on the chair of the angry child mode, but mainly gets frightened?

In their childhood, patients were often punished for expressing anger. In these cases, anger should be validated, modeled, and encouraged. Furthermore, anger can be experienced in a playful or funny way (e.g. the patient and the therapist sing songs against the punitive parent mode and record them).

(8) What can you do when a patient feels guilty after fighting the punitive parent mode?

Guilt feelings following chair dialogues fighting the punitive parent mode usually indicate that this mode has been triggered. It is important to discuss with the patient (in advance, if possible) how they can calm down and counteract guilt feelings. Eventually, you can develop exercises with the patient, helping them to decrease the punitive parent mode following an exercise (e.g. audio files, funny activities).

(9) How are chair dialogues linked with daily life?

It is important to link emotion-focused interventions with behavioral changes. Often, behavioral consequences are self-evident and do not need further discussion (e.g. Eva should work less obsessively for her thesis). Particularly with more severely disordered patients or with very avoidant patients, homework assignments can be quite important. They should be related to behavioral techniques against the punitive parent mode. Most important are building up positive activities, reducing perfectionism, and increasing self-care.

(10) What about patients who fear that they will lose their morality and values when they combat their parental modes?

Some patients express fears that when their punitive or demanding parent is defeated, they will lose their moral compass and no longer know what their values are, they will end up doing nothing, and so on. It is suggested that therapists deal with this type of resistance through empathic confrontation, and by pointing out that eliminating moral rules and values can indeed temporarily create some confusion, but that they will assist the patient in developing their own conscience, which will be healthier—and that this is much better than sticking to such damaging and imposed moral rules and values. A reassuring and firm attitude is important here, otherwise the patient will get more anxious.

9

Strengthening the Healthy Adult Mode

The healthy adult mode is realistic, is able to take responsibility for itself and for others, and balances its own needs and the needs of others. It chooses adaptive actions and has functional attitudes towards needs and emotions. A central goal of schema therapy is strengthening the healthy adult mode. This is partly accomplished indirectly, by reducing dysfunctional modes. When, for example, the punitive parent mode is diminished, patients reduce self-punitive behavior, which is an improvement in itself. However, unlearning does not necessarily imply new learning. Thus, reducing the influence of maladaptive modes gives more opportunity for the healthy adult mode, but does not necessarily imply that healthy attitudes and behaviors will replace the dysfunctional ones. Particularly when the healthy adult part is very weakly developed, therapy should also focus on teaching healthy attitudes and behaviors.

Of course, learning healthy alternatives is already interweaved in many techniques developed to address dysfunctional modes. For example, in fighting the punitive parent, the therapist not only tells the punitive mode that it is wrong, but also brings forward healthier ways of viewing problems. This is not to convince the punitive part (which is so irrational that it won't listen to arguments), but to correct the vulnerable child mode and to build the healthy adult mode. Similarly, when patients learn to express anger adequately (see Chapter 7), the angry child mode is replaced in a stepwise manner by the healthy adult mode. When patients learn to

Schema Therapy in Practice: An Introductory Guide to the Schema Mode Approach, First Edition. Arnoud Arntz and Gitta Jacob.
© 2013 John Wiley & Sons, Ltd. Published 2013 by John Wiley & Sons, Ltd.

comfort their vulnerable child mode, regressive feelings and needs are reduced and they become more adult.

Apart from these indirect techniques, some intervention strategies aim to strengthen the healthy adult mode directly. These strategies are vital for many patients.

9.1   The Therapeutic Relationship

In the therapeutic relationship, the therapist always tries to relate to the healthy adult part of the patient. The following intervention strategies can be used to strengthen the healthy adult mode in the therapeutic relationship. They have the common goal of constructive collaboration with the patient and and the taking of joint responsibility for the therapy process.

1   Relate all interventions to the schema mode model and explain why you have suggested them; thus invite the healthy adult mode to reflect on the therapy process.
2   Discuss emotion-focused interventions with the patient; encourage the patient to participate in shared decision-making regarding these interventions.
3   Include the patient stepwise as a healthy adult in emotion-focused interventions.
4   Record sessions and ask the patient to listen to them at home.
5   Address problems within the therapeutic relationship and find joint solutions with the patient.
6   Ask the patient to change to the healthy adult mode when therapy gets stuck; analyze the problem together.

9.1.1   Relate to the mode model

In every session, we link current problems and therapeutic strategies with the schema mode model. The therapist gives suggestions for emotion-focused interventions and explains the reasoning behind them. However, therapists may also suggest different exercises (particularly when the patient is already familiar with different treatment techniques) and ask the patient for their preferences. Thus, usually all steps in therapy are joint decisions, and the patient takes some responsibility for them. This is particularly true for emotion-focused interventions aimed at comforting and soothing the vulnerable child mode. By giving responsibility to the patient and jointly reflecting on the therapeutic process, the therapist continuously asks the patient's healthy adult mode to be active in therapy. Care for the vulnerable child mode is balanced with some degree of challenge for the healthy adult mode. This is also important with angry-/impulsive child modes and with behavioral change, in which the therapist and healthy adult mode of the patient should work out their plans together.

9.1.2 Discuss emotion-focused interventions

From a psychodynamic perspective, emotion-focused interventions, particularly imagery rescripting exercises, require (and induce) a high degree of regression. To balance this, the healthy adult mode is always involved: the therapist and patient jointly decide upon imagery rescripting exercises, monitor process, and "rewind the tape" if necessary to improve the emotional process. Furthermore, sessions are recorded and the patient listens to them as homework to improve transfer to daily life. Thus regression ($\rightarrow$ vulnerable child mode) is combined with a strong connection to reality and a reflection of regressive emotional processes ($\rightarrow$ healthy adult mode). The connection to reality is sometimes painful for patients, since it highlights the limits of the therapeutic relationship (the therapist cares wonderfully for the patient's child mode in imagery, but does not adopt the patient in reality).

One practical example for this approach is the constant monitoring of the patient's emotional process. The therapist frequently asks how patients feel and what they need; the imagery rescripting process is adapted accordingly. When the emotional process does not take the desired direction, the therapist and the patient together look for ways of improving it. When a patient seemingly does not cooperate in an intervention, the therapist explains why she suggested the intervention and tries to find out which mode is interfering with it.

9.1.3 Include the patient stepwise as a healthy adult in emotion-focused interventions

As described in Sections 6.3.2 (imagery rescripting) and 8.3.1 (chair dialogues), the patient gradually gets into the role of the healthy adult in emotion-focused interventions. Playing this part includes caring for the vulnerable child mode in imagery rescripting exercises, or fighting the punitive parent mode in chair-work exercises, two major tasks of the healthy adult.

Case example: reflecting emotion-focused interventions

Jane, a 28-year-old patient with BPD and avoidant personality disorder (see Section 2.1.3), gets into a detached self-soother coping mode when she feels threatened by others. She uses daydreams as a powerful internal stimulus to distract from external threat. In her daydreams, many wonderful people care for her in her inner world. Imagery rescripting exercises are applied to increase her feelings of safety with other people.

In the rescripting phase of an imagery exercise, the therapist enters the image and asks Little Jane what she would like to do. Little Jane would like to flee and enter her inner world of daydreams. The therapist suggests that this is not a solution, since switching into a coping mode will make the intervention ineffective. Instead, the therapist suggests doing something nice together in the imagery. Jane reacts with irritation.

This disrupts the exercise. The therapist thus asks Jane to briefly open her eyes. She explains that imagery rescripting exercises aim to establish new emotional experiences; therefore, the use of coping modes stands in the way as they block out emotion. The therapist comments that fleeing into an inner fantasy is not a good idea only because it is a coping mode blocking the change process, not because the therapist personally dislikes it. After this explanation, Jane agrees to close her eyes again and continues the rescripting phase with images other than those of her inner world.

9.1.4   Record sessions

Patients with severe personality disorder are particularly recommended to listen again to all therapy sessions at home. This is technically easy, as the patient can record the session with an MP3 player or a cell phone with a microphone function. This strategy aims at consolidating the therapeutic process; furthermore, it requires the patient (or trains them) to be disciplined and independent, two important features of the healthy adult mode. Note, however, that with many severely disordered patients, the healthy adult mode is not strong enough to reliably do this. Therapists have to tolerate this and try not to force patients to do something they are not yet capable of. On the other hand, they should continue to stimulate the patient to do it.

9.1.5 Address problems within the therapeutic relationship

Often patients relate in a dysfunctional way to the therapist, for example with dysfunctional coping modes or with child modes (e.g. angry child, dependent child). When due to such patterns a patient does not make progress in therapy, this is openly addressed. Furthermore, intervention strategies are applied which encourage the healthy adult mode to be more active in therapy (for example, chair-work exercises related to the therapeutic relationship).

> The healthy adult mode is essentially enhanced by all schema-therapy intervention techniques, either indirectly (via reduction of dysfunctional modes and information about healthy attitudes and behavior) or directly (when patients are asked to take responsibility and express their own feelings and needs in a healthy manner).

Case example: reflecting upon a problem in the therapeutic relationship and encouraging the healthy adult mode

Evelyn, a 52-year-old secretary with OCD (see Section 2.1.3), relates to the therapist with a very dependent pattern, since she only feels safe when a professional caretaker is at hand. For example, she is perfectly able to conduct exposure exercises for OCD symptoms together with the therapist, but when she is on her own, she doesn't find even the smallest exercise possible.

The therapist addresses the issue of functional dependency with empathic confrontation and suggests doing a chair dialogue, with one chair for dependent patterns (= compliant-surrender coping mode) and one chair for her taking responsibility and becoming independent (= healthy adult mode). The patient agrees, compliant as always. However, on the healthy adult mode's chair she slumps down and cannot say a word. She helplessly looks at the therapist, asking for support. The therapist does not take over the healthy adult role, but empathically explains that this is obviously a central problem. Evelyn has to weaken the dependent/passive mode and strengthen the healthy adult in order to become able to bear a more fulfilled and independent life. Evelyn is slightly irritated about this "lack of therapist support." But, on the chair of the healthy adult, she can see that she must learn to stand up for her needs herself. In the following sessions, chair dialogues are used to train the expression of Evelyn's emotions, needs, and limits.

9.2   Cognitive Techniques

An important part of cognitive work aimed at strengthening the healthy adult mode is working with the mode model itself. As the mode model is developed together with the patient, patients are made to reflect on their psychological patterns on a healthy adult level from the very beginning of therapy. Later, the joint planning and consideration of (emotion-focused) interventions has the same effect. In psychoeducation, the patient is taught healthy ways of psychological functioning. Socratic questioning can also be used to strengthen the healthy adult, as it puts the patient in a reflective and adult perspective.

When the patient has problems taking the healthy adult perspective, the following questions can be helpful: "What would I or your good granny [= therapist or granny as model for the healthy adult mode; note that you have to name a really healthy person here, adapted to the specific patient] say now?" "If we weren't talking about you right now, but about your friend or your children, what would you say then?" "What would you say if you were able to put yourself in the perspective of the healthy adult mode?"

Cognitive work with the healthy adult mode often deals with motivational issues. Patients whose dysfunctional patterns are highly rewarded (for example narcissistic overcompensator, self-stimulation mode, undisciplined and spoiled child mode) may have little genuine motivation for change. In motivational exercises with the healthy adult mode, the perspectives of the dysfunctional mode and the healthy adult mode are contrasted (if possible, with chair dialogues). Both sides are balanced; sometimes the advantages of the dysfunctional mode beat the advantages of the healthy mode, at least at the given moment. This should be considered and openly discussed—sometimes patients have subjective reason to decide against changing their dysfunctional modes (at least temporarily, and even though the therapist may justly see a need for change). Even if the patient does decide not to change dysfunctional patterns at the moment, the healthy adult mode is included in this decision, and alternative aims for therapy can be considered (e.g. using therapy to increase motivation for

---

Case example: clarifying treatment motivation

Colette, a very attractive 38-year-old businesswoman with narcissistic features (slight self-aggrandizer and strong self-soother modes), has a depressive reaction with feelings of loneliness and sadness after the break-up of her relationship (vulnerable child mode). When intimate relationships are discussed, it quickly becomes clear that Colette often has exciting short sexual affairs related to the self-soother mode, while she has found most of her longer-term relationships rather boring. The therapist discusses the black-and-white perspective on relationships related to this pattern of distinguishing between exciting affairs and boring everyday life relationships. His idea is to develop a model of healthy attachment together with the patient. Colette basically agrees with this concept, but after a couple of sessions she starts another exciting affair and her depressive symptoms disappear. The therapist suggests a chair dialogue between the healthy adult mode and the over-compensation mode related to the affair. It becomes clear that the patient does not suffer from depressive symptoms any longer. Her primary therapy motivation has disappeared, since she came to therapy to improve depressive symptoms. The therapist explains that her current positive feelings might well be caused by the self-soother mode and not necessarily be an indicator of stability. However, the patient prefers to stop therapy and come back if the symptoms return.

change, or stopping therapy for now, but coming back when the motivational situation has changed).

9.3   Emotional Techniques

Emotion-focused interventions aimed at strengthening the healthy adult mode include chair dialogues and imagery rescripting exercises. More detailed explanations can be found in Sections 6.3.2 and 8.3.1. When the patient's progress lags behind realistic expectations, the therapist and the patient should try to understand together which mode is blocking the process. If necessary, interventions are explained and the patient is assisted in taking the perspective of the healthy adult mode. An important imagery technique in this phase is to rescript memories or expected catastrophic future outcomes. Patients are asked to close their eyes and imagine the problematic situation, and to change the negative script by trying out new ways of dealing with it, from a healthy adult perspective. The therapist can assist (e.g. by entering the image and supporting the patient), but gradually the healthy adult mode will take the lead.

9.4   Behavioral Techniques

Over the course of therapy, transfer of emotional and cognitive changes into the patient's everyday life gets increasingly important. That is, patients increasingly adopt the perspective and the behavior of the healthy adult mode in their normal social surroundings. Furthermore, establishing healthy adult activities is a goal for the later phase of therapy. The ultimate goal— apart from reducing symptoms in the narrower sense—is to support patients in organizing life in such a way that their needs are adequately met. This includes issues like establishing or maintaining safe attachment, developing their capacities, developing an interest in study, work or a hobby, and so on. Furthermore, a good balance between obligations and fun, and between caring for their own needs and for the needs of others, should be established. In this later phase of treatment, the patient and therapist set up a plan to reach such goals to such an extent that further healthy development can be expected. This plan involves concrete steps. When indicated, roleplays can be used in preparation (e.g. practicing assertiveness, anger expression, or intimate talk). Taking up the challenges this involves will almost inevitably trigger dysfunctional modes again. It is important that the therapist reflects on these with the healthy adult side of the patient, and frames them as opportunities to deepen learning, and not as relapses. Techniques for specific modes can and often should be used again, so progress is often not linear but cyclic. Nevertheless, the overall trend is that the healthy adult mode gets more and more involved, and takes more responsibility.

9.5 Terminating Therapy

Emotion-focused interventions aimed at vulnerable child and dysfunctional parent modes are usually common in the beginning phase of therapy. Thus the patient is emotionally strengthened and behavioral change is prepared. In the further course of therapy, the focus gradually shifts on to the transfer of these steps into the patients' everyday life and their experiences with changing old patterns. Thus the healthy adult mode moves to the foreground. While parent and child modes are the main target of emotion-focused interventions, (behavioral) transfer of therapy issues into everyday life is largely related to the healthy adult mode. Nevertheless, the behavioral change can be supported by emotion-focused and cognitive techniques.

9.5.1 *Duration of therapy*

The duration of therapy varies a lot depending on the symptoms and problems of the patient, and the strength of the healthy adult. Schema therapy is used for a large variety of patients, and their treatment durations may thus be very different. In patients with BPD and other severe personality disorders, a total duration of 2–3 years is recommended, ideally starting with two weekly sessions. In less severe disorders, schema therapy can be shorter, with lower frequency. Some clients come to therapy to solve a clearly focused problem; in these cases, a few sessions may be sufficient.

We recommend terminating therapy slowly (reducing frequency in a stepwise manner: offer booster session once a month for a while) and staying at least marginally available even after the end of therapy. For example, some patients like to write an email to their former therapist twice a year (and to get a short answer at least); since the therapist offers an intense attachment experience during the actual schema therapy, we recommend fulfilling these kinds of wish, as long as they are adequate and realistic.

9.6 FAQ

(1) Does the healthy adult mode always participate in emotional interventions?

Yes! Strengthening the healthy adult mode is an ultimate goal of therapy, and the healthy adult mode is included in all emotional interventions. Note, however, that depending on the current state of their healthy adult mode, patients may not be able to take on this role at the beginning of therapy themselves; in that case, the healthy adult mode is modeled by the therapist or another suitable model.

(2) What can you do when a patient hardly has any healthy adult mode?

When the healthy adult mode of the patient is very weak at the beginning of therapy, it is modeled by the therapist or by other helping figures. Over the course of the therapy, patients can use different helping persons. For example, they might imagine that their best friend sits on the chair of the healthy adult mode in a chair dialogue, and use the Terminator from the movies of the same name in imagery rescripting exercises. Over time, patients will take on the responsibility of the healthy adult mode themselves.

(3) What can you do when patients come across as very healthy during the session, but obviously don't manage to make corresponding changes in their life?

Given that the patient has serious psychopathological problems in the indication area of schema therapy, the therapist should consider that the patient uses the apparent healthy behavior to prevent activation of other modes, like the punitive parent mode or the vulnerable child mode. The therapist should try to explore with the patient whether this might be the case. Often the healthy appearance is only superficial, and is part of a coping mode (e.g. detached protector, self-aggrandizer). The therapist should then not be distracted by the superficial healthiness of the patient, and should look for vulnerable child modes. Empathic confrontation and an attempt to directly access the child modes are possible approaches here.

References

Arntz, A. (2008). Schema therapy. Keynote delivered at the International Conference on Eating Disorders (ICED), Academy for Eating Disorders, Seattle, May 14-17, 2008.

Arntz, A. & van Genderen, H. (2009). *Schema Therapy for Borderline Personality Disorder*. Sussex: John Wiley & Sons.

Arntz, A. & Weertman, A. (1999). Treatment of childhood memories: theory and practice. *Behavior Research and Therapy*, **37**: 715–740.

Arntz, A., Tiesema, M., & Kindt, M. (2007). Treatment of PTSD: a comparison of imaginal exposure with and without imagery rescripting. *Journal of Behavior Therapy and Experimental Psychiatry*, **38**: 345–370.

Bamelis, L.L.M., Renner, F., Heidkamp, D., & Arntz, A. (2011). Extended schema mode conceptualizations for specific personality disorders: an empirical study. *Journal of Personality Disorders*, **25**: 41–58.

Bernstein, D.P., Arntz, A., & de Vos, M. (2007). Schema focused therapy in forensic settings: theoretical model and recommendations for best clinical practice. *International Journal of Forensic Mental Health*, **6**: 169–183.

Costa, P.T. & McCrae, R.R. (1992). *Revised NEO Personality Inventory (NEO-PI-R) and NEO Five-Factor Inventory (NEO-FFI) Professional Manual*. Odessa, FL: Psychological Assessment Resources.

Farrell, J. & Shaw, I. (2012). *Group Schema Therapy for Borderline Personality Disorder: A Step-by-Step Treatment Manual with Patient Workbook*. Sussex: John Wiley & Sons.

Farrell, J., Shaw, I., & Webber, M. (2009). A schema-focused approach to group psychotherapy for outpatients with borderline personality disorder: a randomized controlled trial. *Journal of Behavior Therapy and Experiential Psychology*, **40**: 317–328.

Giesen-Bloo, J., van Dyck, R., Spinhoven, P., van Tilburg, W., Dirksen, C., van Asselt, T., Kremer, I., Nadort, M., & Arntz, A. (2006). Outpatient psychotherapy for borderline personality disorder. Randomized trial of schemafocused therapy versus transference-focused psychotherapy. *Archives of General Psychiatry*, **63**: 649–658.

Grawe, K. (2006). *Neuropsychotherapy*. Oxford: Routledge.

Gross, E.N., Stelzer, N., & Jacob, G.A. (2012). Treating obsessive–compulsive disorder with the schema mode model. In M. van Vreeswijk, J. Broersen, & M. Nadort (eds.), *Handbook of Schema Therapy: Theory, Research and Practice*. Sussex: John Wiley & Sons. pp. 173–184.

Hackmann, A., Bennett-Levy, J., & Holmes, E.A. (2011). *The Oxford Guide to Imagery in Cognitive Therapy*. Oxford: Oxford University Press.

Hawke, L.D., Provencer, M.D., & Arntz, A. (2011). Early maladaptive schemas in the risk for bipolar spectrum disorders. *Journal of Affective Disorders*, **133**: 428–436.

Hayes, A.M., Beevers, C., Feldman, G., Laurenceau, J.-P., & Perlman, C.A. (2005). Avoidance and emotional processing as predictors of symptom change and positive growth in an integrative therapy for depression. In G. Ironson, U. Lundberg, & L.H. Powell (eds.) *International Journal of Behavioral Medicine*, special issue: Positive Psychology: 111–122.

Kellogg, S.H. (2004). Dialogical encounters: contemporary perspectives on "chairwork" in psychotherapy. *Psychotherapy: Research, Theory, Practice, Training*, **41**: 310–320.

Linehan, M.M. (1993). *Cognitive-behavioral Treatment of Borderline Personality Disorder*. New York: Guildford.

Lobbestael, J., van Vreeswijk, M., & Arntz, A. (2007). Shedding light on schema modes: a clarification of the mode concept and its current research status. *Netherlands Journal of Psychology*, **63**: 76–85.

Lobbestael, J., van Vreeswijk, M., & Arntz, A. (2008). An empirical test of schema mode conceptualizations in personality disorders. *Behavior Research and Therapy*, **46**: 854–860.

Lobbestael, J., van Vreeswijk, M., Spinhoven, P., Schouten, E., & Arntz, A. (2010). Reliability and validity of the short Schema Mode Inventory (SMI). *Behavioral and Cognitive Psychotherapy*, **38**: 437–458.

Nadort, M., Arntz, A., Smit, J.H., Giesen-Bloo, J., Eikelenboom, M., Spinhoven, P., van Asselt, T., Wensing, M., & van Dyck, R. (2009). Implementation of outpatient schema therapy for borderline personality disorder with versus without crisis support by the therapist outside office hours: a randomized trial. *Behavior Research and Therapy*, **47**: 961–973.

Norris, M.L., Boydell, K.M., Pinhas, L., & Katzman, D.K. (2006). Ana and the internet: a review of pro-anorexia websites. *The International Journal of Eating Disorders*, **39**(6): 443–447. doi:10.1002/eat.20305, PMID 16721839.

Oei, T.P.S. & Baranoff, J. (2007). Young schema questionnaire: review of psychometric and measurement issues. *Australian Journal of Psychology*, **59**: 78–86.

Reddemann, L. (2001). *Imagination als heilsame Kraft/Zur Behandlung von Traumafolgen mit ressourcenorientierten Verfahren.* Stuttgart: Pfeiffer bei Klett-Cotta.

Renner, F., Arntz, A., Leeuw, I., & Huibers, M. (2012). Treatment for chronic depression using schema focused therapy. *Clinical Psychology: Science and Practice.* Accepted pending revision.

Rogers, C. (1961). *On Becoming a Person: A Therapist's View of Psychotherapy.* London: Constable.

Schmidt, N.B., Joiner, T.E., Young, J.E., & Telch, M.J. (1995) The schema questionnaire: investigation of psychometric properties and the hierarchical structure of a measure of maladaptive schemas. *Cognitive Therapy and Research*, **19**: 295–321.

Smucker, M.P., Dancu, C., Foa, E.B., & Niederee, J.L. (1995). Imagery resctipting: a new treatment for survivors of childhood sexual abuse suffering from post-traumatic stress. *Journal of Cognitive Psychotherapy: An International Quarterly*, **9**: 3–17.

Taylor, C.T., Laposa, J.M., & Alden, L.E. (2004). Is avoidant personality disorder more than just social avoidance? *Journal of Personality Disorders*, **18**: 571–594.

Young, J.E. (1990). *Cognitive Therapy for Personality Disorders: A Schema-focused Approach.* Sarasota, FL: Professional Resource Exchange.

Young, J.E., Klosko, S., & Weishaar, M.E. (2003). *Schema Therapy: A Practitioner's Guide.* New York: Guilford.

Index

Schema Therapy in Practice: An Introductory Guide to the Schema Mode Approach, First Edition. Arnoud Arntz and Gitta Jacob.
© 2013 John Wiley & Sons, Ltd. Published 2013 by John Wiley & Sons, Ltd.